*Chickamauga, Andersonville, Fort Sumter
and Guard Duty at Home:
Four Civil War Diaries by Pennsylvania Soldiers*
(McFarland, 2005)

The Battle of Perryville, 1862

Culmination of the Failed Kentucky Campaign

ROBERT P. BROADWATER

McFarland & Company, Inc., Publishers
Jefferson, North Carolina, and London

Acknowledgments

I would like to express my gratitude to the staffs of several repositories for their valuable assistance in locating information for the compiling of this book. Your knowledgeable advice and friendly help has been greatly appreciated. My thanks go out to: Alabama State Department of Archives, Duke University, the Filson Historical Club, Indiana Historical Society, Minnesota Historical Society, Tennessee State Library, University of Georgia, and Western Reserve Historical Society.

I would also like to acknowledge Mr. Richard Heiler for the invaluable assistance he has provided to me over the years, and for the friendly and gracious manner with which he has always treated me.

LIBRARY OF CONGRESS CATALOGUING-IN-PUBLICATION DATA

Broadwater, Robert P., 1958–
The Battle of Perryville, 1862 : culmination of the
failed Kentucky campaign / Robert P. Broadwater.
p.   cm.
Includes bibliographical references and index.

ISBN 0-7864-2303-X (illustrated case binding : 50# alkaline paper) ∞

1. Perryville, Battle of, Perryville, Ky., 1862.
2. Kentucky — History — Civil War, 1861–1865 — Campaigns.
3. United States — History — Civil War, 1861–1865 — Campaigns.
I. Title.
E474.39.B76 2006   973.7'33 — dc22   2005025348

British Library cataloguing data are available

On the cover: Battle of Perryville reenactment, October 5, 2002
(photograph by Frank Becker, www.reenactmentphotography.com)

Manufactured in the United States of America

McFarland & Company, Inc., Publishers
Box 611, Jefferson, North Carolina 28640
www.mcfarlandpub.com

To Kolby and Quinn,
my grandsons

Contents

Contents

Preface

The purpose of this work is to spotlight the largest battle to take place in Kentucky during the Civil War. I was attracted to the subject by virtue of the battle's significance in shattering the hopes of the Confederacy to take the war to Northern territory and to gain foreign recognition through victories on the battle-field. I was also drawn to the battle because, after a full year of war, so many of the Union troops and officers were completely green to the service, or to their responsibilities of rank. To me, it seemed to be almost a second Shiloh, on the Northern side, where the grit and determination of the men in the ranks took the place of training and experience.

I have drawn on many first-hand sources in the creation of this book, using a number of accounts written for magazine articles and periodicals in the years after the war — letters, diaries, and regimental histories — and I have tried, as much as possible, to tell the story of this battle through the words of the men who fought it. It is my intent that, using the soldiers' memories, the reader may be guided through the action in a first-person manner. Appropriate narration and historical background have been added to weave together the eyewitness accounts and add flow to the book.

The main focus of this book is the battle of Perryville. However, appropri-ate portions of the Kentucky campaign have been included, in order to provide the reader with a solid background regarding the events leading up to the battle, as well as the consequences of its being fought. The book begins with the Con-federate plans to wrest Kentucky away from the Union, and follows the move-ments of the opposing armies, through the battles of Richmond and Munfordville (usually spelled "Mumfordville" or "Mumfordsville" in letters and diaries of the period), to the decisive struggle of the campaign, at Perryville. It then follows the retreat of the Confederates back into Tennessee. The work discusses both the tactical and strategic elements of the campaign, and addresses the many blunders and missed opportunities on both sides.

At the time that I first began researching and writing this book, there were no published histories devoted specifically to Perryville. Since that time, there have been three very good histories offered to Civil War enthusiasts by accomplished historians. I hope that this book serves to enhance and broaden the study of the battle of Perryville, and that historians of Perryville, the Civil War in Kentucky, and the Western campaigns may find it a worthy addition.

Introduction

The battle of Perryville culminated the Kentucky campaign of 1862, and ensured that Union forces would continue to control all of the Bluegrass state, as well as a major portion of Tennessee. Confederate efforts to wrest these states away from Federal domination disappeared even as the smoke was clearing from the battlefield of Perryville.

The invading Confederates had hoped for an outpouring of support, in both men and materials, from Kentucky, but Kentuckians withheld both, particularly in regard to manpower, seeming to revert to the stance of neutrality they had adopted in the opening phases of the war. The majority of Kentuckians, though Southerners by culture, waited to see how the campaign would come out before they threw in their lot with the Confederacy. They were not anxious to enlist in the army if it meant leaving their homes and families behind in a Federally occupied Kentucky. So, they watched and waited, and reserved their support, to see if the Confederate army was there to stay, or was merely passing through. In the end, it proved a catch-22. The Confederate army could not hope to remain in Kentucky without the active support of the people of that state, but the Kentuckians would not support the Confederacy unless the army planned to stay.

The story of the battle of Perryville is filled with strange and interesting facts. The acoustic shadow that prevented the Union's Major General Don Carlos Buell from hearing the battle, though he was but four miles distant, was a scientific phenomenon that placed Buell under severe criticism, and helped to foster the allegation that he was, at heart, a Southern man. Buell's army was made up largely of raw recruits who had answered Lincoln's latest call for 300,000 volunteers. Though he did his best to disperse these green regiments throughout his brigades, Buell's army would fight the battle of Perryville with close to 20,000

3

untried men. Thirty-five of his 125 regiments that made up the army had been in the service a month or less when the campaign began.

The lack of battle experience would make this engagement very similar to Shiloh. It wasn't only the men in the ranks who were green. Many of the top Union commanders were new at their positions, with two brigade commanders and one corps commander being promoted into their new assignments as generals immediately prior to the battle. All three of these had previously been only captains, not even holding field-grade commissions before their promotions. The campaign witnessed the murder of a Union general by a brother officer, and the battle saw Phil Sheridan begin to show the leadership qualities that would make him one of the North's leading generals. Possibly the strangest feature in this battle filled with oddities was the fact that only about one-third of the Federal force was actually engaged in the fighting. Another third of Buell's army, though formed in line of battle, watched as the Confederates threatened to sweep their comrades off the field, without coming to their assistance. Breakdowns in command caused these troops to become spectators to some of the bloodiest fighting of the war, but they were not permitted to become participants.

On the Confederate side, Perryville is a story of missed opportunities and squandered chances. General Braxton Bragg incurred public censure, as well as the open hostility of many of his subordinate generals, as a result of the failure of the campaign. Though Bragg was deserving of criticism for many of his failures later in the war, at Perryville it seems he was unjustly accused. In fact, the Kentucky campaign was possibly Bragg's best planned operation of the war. Bragg lacked the support and cooperation he had been promised by Kirby Smith, Earl Van Dorn, and Sterling Price. He was also badly served by several of the generals in his own army. He had the right force in the right place at the right time to have altered the course of history, but he could not bring about cohesive action between the various commands. Had he received the cooperation he expected and deserved, Braxton Bragg might well have succeeded in dealing the Union a crushing defeat in Kentucky and entering his name along with Lee, Jackson, and Stuart on the Confederacy's roll of heroes. Instead, the battle of Perryville became the first of a number of failed campaigns credited to Bragg.

Like so many battles in the Civil War, Perryville came about by accident. Neither side planned to fight upon that ground. In fact, the battle was initiated in large measure by a long dry spell that had created a shortage of water. When the lead elements of both armies came into contact at Perryville, the few existing pools of water became a point of contention. Skirmishing over the precious pools touched off a battle and brought the ill-fated Confederate invasion of Kentucky to a close.

Veteran soldiers on both sides described Perryville as the bloodiest struggle of the war. Though the casualties of the battle are far below those of other engagements, when one looks at the relatively small number of men engaged, and at the fact that the entire battle was fought in only about four hours, one can begin to understand the savagery of the fighting. Like Shiloh, Perryville was a test of wills between the opposing soldiers, a bloodbath where the victor suffered as much as the vanquished. Confederate Private Sam Watkins stated: "When the accounts of the hard battles fought during the war are rendered by the true historian, it will be found that the battle of Perryville was one of the hardest contested and one of the most sanguinary during the war. It was like two huge monsters together in one death-grasp, and each trying to drink the last drop of the other's blood. It was the only battle in which bayonets and butts of guns were used with death-dealing effect."[1] Though Watkins' last sentence is inaccurate, this soldier fought in all of the major battles of the Western Theater, and his assertion that Perryville was the most severe must be credited.

In the end, Perryville did little to advance the cause of either side. It simply added names to the ever-growing casualty list of the war. Though a few officers, like Joe Wheeler and Phil Sheridan, were able to spotlight their leadership abilities during the campaign, many more suffered blots on their records that would follow them for the rest of the war, and Buell was relieved of command and forced to defend his actions to Congress. Perhaps Lieutenant Colonel Charles Kerr best summed up the situation with these remarks: "The summer and fall of 1862 was perhaps the darkest period of the War of the Rebellion. Corinth, through the imbecility of Hallock [sic], had been evacuated instead of captured; the line dividing the contestants in the East had been pushed north of Maryland, a State that had not seceded, and there seemed imminent danger of our losing in the West most of the territory our armies had gained.

"Grant truly remarks in his 'Memoirs' that many loyal people despaired in the fall of 1862 of ever saving the Union."[2]

Robert E. Lee's withdrawal from Maryland and Braxton Bragg's retreat from Kentucky were both the results of drawn battles, but the North was able to claim victory in both instances because the invading Confederates had been forced to return to their own territory, foiled in achieving their goals in the campaigns. Gettysburg is commonly referred to as the high tide of the Confederacy, but Southern fortunes began to crumble with the failed Maryland and Kentucky campaigns of 1862. Victory was on the horizon for the South in September and October of 1862, and victories in the Maryland and Kentucky campaigns could have led to foreign recognition and placed the war-weary citizens of the North in a position to sue for peace. The failed campaigns instead gave new heart to the Union, and gave the North the ability to bring its overwhelming resources to bear in a long war that it could not lose.

CHAPTER ONE

Kentucky Invaded and On to Richmond

On July 12, 1862, under a flag of truce, Colonel Philip H. Sheridan visited the camp of the Confederate army, then located between Rienzi and Guntown, Mississippi. He was greeted by Colonel Joseph Wheeler and Colonel E.D. Tracy, of the 19th Alabama Infantry; Captain T.M. Lenoir, a staff officer of commanding general Braxton Bragg; and Captain F.H. Robertson, of the artillery. Such informal truces were still quite common at this stage of the war, and these comrades from the old army took advantage of the opportunity to engage in a wide variety of topics as they exchanged pleasantries. Wheeler and his companions seemed to have loose tongues indeed, as they let slip numerous pieces of military intelligence to their adversary. They informed him of how General P.G.T. Beauregard had been relieved of command of the army, in disgrace, and how the new commander, Braxton Bragg, was now hard at work to reorganize the command. When the subject of upcoming operations was discussed, they told Sheridan that Bragg would not move at all until after the harvest had been completed, so as to be sure of having sufficient sustenance for the horses and men. They added that when the Confederate army did move, it would be west, toward Holly Springs, Mississippi, and West Tennessee. Sheridan could not know that he was being intentionally misinformed through the statements of these Confederate officers. The information that he would take back to his own high command was being deliberately planted in an effort to mask the real intentions of the Confederates, and the deception would work, as planned, when the Southern forces broke camp and set out to challenge Union control of the area.[1]

In fact, General Bragg had already formulated the initial phases of his upcoming campaign, and though he intended to march his army north, they would be heading northeast, not northwest. Bragg had few reasonable options open to him. The Union forces, under the command of Major General Ulysses S. Grant, at Corinth, Mississippi, were too strong for his army to attack. If he invaded West Tennessee, as Wheeler and his conspirators had led Sheridan to believe, it would open Alabama and Georgia to Union invasion. An assault against Nashville would put Bragg's army between Grant's army and one commanded by Major General Don Carlos Buell, each of which was superior to his own in numbers. The only viable option seemed to be a rapid thrust toward Chattanooga, Tennessee, followed by a drive into Middle Tennessee, and possibly Kentucky.[2]

Bragg, a North Carolinian, had graduated from West Point in the class of 1837. He distinguished himself in the Mexican American War and in the fighting against the Seminoles in Florida, rising to the rank of lieutenant colonel. After a 20-year career, he resigned his commission in 1856 to become a planter in his native state. He was appointed to be a brigadier general in the Provisional Army of the Confederacy in 1861, and was assigned to command a coastal district that encompassed Pensacola, Florida, and Mobile, Alabama. In September of that year, he was promoted to major general and was assigned to the command of Albert Sidney Johnston's 2nd Corps, and with that body he took part in the battle of Shiloh. In June of 1862, he received orders to assume command of the Army of

General Braxton Bragg, commander of the Confederate Army of Tennessee. Though commander for only a short period of time, he adopted the bold plan of invading the North and trying to bring Kentucky into the Confederacy. (Courtesy of the United States Army War College.)

Tennessee, replacing Beauregard in that assignment. Bragg was still relatively new at his command assignment when he envisioned a strike against the Union forces in Tennessee and Kentucky, and his officers and men were still just getting to know him.[3]

Brigadier General John Hunt Morgan had departed on July 4 for a twenty-four-day raid in his native Kentucky, and he was reporting that the area was ripe for invasion and could easily be taken away from the Union. Morgan's raid took him through a large portion of the state east of the Louisville and Nashville Railroad. His cavalry traveled over 1,000 miles, captured 17 towns, and took approximately 1,200 Union prisoners, who were all released on their parole not to again take up weapons against the Confederacy until duly exchanged, all at the cost of only 90 of his own men. Morgan was positive that Kentucky was Bragg's for the taking, and he assured the Confederate chief that the natives of the Bluegrass state would rise up to assist any Southern army that came to deliver it from the control of the Union. Morgan had already earned for himself and his command the fame that would make him the western rival of J.E.B. Stuart, by means of his legendary raids into

Colonel Joseph Wheeler. Wheeler's misinformation to Union officers kept the Northern high command off balance, as they planned for an anticipated Confederate thrust against Nashville. Wheeler would shine during the Kentucky campaign, earning overall command of the cavalry detachment and a general's stars. (Courtesy of the United States Army War College.)

enemy territory. He had been promoted to colonel in April of 1862, and would win a general's star before the year was over.[4]

Colonel Wheeler was to be given another assignment in the name of deceiving the Union commanders, and in covering the real purpose of Morgan's raid into Kentucky. Bragg ordered Wheeler to take his new brigade on a feint toward West Tennessee. Given the fact that misinformation concerning Confederate intentions had already been planted with Sheridan, this move would strengthen the Union's belief in that information. It would also draw attention away from

Morgan, who was known for making dramatic raids, and convince the Federals that Morgan's activities were nothing more than that, a raid, not a reconnaissance for future operations. Wheeler set out with his command, about 1,000 strong, in the latter part of July, and made for Holly Springs, Mississippi, where he received infantry reinforcements from Brigadier General John B. Villepigue's brigade. The combined force then struck for Grand Junction, Tennessee, with the intention of attacking the Union garrison stationed there. But Wheeler found the town deserted by the Federals, and had to content himself with destroying the 200 bales of cotton they had left behind. He then determined to threaten the Federal position at Bolivar, followed by attacking the Yankees at Jackson. But General Villepigue recalled his infantry, and Wheeler did not feel his own cavalry force sufficient to undertake the operation. He advanced no farther than Bolivar, where he was once again forced to content himself with the destruction of some 3,000 bales of cotton, gathered there to be sent north.[5]

Wheeler's ruse had the desired effect, however, and Union command took the bait. It was expected that any move by the Confederates would be into West Tennessee, with Nashville being a possible target. With the Federals essentially frozen in position, guarding against a perceived threat against Nashville, the Confederate army was given its marching orders on July 21 for Chattanooga. The infantry was conveyed by train, via Mobile, Alabama, while the artillery and its trains moved overland, through northern Alabama, on the most direct route. Bragg preceded his army and had a meeting with General Edmund Kirby Smith at Chattanooga, Tennessee, on July 31, to come up with a combined operation of the two commands. Though Bragg was senior to the commander of the Department of East Tennessee, he was hesitant to issue any orders to Smith. Instead, he preferred to plan the operation as a joint venture, allowing Smith to conduct what was virtually an independent operation within the overall campaign, which Bragg described as "measures for mutual support and effective co-operation." This loosely tethered arrangement would prove to be anything but effective.[6]

Edmund Kirby Smith had been born in Florida and, because of that, was tagged with the nickname Seminole when he attended West Point. He graduated in the class of 1845, just in time to take part in the Mexican War. Smith exhibited conspicuous gallantry at Cerro Gordo, winning a brevet of captain for his heroism. His pre-war service included a stint as an instructor at West Point, as well as serving as major of the famed 2nd U.S. Cavalry. He was commissioned a brigadier general in the Confederate army in June of 1861, and took part in the fighting at First Manassas, where he was severely wounded. In October of 1861, he was promoted to the rank of major general and sent to command the District of East Tennessee. Smith had had almost a year to familiarize himself with his district and his army, and was used to exercising independent command. Bragg's deference toward Smith was undoubtedly due to the fact that he felt somewhat uncomfortable in being the new commander of an officer who had been conducting his own affairs for such a long time.[7]

Though its numbers would increase as the campaign progressed, Bragg's command totaled some 20,000 men at the outset of the operations, while Kirby Smith's available force totaled around 15,000. General Buell described Bragg's army as being "composed of veteran troops ... and thoroughly inured to hardships." They were surely a hardy lot, and were eager to avenge the military reverses they had suffered during the last year. Many in the ranks were armed

Major General Edmund Kirby Smith. Smith would command a separate Confederate army in what was to be a joint operation between himself and General Bragg in Kentucky. His smashing victory at Richmond boosted morale, and gave promise for a stunning campaign, but the lack of cooperation between the two commanding generals doomed the operation almost before it had begun. (Courtesy of the United States Army War College.)

with old unrifled muskets, and they carried buck and ball cartridges in their cartridge boxes. The Union army they would face would outnumber them, and would be equipped with modern rifled muskets. Nevertheless, the Confederates in the ranks were confident of their ability to whip the Yankees wherever they found them.[8]

The bulk of the Confederate army reached Chattanooga in the first part of August, and Bragg spent the remainder of the month completing his plans and organizing for the campaign. Kirby Smith was the first to initiate the offensive. Reinforced by Brigadier General Patrick Cleburne's brigade, under the command of Colonel B.J. Hill, and Preston Smith's brigade, both under the overall command of General Cleburne, Kirby Smith advanced his army from Knoxville, Tennessee, on August 14, and began his drive for Kentucky. In a series of rapid marches, he bypassed the Union stronghold at Cumberland Gap and struck straight for the Bluegrass region. Smith had intended to capture Cumberland Gap, and the division of Union troops stationed there, under the command of Brigadier General George W. Morgan, until he learned that the Federals were amply provisioned to withstand a siege. Smith knew that it would be extremely difficult to provision his own army in the rugged and barren terrain around the gap, and rather than take the chance of bogging down the entire campaign, he opted to head for central Kentucky, a bountiful area that he knew could support his troops.[9]

Smith's route took him through Barbourville and Crab Orchard as he headed north, in the general direction of Lexington. One Confederate soldier described this portion of the march, and the search for water that would become all too important a part of the campaign:

> We entered the State at a little town called Barboursville, in the southern portion of the state. On the second day's tramp, after leaving Barboursville, having extended our day's march into the night, our pathway was lighted only by the jeweled stars of the firmament, which from their empyrean heights shone in all their pristine glory and splendor. It must have been 9 p.m., and we were still trudging along, footsore, weary, and hungry, when I espied a strong, masculine-looking woman standing in the doorway of a little one-room cabin that stood several yards back from the road. She was shading her eyes with her hands from the light that came from some lightwood fagots, which were burning in the broad, deep fireplace of the cabin, and as she peered out into the darkness, attracted by the rumbling, rustling noise made by the patter of the many feet, endeavoring to detect what it was, I could see her much more plainly than she could see me. As she stood directly between me and the burning lightwood knots, she did not see me until I was within a few steps of her. I made as stately a bow as I could and raising my greasy wool hat said: "Madam, will you be so kind as to inform me how far ahead will it be before we find a stream of water?" Seeing my garb and judging that we were the Southern army, she, doubtless the wife of one of those bushwhackers who had given us no little trouble ever since we reached the mountainous region of East Tennessee and Southern Kentucky and who was then in all probability lurking dangerously near seeking an opportunity to give us one of his murderous bullets, with a scornful, contemptuous look, answered me in a snappish, petulant manner: "I guess you will find it in the Ohio River."[10]

12

By August 29, the Confederates had reached Kingston, some five miles south of Richmond, where Smith's cavalry, under the command of Colonel John S. Scott, encountered a force of Union infantry that gave every indication of making a stand and opposing the further advance of the Southerners. Kirby Smith lost no time in deciding upon a course of action. Scott's cavalry was ordered to skirmish with and develop the Union position, while Cleburne was sent instructions to advance his two brigades straight up the Richmond Road, where he was to serve as the infantry advance of the army. At 5:00 p.m., Cleburne's troops heard the distinctive roar of artillery in front of them, as Federal batteries opened on Scott's cavalry and began driving it from the field. With darkness coming on, Cleburne opted to halt his march and make camp. As a precaution, he ordered that his brigades be formed in line of battle before bedding down for the night. Colonel Scott ordered his cavalry to make camp immediately in

Brigadier General Patrick Cleburne. Cleburne received a painful wound to the mouth at Richmond, but he returned to the army in time to take part in the battle of Perryville. (Courtesy of the United States Army War College.)

front of the infantry, and he rode back to inform Cleburne of that fact, lest there be any confusion about whether it was friend or foe who was moving about in the darkness. The Confederate infantry was more than ready to go into camp. As one gray-clad soldier put it, this march had been "the most dreary, desolate, and fatiguing" that he could "ever remember making during my three years of soldier life." In the three days preceding their arrival at Richmond, the footsore Confederates had marched a distance of approximately 90 miles.[11]

But the weary foot soldiers were to be permitted little peaceful slumber that night. Cleburne had barely finished issuing instructions to his regimental commanders regarding their assigned positions, should a cause for alarm arise during the night, when the sounds of musketry and yelling men became distinguishable in their front. This was closely followed by retreating members of Scott's command, who were being driven, helter-skelter from their camp by Union cavalry. As the Confederate troopers passed through Cleburne's forming lines, the hoof beats of their pursuers were distinctly audible to the infantry. The 48th Tennessee stood directly in the path of the Federals, and when the Union horse reached a point approximately 75 yards in their front, two companies of the regiment were ordered to fire a volley. The Union advance halted, at once, as the stunned troopers tried to reorganize from the shock of the volley. They were not to be given the opportunity to regain their composure, however, for several sharpshooters were pushed forward, from the main line, and when they opened fire on the already stunned and confused cavalrymen, it caused them to break and retreat from the field. Though there are no reports of the killed and wounded on the Federal side during this little skirmish, General Cleburne reported that the 48th Tennessee captured 30 prisoners, 100 stand of arms, and several horses, all at the loss of only one man wounded.[12]

At dawn on August 30, Cleburne began moving his two brigades forward, with B.J. Hill taking the lead. Preston Smith's men followed, a quarter mile behind the front line, in easy supporting distance. A company of cavalry, the Buckner Guards, was sent out ahead of the infantry to find and develop the position of the enemy. They struck the Union skirmish line one-half mile north of Kingston, and could see that the main line was approximately 500 yards north of that, straddling and perpendicular to the Richmond Road. This Union force was under the nominal command of Major General William Nelson, a longtime officer in the old navy, who had left the rolling deck of a ship behind to become an army officer only at the direct request of President Lincoln. But Nelson was not at Richmond when the Confederates were about to attack. Instead, he was at Lexington, some 40 miles away. The Union force was composed of the brigades of Generals Mahlon Manson and Charles Cruft. Manson, being the senior brigadier of the two, assumed overall command of the combined force.[13]

Manson had been informed of the approach of the Confederates, but the Rebel advance had been well screened by Kirby Smith's cavalry, and the Union commander believed that he was facing little more than the nuisance of another raiding party. He immediately issued orders for the two brigades to march south from Rogersville, with Richmond being the objective. When his advance met Scott's cavalry, a few miles south of the town, Manson assumed that this cavalry comprised the sum total of the Confederate force. The actions of Cleburne's infantry, on the night of August 29, disabused Manson of this notion, and he set his men to preparing the defensive position the Buckner Guards reported the following morning. Though Manson was now uncertain of the exact composition or number of the force in his front, he was still responding to the situation as if it were a raiding force that he could easily deal with. Daylight would bring the first clear picture of the situation. Manson discovered that he was facing not a raiding party, but an entire Confederate army, and having already advanced beyond any possible support, he had little choice but to fight it out on this ground.[14]

Cleburne ordered his own brigade, under the direct command of Colonel Hill, to assume a position behind the crest of a low hill, approximately 500 yards in front of the Union line. In the center of this line, he placed Douglas's Arkansas Battery, atop the crest. Smith's Brigade was formed behind Hill's, on the back side of the next low ridge, but still within easy supporting distance. When Douglas's artillery opened, it drove off a group of Yankee cavalry in between the lines, and succeeded in unmasking a Federal battery located on their main line. A brisk artillery duel ensued, as the Confederates sent out skirmishers to protect the right and left flanks. A second advantageous position for artillery was found on the ridge occupied by Hill's men, and Martin's Battery, of Preston Smith's Brigade, was ordered to place their guns there and open fire on the Union line. A real fight was shaping up, and Cleburne was preparing an assault with his men when he received word from Kirby Smith that he was not to bring on a general engagement until Major General Thomas J. Churchill's Division had arrived on the field. Cleburne directed his infantry troops to hold fast to their positions, and instructed the artillery to decrease its rate of fire so as to conserve ammunition for the main battle. For the next two hours, the engagement was reduced to skirmishing and slow, sporadic artillery fire.[15]

Emboldened by the apparent reluctance of the Confederates to attack him, Manson mounted an attack of his own, on Hill's right flank, driving in the skirmishers and threatening to turn the line. The 154th Tennessee, of Smith's Brigade, was ordered to the support of Hill, and was sent to the right of the line to secure the flank. Federal pressure was so extreme, however, that the 13th and 15th Arkansas, under the command of Colonel Lucius E. Polk, had to be hurried to the right to prevent its collapse. The battle was now fiercely joined, and, feeling that Churchill must surely be within supporting distance by this time, Cleburne ordered Smith to advance the remaining three regiments of his brigade, extending Hill's line to the right. The Federals were throwing everything they had into this attack against the Confederate right, and Cleburne correctly assumed that they had weakened their own center in the process. He was sure that his dispositions would ensure the safety of his right flank, leaving Hill's Brigade free to punch a hole in the center of the Union line. Once Smith was in position,

15

Cleburne rode to Hill's portion of the line to personally supervise this assault. He stopped to speak to Colonel Polk, who had been wounded while leading his two regiments to Hill's support, when Cleburne was struck in the left cheek by a minie ball that carried away his teeth on that side. Luckily, he was in the middle of answering a question from Polk when he was hit, and the ball emerged through his open mouth. Though not seriously wounded, Cleburne soon lost the ability to speak, and Preston Smith assumed overall command of the two brigades. Cleburne was taken to a private home near the battlefield, where he received such good treatment that he was well enough to rejoin his command by the beginning of October.[16]

Cleburne was out of the battle, but his plan was followed to perfection by Smith and Hill. Churchill's Division was now on the field, and it extended the Confederate line to the left, joining in Hill's attack against the weakened Union center. Though the Confederates were forcing the Federal troops to give ground, they were not having an easy time of it. Manson's command was outnumbered two to one, and the vast majority of his men had never before seen a battle, but they were providing stiff resistance, contesting every foot of ground. These Union recruits rallied continuously, to the very edge of town, where they planned to make their final stand. One Rebel soldier described the action:

> After driving the Federals some three or four miles, they made another stand. When we came up to where they were, the order to charge was again given, they staying only long enough to give us a volley or two, when they precipitately and in great disorder retreated again. We killed, wounded, and captured a great many of them, while they killed and wounded some of us. As fast as we could we followed them up. It was the month of August and very hot. Often in making a flank movement we would have to go through a cornfield, the sun streaming down on our defenseless heads, the corn completely shutting out any air that might be stirring, and it seemed that we would suffocate.
>
> It must have been about three o'clock in the afternoon when the Federals made their third and last stand, the spot they had selected for that purpose being in the little cemetery just at the outskirts of the town of Richmond, Ky. They sheltered themselves behind the tombstones. We had to approach them through a field of corn which was very tall and in full ear and was enclosed by a high rail fence.... The Federals showed strong and stubborn resistance; but seeing that we steadily advanced toward them, after giving us two or three rounds, they broke into a deep run, showing that they were in a wild and ungovernable panic. Then it was that we charged them with a double-quick, killing, wounding, and capturing many of them.[17]

The 2nd and 48th Tennessee Regiments were leading the charge. Colonel Nixon, of the 48th, was struck in the breast by grapeshot, and the men around him felt that the wound must be fatal. He had been thrown to the ground, but was seen to be struggling to rise up on his knees. Kneeling there, amid the charging men, his voice could be heard above the din of battle: "Forward, Forty-eighth!" The colonel had escaped death. In his breast pocket had been a watch and a pocket Bible, and the grapeshot had struck them both, knocking the wind out of him, but doing him no real harm. Others in the regiment were not so lucky. One hundred twenty-eight men of the 48th Tennessee were killed or wounded in making the attack.[18]

The field—and with it, the spoils—belonged to the Confederates. "The Federals, having relieved themselves of their blankets and extra luggage, left them all in a heap to one side, intending, it is supposed, to replace them as soon as they had driven us back," reported Captain Frank Ryan, "but as the result proved that we did the driving, and not stopping long enough to claim their baggage, it fell to us. In following the retreating Federals we came across a pile of their plunder. Seeing an especially fine and handsome blanket and having a very common one, I selected this one, which was a regular Mackinaw, solid mouse color. In one corner was sewed a piece of red morocco upon which the owner had inscribed his name. I carried it with me all through the Kentucky campaign and intended the very first opportunity to have a coat made of it."[19]

General Manson tried to retreat from the field, but Kirby Smith had sent his cavalry around the Federals to block their means of escape. Manson attempted to break out of the encirclement, but the Confederate horse would not be brushed aside, and he was forced to surrender himself, along with the 3,000 men who were still with him. W.E. Yeatman, a soldier in the 2nd Tennessee Infantry, describes the final phases of the battle. "As we joined our regiment the Federals were in retreat. A rapid pursuit was made by our army in full line of battle. We swept on for several miles. As we emerged from a wooded pasture to the next open field we found the Federals in line a few hundred yards ahead. Immediately to our left their artillery posted with their right, raked our line. We were here the center, our left came up in a few minutes attacking their right with a rush, the tall corn having concealed their approach. The Federal line broke at all points, then we had a race to Richmond." General Nelson had arrived from Lexington, and though he made it to the field in time to see the battle taking place, receiving a painful leg wound in the process, he was far too late to affect the outcome in any way. Nelson could do little but flee toward Lexington, along with the few remaining members of Manson's command. Indeed, many members of Manson's beaten command did not halt their retreat until they reached the Ohio River at Cincinnati, nearly 300 miles away. The retreat was covered by the 9th Pennsylvania Cavalry, under order of General Wright. It was one of the few veteran regiments he had in the area, but their time in service did not make up for a severe disparity in weaponry. The vast majority of the troopers of the 9th Pennsylvania were armed only with sabers and revolvers. They had been issued smoothbore Belgian muskets, which their commander referred to as "the most ineffective arms ever placed in the hands of men." He stated, "Some companies of my regiment have been compelled to turn them over. Nipples blowing out and cast iron hammers (breaking) render them unfit for any service. We have loaded them and attempted to fire by companies. Sometimes three would go off out of sixty or seventy. Many have to be snapped four or five times before the cap will explode." The entire regiment had only 41 Sharps and 13 Maynard carbines. The regiment was successful in carrying out the rear-guard action, mostly because of the fact that the Confederate pursuit was halfhearted. Even so, Company K was captured, almost in its entirety, and was not exchanged until the campaign in Kentucky was ended.[20]

On August 31, Major General Horatio G. Wright, commanding the Department of Ohio, telegraphed Major General Henry Halleck in Washington: "The force engaged in the battle in front of Richmond was utterly broken up, and after all the exertion to collect stragglers only some 800 or 900 could be found. The remainder were killed, captured, or scattered over the country."[21]

The battle of Richmond was one of the most lopsided victories of the war. Casualties to Kirby Smith's army were mostly from Cleburne's Brigade, and were relatively light. Losses on the Federal side were 1,050 killed and wounded, and 4,303 captured, for a total of 5,353. In addition, nine pieces of artillery, 10,000 stand of small arms, and a large quantity of military supplies stored in Richmond fell into the hands of the Confederates. Nelson, the top Federal commander in the region, had been wounded, and his second in command, General Manson, had been captured.[22] The complete success achieved in the battle should have infused Kirby Smith with a killer instinct to finish off his foe, but the battle seemed to have the opposite effect. Smith had previously maintained a low opinion of the Union troops he would be facing from the time he first entered Kentucky. After all, they were mostly green, untried recruits, and Smith expected them to retreat at the first sight of a veteran Rebel army.

Though he had delivered a crushing defeat to the Federals at Richmond, Smith seems now to have become imbued with a healthy respect for the Union recruits. Outnumbered two to one, they had not fled at the first volley, but had held their ground as tenaciously as veterans, and had given up the contest only when they were completely surrounded and cut off. Smith had been forced to reevaluate his estimation of the fighting spirit of the enemy he faced. Instead of being flushed with success, and emboldened, Smith became cautious after

Richmond. That caution would have far-reaching effects on the outcome of the campaign.

For the men in the ranks, the end of the battle ushered in a well deserved period of rest. Richmond was filled with military supplies of all kinds, and the conquering Confederates lost little time in confiscating them for public or personal use. "They had a great quantity of stores and munitions of war at this place," reported one soldier, "which seemed to have been a distributing bureau; and here I first saw how they were being fed — canned fruits of all kinds, condensed milk (the first I ever saw), cheese, and other edibles. They also had large quantities of clothing, shoes, hats, etc., all of which we put to good use. I well remember the supper I sat down to the night after the battle. It would grace any gentleman's table in this day and time. Asking no questions as to where it came from, as I was in charge of the guard, I merely sat down and ate heartily." Several days were spent in Richmond, burying the dead, paroling prisoners, and gathering transportation with which to haul the captured stores. The completeness of the victory was apparent to the men. They had met their first test of the campaign and had annihilated the enemy. Captain Ryan spoke for many when he said: "So, taken all in all, it was a grand and a most signal victory, having the effect of raising the morale of the army to a very high state, so that when we left Richmond for our northward march we believed fully that we were invincible."[23]

The capture of clothing was especially beneficial to Smith's army. "We were all nearly naked," wrote one Confederate. "The pants I wore (coat I had not) were made of some thin material, and my canteen, haversack, and belt had worn holes through on both sides, and in a short time they would not have held together. I confiscated a pair of blue pants, a gray army shirt, a pair of excellent shoes, and hung my old ones out on a fence."[24]

Smith's next concern would be the Union division of Brigadier General George W. Morgan, stationed in the stronghold of Cumberland Gap. The position had originally been bypassed, but Smith now reversed his decision and decided to move against the bastion. Brigadier General Carter L. Stevenson's Division was assigned to deal with Morgan, assisted by Brigadier General Humphrey Marshall's Brigade, of 4,000 infantry and a battery, which had entered the state from western Virginia, and John Hunt Morgan's cavalry. George Morgan had been concerned that Stevenson would attack his position as early as August 17. The area around Cumberland Gap had been stripped of Union soldiers to oppose Bragg's advance, and Morgan's Division served as the only Federal presence in that region. Though he held a strong position, Morgan did not think he could defend it against the superior force that was being gathered to attack him, and he knew that he could not outlast a siege. On September 16, he determined to evacuate the position and try to make his way to the Ohio River. A large wagon train, accompanied by the 33rd Indiana, two companies of the 3rd Kentucky, and the 9th Ohio Battery, started that day toward Manchester, as Morgan made preparations to retreat with his main body. He was in the act of destroying military stores when a body of Confederates was seen approaching with a flag of truce. Morgan sent a small party of officers to meet the flag, outside of his own picket line. While the officers were talking to the Confederates, a large plume of smoke was seen to be rising from the Union position. The Confederates inquired as to its meaning, and asked if Morgan was preparing to evacuate the gap. Lieutenant Colonel Gallup, the leader of the Union party, was quick to come up with a response that concealed the true meaning of the smoke. When asked if the Yankees were evacuating, he replied: "Not much. Morgan has cut away the timber obstructing the range of his guns, and they are now burning the brush on the mountainside." The Confederates seemed to be satisfied with the answer, and returned to their own lines with news that Morgan planned to make a determined defense of the gap. In the meantime, the Federals made every preparation to slip out of the place that night.[25]

General Morgan's intention seemed to be to reach Maysville, on the Ohio River, via Manchester, Booneville, and Mount Sterling. Colonel John Hunt Morgan's Confederate cavalry, some 900 strong, was in his front, trying to delay his movements until Marshall, advancing from eastern Kentucky, or Stevenson, pursuing from Cumberland Gap, could overtake the Union column and attack it. On September 21, fearing entrapment by the Confederates, Morgan changed his line of march to the east, and John Hunt Morgan spent the next two days trying to get his cavalry back in a blocking position in front of the Federals. Though John Hunt Morgan's delaying tactics allowed the Federals to advance only 30 miles in six days, neither Marshall nor Stevenson was able to get within striking distance. The Confederate attack was reduced to merely the skirmishing and forays of Morgan's gray-clad troopers. On October 1, John Hunt Morgan received orders to rejoin Kirby Smith's main body, and the pursuit was given up. George Morgan was allowed to escape with his command, having suffered only eighty casualties in the process.[26]

The Union authorities were duly concerned about Kirby Smith's presence in the Bluegrass region of Kentucky, but they were still considering Braxton Bragg's army to be the main threat. Nothing Kirby Smith had done had changed the opinion of the Federal top brass that Nashville, or possibly Memphis, was to be the real objective of the Confederates, once the campaign began in earnest. Smith's movements were viewed as a feint, calculated to throw off the Union army and cause it to take to the field to oppose him, thus uncovering Nashville, or Memphis, to Bragg's army for easy capture. Don Carlos Buell was a cautious man. He would wait to see what movements Bragg made before committing himself to any particular plan of action.

Back in Chattanooga, Bragg had been busy finalizing plans for his own invasion of Kentucky. By August 21 everything was in order, and he directed his army to cross the Tennessee River at Harrison's Ferry, some nine miles above the city. Since there was but one transport available, it took several days to get the entire army across. The soldiers took advantage of this delay, "which allowed the boys in gray an opportunity of bathing."[27]

By September 5, Bragg's army had reached Sparta, Tennessee, and he received information detailing the battle of Richmond, as well as a letter from Kirby Smith requesting him to turn north immediately and join in the invasion of Kentucky. Bragg was elated by the news, and the troops were exuberant. That same day, as the Confederate column moved forward, it was greeted by a

Brigadier General George W. Morgan. His Union troops held the important pass at Cumberland Gap. Though Kirby Smith opted to bypass this stronghold in his initial advance, it later gained the full attention of his army. (Courtesy of the United States Army War College.)

large sign, nailed on a tree by advanced members of the pioneer corps, upon which was written: "You now cross from Tennessee to Kentucky." The seat of war had been moved to Kentucky, and "well did the boys in 'dirty gray' make the welkin ring as they at one step bounded across the narrow but visible line drawn for their observation and exultation."[28]

Braxton Bragg commemorated the symbolic step into Kentucky by issuing a proclamation to the troops:

> I. The signal triumph of our arms in Virginia over the combined forces of McClellan and Pope had hardly been announced to the whole of this

command before we are again called upon to rejoice and give thanks to God for a victory as brilliant and complete achieved in our own campaign by the troops under Maj-Gen. E. Kirby Smith at Richmond, Ky., on the 30th ultimo. The enemy, under Major-General Nelson, was completely routed, with the commander wounded, one general killed, and one captured, with 3,000 other prisoners. Not the least important of the fruits secured was the whole of the enemy's artillery, small-arms, and transportation.

II. Comrades, our campaign opens most auspiciously and promises complete success. Your general is happy and proud to witness the tone and conduct of his army. Contented and cheerful under privations and strictly regardful of the rights of citizens, you have achieved a victory over yourselves which insures success against every foe. The enemy is in full retreat with consternation and demoralization devastating his ranks. To secure the full fruits of this condition we must press on vigorously and unceasingly. You will be called on to make greater sacrifices still, to suffer other, perhaps greater, privations, but your generals will share them and a grateful people will reward you. Alabamans, your state is redeemed. An arrogant foe no longer treads her soil. Tennesseeans, the restoration of your capital and State government is almost accomplished without firing a gun. You return to your invaded homes conquerors and heroes. Kentuckians, the first great blow has been struck for your freedom. The manacles will soon fall from your limbs, when we know you will arise and strike for your freedom, your women, and your alters. Soldiers from the Gulf, South Carolina, Georgia, and Arkansas, we share the happiness of our more fortunate brothers, and will press on with them, rejoicing in the hope that a brighter future is in store for the fruitful fields, happy homes, and fair daughters of our own sunny South.

Braxton Bragg,
General, Commanding.[29]

Some of Bragg's men had celebrated the invasion of Kentucky a bit more than they should have. One Alabamian with the army told of how he and some comrades had been detailed to ensure that there was no whiskey brought into the camps. It was quiet enough in the early part of the night, but about midnight two fellows came riding in on wagon mules they had "borrowed" from a teamster. When halted they said they had been out foraging, and their wagon had broken down and they were returning to camp for repairs. One carried a jug and the other had more than his share of canteens, which looked suspicious, and on examination they were found to contain apple brandy instead of the buttermilk they claimed.

> Our orders were positive, and we had to arrest them, but were not as honest as "Si and Shorty" when they arrested the smugglers in Middle Tennessee and broke the bottles. Instead, we proceeded to destroy the brandy in a different

way, assisted by the prisoners, who took the matter good-naturedly, and seemed willing to divide.

In a short time we heard coming from the same direction more who evidently had been imbibing pretty freely, judging from the noise they made yelling, laughing and singing merry songs. They ran right into our trap, entirely oblivious of danger lurking in front, and very much surprised as they had passed out on the same road before we were posted. They, too, were loaded down with canteens all filled with apple brandy; and from that time the boys were coming in at intervals the remainder of the night.[30]

The next morning, the entire company, officers and privates, was placed under arrest for their celebration. Though the privates were released from arrest in three days, the officers were not pardoned until October 8.

Thus far, all seemed to be going well with the campaign. Smith had won a brilliant victory, and Bragg had his army in the state, ready to initiate joint operations. But events were already taking place far behind the Confederate advance that would affect the final outcome. Generals Sterling Price and Earl Van Dorn had been counted on to provide support for Bragg's offensive, both by supplying manpower and by pinning Union forces in their area down so that they could not shift troops to Buell's army to assist in opposing Bragg. Union Major General William S. Rosecrans did not intend to be tied down, however. He moved against Price's position at Iuka, Mississippi, and the result was that Price himself was pinned down. Bragg headed west, toward Carthage, Tennessee, arriving at that place on September 9. Colonel Joe Wheeler and his cavalry had been harassing the Federal forces at Altamont, and the overall impression given by Bragg's army was that Nashville was indeed its target. Military Governor Andrew Johnson was in the city and was fully taken in by Bragg's movements. When he learned that Buell's plan was not to prepare for a vigorous defense of Nashville, but rather merely to resupply his army before going out in search of Bragg, Johnson made known his objections in a letter to the general dated September 14:

> It is all important that Major-General Thomas and his forces, as now
> assigned, should remain in Nashville. There is the utmost confidence in
> his bravery and capacity to defend Nashville against any odds. I am advised
> that, including your division of the army, there are not less than 75,000
> men in Kentucky and the number increasing, so you will be enabled to meet
> Smith and Bragg successfully. I was reliably informed on Yesterday that a
> portion of Bragg's forces were lingering about Carthage and the Cumberland
> River. Bragg no doubt with them, daily informed as to the number of our
> forces passing into Kentucky and the force left here. If our strength is much
> reduced at this point they will be induced to attack Nashville as a matter of
> course. In conclusion I express the strong and earnest hope that the present

assignment of forces under General Thomas for the defense of Nashville may not be disturbed.[31]

Johnson's opinion of the military situation was already outdated by the time he wrote this message to Buell. True, Carthage was only 50 miles from the Tennessee state capital, but the Confederates were coming no closer. Bragg had already turned his army north, and by September 12 it was in Glasgow, Kentucky. Buell now had definitive proof, for the first time in the campaign, that Nashville was not the target. He therefore left a small but substantial garrison to defend the city and quell the fears of Governor Johnson, and with the rest of his army, he set out on a march that paralleled that of Bragg. Buell's shadowing of the Confederate army was to be a cautious enterprise. Though the Union commander was now sure that Nashville was not the objective of the Rebel army, he had no clear information as to what the intended objective was, so Buell organized his forces, marched as the Confederates marched, and tried to decide on his own course of action.

CHAPTER TWO

Delay at Munfordville

The route Braxton Bragg chose for his army in Kentucky was dictated by his need to secure forage and supplies. Bowling Green was a possible source for capturing the needed supplies, but Bragg felt that that place was too heavily fortified by the Federals to risk an attack. Reports had come in that a large quantity of Federal stores were to be found at Glasgow, so Bragg opted to make that the first destination for his army, while he tried to make up his mind what the final objective of the campaign would be.

Louisville and Cincinnati were both possible targets, and each had merits. The capture of Louisville, the capital and largest city in the state, would enable the Confederates to claim the seat of government and add legitimacy to the installation of a Southern government. If Cincinnati was seized, the Confederates would be taking the war to the North, and the political benefit that would be derived from capturing a Northern city could be significant in the Confederacy's negotiations with European powers. In either case, the Confederates would be assured of acquiring a large amount of captured stores and munitions from these Federal staging areas. But the decision as to a final objective was more in the hands of fate than it was in the hands of Bragg. His arrangement with Kirby Smith provided for a loose command structure that was already beginning to hamper the Confederate invasion. Communication between the two commands was minimal, and Bragg was uncertain, most of the time, as to the exact location, or intentions, of Smith's army. In addition, he was receiving reports that General Buell's army had left Nashville, and he could be certain that Buell's Federal army intended to intercept his force and bring it to battle. The shortage of supplies may have dictated that Glasgow become Bragg's first objective in the invasion, but even as his army marched toward that place events were taking shape that would ensure that Bragg would largely be reacting to the situation, not controlling it.

Buell was being prodded and pressured, but he was in a better position to influence his own destiny than was Bragg. Having received large reinforcements from the armies of Major Generals William S. Rosecrans and Ulysses S. Grant, Buell would have a numerical supremacy to Bragg's army when he eventually brought that force to battle. But then the numbers had been on the side of the Federals even before the campaign began. Counting the armies under Buell, Grant, Rosecrans, and Wright, and with the commands at Cumberland Gap, Bowling Green, and throughout central Kentucky, Bragg and Smith would be facing an available Union force that outnumbered them by a three-to-one margin. The Confederates had to win victories, and had to win them quickly before all of the available Union manpower in the area could be collected and brought against them. Buell, on the other hand, could afford to be more cautious. He commanded an army that was, in numbers, more than a match for the Confederates arrayed against him, and he was assured of receiving support from many different quarters, should it become necessary. The longer the campaign lasted, the more lopsided would become the Federal advantage in manpower.

But the pressure from Washington was extreme. On August 18, Buell received a message from General Halleck that let him know how displeased the administration was with his actions to date. "So real is the dissatisfaction here at the apparent want of energy and activity in your district, that I was this morning notified to have you removed, I got the matter delayed till we could hear further of your movements."[1]

Don Carlos Buell was a member of the West Point class of 1841 that saw 21 of its graduates become general officers in the Civil War. In the 20 years that preceded the Civil War, Buell had seen action against the Seminoles in Florida and had fought in the Mexican War. He had been seriously wounded at Churubusco, but the gallant manner in which he led his men earned him the brevet of major. Following the Mexican War, Buell had been assigned to the adjutant general's department, and was serving in that capacity, with the rank of lieutenant colonel, in San Francisco, when the war broke out. He was commissioned a brigadier general of volunteers in May of 1861, and was ordered east, joining George B. McClellan's Army of the Potomac in September of that year. After a brief stint with the Army of the Potomac, McClellan chose Buell to command the Army of the Ohio, and assigned him to lead that army from Kentucky into East Tennessee. He was responsible for capturing Nashville, Tennessee, and had been instrumental in saving the Union army from disaster at Shiloh. He served under Major General Henry Halleck during the Corinth campaign, and was promoted to major general in March of 1862. In June of 1862, he had been charged with the mission of trying to take Chattanooga, Tennessee. Bragg's offensive upset the

Union plans to capture Chattanooga, and forced Buell to adapt to the changing situations. The general had achieved success thus far in the war, but he was also a close friend of McClellan's and was married to a Southern girl, both of which provided ammunition for his detractors.[2]

Buell's decision was to march his army for Murfreesboro, Tennessee, and assume a position from which he could monitor Confederate movements and plan for future operations. In this, he was quite correct. At Murfreesboro, he had his army in an optimum position to react to whatever moves the Confederate army might make. Should the Southerners head west, toward Nashville, he would be in position to block them and offer battle. If the Confederates kept heading north, into Kentucky, he was also in a favorable position to intercept them before they reached Lexington or Louisville. Though Buell received severe criticism from both the War Department and from General Halleck for not rushing out and offering battle to Bragg's army immediately, it

Major General Don Carlos Buell. The Union army Buell would lead was largely made up of new recruits and newly promoted officers. Its mettle would be sorely tested in the Kentucky campaign. Buell's own performance was severely criticized, and his reputation ruined, as a result of the Confederate invasion. (Courtesy of the United States Army War College.)

would seem that his course of action was exactly correct, given his lack of reliable information as to the Confederate intentions. He placed his army in a position where it could react quickly to any exigency the situation might offer as the Southern plans unfolded before him. Buell knew that time was on his side and he did not wish to hastily commit his army.

During this time, Buell seemed to be the only Union officer who was confident about the disposition of his forces. By the time Bragg's army had reached

Sparta, Tennessee, it had thrown Northern leadership into somewhat of a panic. Major General Horatio Wright had sent a frantic message to the governor of Indiana requesting reinforcements from that state, asserting that Cincinnati was in immediate danger. News from the front was slow in reaching Washington, and for all President Lincoln knew, Bragg's army had disappeared and was likely to turn up anywhere. Lincoln wired Brigadier General Jeremiah T. Boyle, at Louisville, requesting current information as to the last known whereabouts of the Confederates, and Boyle was forced to answer that he had no idea where Bragg's army might be. Lincoln next wired Wright, in Cincinnati, and asked, "Do you know to any certainty where General Bragg is? May he not be in Virginia?" Wright's response was simply, "Nothing reliable about Bragg." Buell seemed to be the only Union officer in the area with any definite information as to the location of the Rebel army. Colonel Wheeler, in advance of the main body, had driven in the Union outpost at Altamont, and had destroyed railroad and telegraph lines north of Nashville. Buell was able to give Lincoln some idea as to the status of the Confederates when he telegraphed that, "Bragg is certainly this side of the Cumberland Mountains with his whole force, except what is in Kentucky under Smith. His movements will probably

General John C. Breckinridge. Breckinridge was a former vice president of the United States, and leader of the famed "Orphan Brigade." Kentuckians were well aware of how the men in this brigade had been detached from their homes and families by joining the Confederate army. Unwilling to suffer the same fate, most Kentuckians waited to see if the Southern army was in their state to stay, before enlisting in the army. (Courtesy of the United States Army War College.)

depend upon mine...I shall endeavor to hold Nashville, and at the same time drive Smith out of Kentucky."[3]

Bragg had few of the assurances with which Buell could comfort himself and with which he could hedge his bets in the coming campaign. Aware of the disparity in numbers between the two armies, Bragg had sought to augment his force by receiving detachments from the armies commanded by Major Generals Earl Van Dorn and Sterling Price. With troops from these armies, as well as the Kentuckians under the command of Brigadier General John C. Breckinridge, Bragg felt that he could hold his own against anything the Federals might throw at him.

But Bragg's overall strategy was already beginning to fall apart by the time he reached Sparta, Tennessee. Price and Van Dorn were to provide reinforcements to Bragg's army, while at the same time keeping the Union armies, under Grant and Rosecrans, from doing the same. The opposite occurred. Grant and Rosecrans kept the Confederates occupied at Iuka and Corinth, and though Price appeared more than willing to cooperate with Bragg, Van Dorn seemed to have other plans. Once Richmond placed Van Dorn in overall command of the two armies, Price could do little but obey the orders of his superior.

Brigadier General Nathan Bedford Forrest joined Bragg at Sparta with his cavalry command. Being the only brigadier general of cavalry in the area, Forrest expected to be given command of that arm in the coming campaign. His rank and accomplishments to date should certainly have warranted such an appointment, but Bragg failed to bestow it. Bragg permitted Joe Wheeler to retain his command, and to operate independently of Forrest. At first, Forrest did not object to the arrangement, but when he began to criticize Bragg's movements in Kentucky, he was detailed back to Tennessee with his command. Wheeler would command the cavalry of Bragg's army. This was to be the first of several altercations that would take place between Bragg and Forrest in the course of the war.[4]

When Bragg reached Glasgow, Kentucky, he decided to test the reports that had been received from John Hunt Morgan that Kentuckians would rally to the Confederate banner in hordes. With no help coming from Price or Van Dorn, the army needed to be augmented by some means, so Bragg issued a proclamation to the people of Kentucky on September 14 that read:

> Kentuckians, I have entered your State with the Confederate Army of the West, and offer you an opportunity to free yourselves from the tyranny of a despotic ruler. We come not as conquerors or as despoilers, but to restore to you the liberties of which you have been deprived by a cruel and relentless foe. We come to guarantee to all the sanctity of their homes and alters, to

punish with a rod of iron the despoilers of your peace, and to avenge the cowardly insults to your women. With all non-combatants the past shall be forgotten. I shall enforce a rigid discipline and shall protect all in their persons and property. Needful supplies must be had for my army, but they shall be paid for at fair and remunerating prices. Believing that the heart of Kentucky is with us in our great struggle for constitutional freedom, we have transferred from our own soil to yours not a band of marauders, but a powerful and well-disciplined army. Your gallant Buckner leads the van. Marshall is on the right, while Breckinridge, dear to us as to you, is advancing with Kentucky's valiant sons to receive the honor and applause due to their heroism. The strong hands which in part have sent Shiloh down to history and the nerved arms which have kept at bay from our own homes the boastful army of the enemy are here, to assist, to liberate you. Will you remain indifferent to our call, or will you not rather vindicate the fair fame of your once free and envied State? We believe that you will, and that the memory of your gallant dead who fell at Shiloh, their faces turned homeward, will rouse you to a manly effort for yourselves and posterity.

Kentuckians, we have come with joyous hopes. Let us not depart in sorrow, as we shall if we find you wedded in your choice to your present lot. If you prefer Federal rule, show it by your frowns and we will return whence we came. If you choose rather to come within the folds of our brotherhood, then cheer us with the smiles of your women and lend your willing hands to secure you in your heritage of liberty.

Women of Kentucky, your persecutions and heroic bearing have reached our ear. Banish henceforth forever from your minds the fear of loathsome prisons or insulting visitations. Let your enthusiasm have free rein. Buckle on the armor of your kindred, your husbands, sons, and brothers, and scoff with shame him who would prove recreant in his duty to you, his country, and his God.

Bragg supplemented this proclamation with an appeal directed at the Kentucky Home Guard:

To the Home Guard of Kentucky:

The officers and members of the Home Guards are hereby required to report and deliver up to the nearest commanding officer of this army all arms in their hands. Those complying with this order will be regarded as noncombatants; all failing to do so will be considered as enemies and treated accordingly. Captains of your companies will be held responsible for the execution of this order, and will report to these headquarters all who refuse to comply herewith.

Braxton Bragg,
General, Commanding[5]

Bragg's proclamation lacked the persuasive or assuring tenor necessary to stir the passions of the people of Kentucky. His comments concerning Kentuckians choosing the Federal side make the statement convoluted, and the overall tone seems to be more begging than rallying. Then, in the supplement to the Home Guard, he flip-flops, and destroys all of his intended good in proclaiming that the Confederate army is in Kentucky as liberators, not conquerors, when he demands that all organized Home Guards within the state turn in their weapons. Kentuckians were wary of leaving their homes to join the Confederate army in the first place. Though the brigade of Kentuckians under Breckinridge had already won everlasting fame within the state, their moniker of the "Orphan Brigade" was one that made men stop and think. Possible recruits were watching to see if the Confederate army was indeed here to stay before they made up their minds to cast their lots with the Confederacy. They had no desire to join Bragg's army if that meant they would not only be leaving their homes, but also would be leaving Kentucky, as had the men of the "Orphan Brigade," in the hands of the Federals. The result was a sort of standoff. Kentuckians were hesitant to join the Confederate army if Bragg did not intend to stay in Kentucky, but Bragg could not hope to maintain his army there unless Kentuckians rallied to it in droves. His proclamation did little to encourage the people of the state that he was there to stay, and enlistments were accordingly few. Ten thousand muskets had been procured with which to arm the recruits Bragg had been led to believe would join his standard. All told, a brigade, or approximately 3,000 men, actually volunteered from Kentucky, but even that number was deceptive. Many of those who volunteered joined existing units, so that their numbers were swallowed up. There were not the Kentucky regiments and brigades to point to as a ground-swelling of support. The majority of the volunteers joined Kirby Smith's army, rather than Bragg's, further adding to the commander's disappointment. Bragg stated to his aide that: "The people here have too many fat cattle and are too well-off to fight." Kirby Smith echoed that sentiment when he stated: "The Kentuckians are slow in rallying to our standard. Their hearts are evidently with us, but their blue-grass and fat-grass are against us." If the Confederates were going to stay in Kentucky, they would have to do so without large-scale reinforcements from any sector.[6]

Lack of anticipated support was the first bedevilment to Bragg's plans, but a stubborn Union colonel was about to cause a costly delay in the Confederate advance. General Buell had learned of the true intent of the Confederates while his army was positioned at Murfreesboro, through a captured Southern dispatch. Buell now had proof positive of Bragg's intentions, and he was at last ready to commit his army. He returned to Nashville to organize for the coming campaign.

Leaving a sizeable detachment under the command of Major General George H. Thomas to defend the city, he started out for Louisville on September 7, with five divisions. It would be a race to see which army could get to that city first, but Buell was to receive a five-day start due to the Confederates being delayed before Munfordville.[7]

Colonel John T. Wilder left Louisville on September 1 with 214 newly recruited replacements for his 17th Indiana Infantry Regiment. They were bound for Nashville, where they would join the rest of the regiment, then serving with Buell's army. When the party reached the Red River Bridge, near Clarksville, Tennessee, they found that the bridge had been burned by raiders from John Hunt Morgan's command. Wilder was informed that a culvert had also been destroyed in their rear, effectively eliminating the possibility of using the railroad to go forward or backward. Darkness had fallen, and though the Yankees could not see them, a detachment of Morgan's Confederates were known to be behind the Federals. Wilder took command of the situation and decided on a bold course of action:

> My recruits were unarmed. There were about twenty armed convalescent soldiers on the train, returning to their commands from the hospital at Louisville.... I immediately formed the armed convalescents as a line of skirmishers (it being quite dark) across the line of the railroad, and the recruits in line in their rear, and advanced in front of the railroad train toward the destroyed culvert. The enemy, supposing my force all armed, fell back when the skirmish line opened fire on them, and the culvert was soon repaired, and we went with the train to Bowling Green, Ky.[8]

When Wilder reached Bowling Green, he was directed to take the men that were with him and make for the bridge at the Green River, near Munfordville. General Wright issued these orders with the caution that Bragg was about to invade Kentucky and Wilder was "to hold the post to the last if attacked."[9]

Wilder arrived at Munfordville on September 8, and immediately assumed command of the defenses at the bridge. His 214 new recruits were now armed, and they would augment "some two hundred Kentucky recruits, also the Sixty-seventh and Eighty-ninth Regiments of Indiana Infantry, of some seven hundred men each." The defenses consisted of only a log stockade and some trenches, situated south of the bridge. Wilder described the stockade as being weak, and capable of holding only about 50 men, and he felt that the trenches were totally inadequate for the defense of the bridge. He set his command to work, at once, to strengthen the fortifications. A large, star-shaped earthwork was constructed a half mile upriver, at Woodsonville, on ground that commanded the approaches to the bridge and would provide covering fire for the entrenchments. This work, named Fort Craig, would hold 200 men, and its firepower was increased by adding two cannon. A line of trenches and rifle pits was dug to connect the stockade and Fort Craig, and a field of fire was created in front of the position by the cutting of trees and brush, from which entanglements were constructed to hopefully impede the advance of the enemy.[10]

Wilder's command was joined by a number of men from the 33rd Kentucky Home Guard. These troops were unarmed, but since they were mostly locals, Wilder ordered that they be sent out into the countryside to scout for Bragg's army. The Kentuckians did exemplary service in their scouting assignment, providing Wilder with news of Bragg's advance when it was still 50 miles away.[11]

On September 12, Bragg sent Brigadier General James R. Chalmers' brigade of Mississippians to Cave City, in advance of the main body, to secure the railroad, where he could be in a position to intercept and cut off the Union forces under Buell, should they decide to pass that way. Chalmers was successful in capturing the depot, but all trains and rolling

Colonel John T. Wilder. Wilder's staunch resistance at Munfordville cost the Confederate army precious time, and enabled Buell to be able to consolidate his forces for a decisive battle with Bragg. (Courtesy of the United States Army War College.)

stock had been removed prior to his arrival. It was at Cave City that Chalmers received information that there was a force of some 3,000 Federals guarding a bridge at Munfordville. He was told that the Federals were largely new recruits, and saw an opportunity to bag the lot of them with his veteran brigade. One of Chalmers' officers, Major E.T. Sykes, of the 10th Mississippi, had a more disparaging opinion of Chalmers' motives when he stated that "Chalmers considered it a fine opportunity to win a Major-Generals star."[12]

Chalmers started his column toward Munfordville on the night of September 13, at approximately the same time Wilder's garrison was receiving its first demand to surrender. Colonel John S. Scott, whose 1st Louisiana Cavalry was performing detached service from Kirby Smith's command, sent this first demand at around eight o'clock on the evening of the 13th. Scott, like Chalmers, had heard that the garrison consisted of green men, and he estimated that the garrison would surrender at the first show of force from the Confederates. But Scott was misinformed, as well as being brash and arrogant. The garrison was made up mostly of veteran men, and even if Scott's information had been correct, his regiment numbered only about 900 men. The Federals outnumbered him almost two-to-one, and would be fighting from behind reasonably strong works. Scott's demand was more bluff and bravado than anything else. Wilder wired headquarters in Louisville that, "I peremptorily refused. He claims to have me cut off and surrounded. I shall fight anything that comes." In the end, Scott was forced to watch the garrison from a respectful distance as he waited for the arrival of Chalmers' brigade.[13]

Chalmers' brigade arrived in front of the Federal works at sunrise on the morning of September 14. After driving in the Union pickets, the brigade was formed with the 29th Mississippi on the right and the 10th Mississippi on the left. The Confederate line advanced "through an open field three-quarters of a mile under fire of the enemy's artillery and small arms from behind formidable entrenchments and earthworks." Initially, the attack seemed to be going well for the Confederates. Colonel Edward Walthall's 29th Mississippi had reached Fort Craig, and was in the process of bridging a ditch around the earthwork. At this moment, Colonel Scott's cavalry mistakenly fired on Walthall's men, causing the regiment to retire. The 10th Mississippi advanced to within 50 yards of the Union right flank, where they were held up by a ravine filled with abatis. The regiment became pinned down in this position, and for the next two hours they slugged it out with the fort's defenders, unable to see, because of the lay of the ground, that the 29th Mississippi had already retired.[14]

Federal resistance was dogged and determined. Colonel Wilder estimated that he had around 2,100 men in the works, but he had only 1,241 muskets, so only slightly more than half his men were armed. Major Abbott, of the 67th Indiana, commanded at Fort Craig, along with 200 of his men and two 12-pounder cannon. During the hottest part of the fight, the regimental flag was shot away. Major Abbott leapt to the top of the parapet, sword in hand, to defend the banner, and was instantly shot dead. He fell on the flag, staining it with his blood. Lieutenant Mason, also of the 67th Indiana, was in charge of the two cannon in the works. Fire from the Southern infantry became so hot as to drive his cannoneers from their post, or pin them down, unable to service their guns. Lieutenant Mason kept his cannon in the fight single-handedly, and poured such a deadly fire of canister into the approaching ranks that he was instrumental in thwarting the attack. Once the Confederates had been repulsed, the regimental flag, and the body of Major Abbott, was retrieved. The banner had been pierced by 146 bullets, and the flagstaff had been struck 11 times.[15]

Wilder had been led to believe that he was facing a vastly superior force. He was still of that opinion more than 40 years later, when he wrote his memoirs of the battle, stating that he was facing nearly an entire Confederate division. Chalmers was largely responsible for this illusion. Failing to capture his objective by force, he tried to do so through deception and bluff. Following the repulse of his troops, Chalmers sent the following message through the lines to Wilder:

> Colonel J.T. Wilder, Commanding United States Forces at Green River:
> You have made a gallant defense of your position, and to avoid further bloodshed I demand an unconditional surrender of your forces. I have six regiments of infantry, one battalion of sharp-shooters, and have just been reinforced by a brigade of cavalry under Colonel Scott, with two batteries of artillery. I have two regiments on the north side of the river, and you can not escape. The railroad track is torn up in your rear, and you can not receive reinforcements. General Bragg's army is but a short distance in the rear,
> James R. Chalmers,
> Commanding First Brigade of Right Wing, Army of the Mississippi.[16]

Chalmers was overstating his own strength, and even Wilder must have realized this by his statement about "recently" being reinforced by Scott. Scott had been on the scene since the previous evening, and had been the first one to demand the surrender of the position. His confidence buoyed by the successful defense of his works, Wilder sent back a rather taunting reply:

> Brigadier-General James R. Chalmers, Commanding First Brigade,
> Right Wing, Army of the Mississippi:
> Your note demanding the unconditional surrender of my forces has been received. Thank you for your compliments. If you wish to avoid further bloodshed, keep out of the range of my guns. As to reinforcements, they are now entering my works. I think I can defend my position against your entire force; at least I shall try to do so.
> J.T. Wilder, Colonel, Seventeenth Indiana Volunteers,
> Commanding Force at Green River.[17]

At approximately 9:30 A.M., General Chalmers proposed a truce for such a period as was necessary for each side to remove their dead and wounded. Wilder not only agreed to the truce, but sent some of his men to help remove those Confederates who had fallen near his lines. They loaded the wounded Southerners who were too badly injured to be rudely moved onto two railroad flatcars and pushed the cars by hand a distance of almost two miles to the Confederate lines.

In addition, Wilder provided the services of some of the surgeons he had under his command.[18]

In many ways, the truce was just a continuation of Chalmers' ruse. Yes, he wanted to carry his dead and wounded off the field, but he also had other, more military reasons for proposing the cease-fire. During the cessation of hostilities Chalmers was able to extricate his troops that had been pinned down by the abatis-filled ravine, and by the fire from the Federal works.[19]

The engagement proved a lopsided victory for the Federals. The attacking Confederates had lost a total of 228 men in killed and wounded, as compared to 37 for the Union. One company of the 10th Mississippi lost 32 men. The balance of power was also swinging toward the Federals again. Colonel Cyrus L.

Dunham arrived from Louisville after the battle with six companies of the 50th Indiana Infantry and a company from the 78th Indiana Infantry. Dunham was senior in rank to Wilder, and was authorized to assume command upon reaching the fort, but this he declined to do. Feeling that Wilder was the most capable officer to defend the fortifications he had built, Dunham opted to wait till the present emergency had passed before taking over command.[20]

Both Bragg and Buell were being informed of the events at Munfordville as they transpired. Buell had wired General Halleck of his intentions to move on the Confederate forces in Kentucky, while at the same time opening and holding the railroad line to Louisville. Halleck's response was terse and to the point: "March where you please, provided you will find the enemy and fight him."[21] Buell knew the location of the Southern army. Wilder had been sneaking messengers through the Confederate lines ever since they first appeared before his works, but Buell sent back no responses, and gave no indication that he intended

Major General Simon B. Buckner. Colonel Wilder's manly and honest request for advice concerning his course of action so touched Buckner that he was moved to counsel his enemy on his options. It was Buckner who finally negotiated the surrender of the Union forces at Munfordville without the useless loss of blood. (Courtesy of the United States Army War College.)

to march to the aid of the garrison. His failure to act caused many in the ranks to question both his motives and his loyalties. A rumor was circulated throughout the army that the reason a decisive battle with the Confederates was not being actively pursued was that Buell and Bragg were brothers-in-law and had made a pact to avoid fighting one another. One Union soldier recorded in his diary: "Old Buell is a coward or a Rebel. Shoot him. Let us go."[22] Wilder was to receive no assistance from the Federal main body. Buell was not marching toward Munfordville, but Bragg was.

Bragg was furious when he learned of the actions taken by Chalmers. Buell was reported to be near Bowling Green with his entire army, only about 40 miles from Munfordville. Bragg feared that Chalmers' aggressiveness would bring on a general engagement before the Confederates had a chance to unite their forces, giving the Federals the opportunity to defeat the two armies in detail. But the hand was already dealt, and Bragg felt he must play it. The garrison had to be taken, and Bragg issued marching orders for his army to concentrate on Munfordville. For Major General Simon B. Buckner, commanding one of Bragg's divisions, it would be a visit home, as Buckner was originally from the Munfordville area. It was Buckner who dissuaded Bragg from making a frontal assault when they reached Munfordville. He cautioned against such a move, and advised that the Confederates instead surround the works and compel the defenders to surrender. Sparing the useless loss of life in storming the works was undoubtedly a motivating factor in Buckner's arguments, but so was his desire to spare his hometown area from being destroyed in a pitched battle.[23]

The main body of the Confederate army arrived on September 16, and Bragg immediately took steps to place a ring of fire around the Union position. Major General Leonidus Polk was ordered to cross the river with his division, eight miles upstream from the Union position and to place his men and guns on ground that would command the Union works from the rear. Major General William J. Hardee placed his division facing the works, and by six o'clock that afternoon, the Confederates had Wilder and his men surrounded and ringed by over 60 cannon. At that time, General Bragg sent yet another demand for the surrender of the works that read: "Sir, surrounded by an overwhelming force, your successful resistance or escape is impossible. You are therefore offered an opportunity by capitulation of avoiding the terrible consequences of an assault."[24]

Colonel Dunham had finally assumed his rightful position of commander of the works by the time Bragg's army had shown up, and the surrender demand was delivered to him at 6:00 P.M. Dunham felt the situation to be hopeless if reinforcements did not arrive from either Buell's army or Louisville, but he attempted to stall the negotiations, hoping that such help would arrive before it was too late. At 9:00 P.M., he held a council of his officers to canvas their opinions of the situation, and all seemed to be in agreement that if the Confederate main army was up, further resistance was useless. Dunham telegraphed the result of his council-of-war to headquarters in Louisville, and he received a reply ordering him to turn over command of the post to Wilder. When Dunham protested serving under a junior officer, he was ordered to report to Wilder under arrest.[25]

Wilder had actually taken the responsibilities of command upon himself a few hours previous to the telegraph ordering Dunham to turn over command. The consensus of the Union officers was that the position was untenable, provided the Confederates had the force they claimed to have in place. Owing to the fact that prior demands for surrender had been sent with exaggerated claims of troop strengths, it was decided that the position would be surrendered only if it could positively be ascertained that Bragg's army was there in force. Wilder sent a message through the lines, at approximately 7:00 P.M., stating that the position would be surrendered if Bragg would give proof of "your ascertions [sic] of largely superior numbers, so as to make the defense of this position a useless waste of human life." The whole affair was beginning to make Bragg testy. Anxious to bring the matter to a close, he fired back the following response: "An unconditional surrender of your whole force, etc., is demanded and will be enforced. You are allowed one hour in which to make known your decision."[26]

Wilder was in a quandary as to his proper course of action. If the Confederates really did have their main force up, it would be tantamount to committing murder to sacrifice his men in a useless defense of the position. On the other hand, if this was another bluff, if the Confederates were exaggerating their numbers again, then it would be dereliction of duty for him to capitulate and give up such a vital stronghold. Unsure of what his course of action should be, Wilder determined to take a most peculiar approach. He went to an outpost where he had been informed Confederate Major General Simon B. Buckner could be found, to ask his opinion of the situation. Buckner's reputation was such that Wilder felt Buckner would give him good advice, so he made his way through Rebel lines to ask one of the leading generals of the enemy army what he should do. Buckner protested, when the Union commander asked his opinion. This was simply not the way things were done. But Wilder's frank, candid manner soon won Buckner over. "It appealed to me at once," Buckner would later write. "I wouldn't have deceived that man under these circumstances for anything." Wilder said that Buckner "Assured me that Bragg's whole army had us entirely in their power, with sixty cannon in position to crush us with their fire. I answered him that if this was the case, there could be no reason why I could not go around and see this overwhelming force; that we had been summoned four times to surrender, with like assurances of their power to compel it, and we at each time repelled their attacks, and I would not surrender to any one without absolutely knowing by observation of our inability to resist."[27]

Buckner agreed to allow the inspection to take place, and he took Wilder on a tour of the Confederate position. The Union commander counted 45 cannon on the south side of the river, with many more in place on the north side. Wilder had only 10 cannon with which he could respond to this overwhelming firepower, and he quickly realized that the Confederates could blast his command into submission without having to resort to an infantry attack. Despondently, he announced that it seemed as if his only option was surrender. Buckner was so taken with the innocent and honorable actions of his adversary that he could not help but reciprocate. He stated Wilder's options and duties quite plainly when he said: "If you have information that would induce you to think, that the sacrificing of every man at this place would give your army an advantage elsewhere, it is your duty to do it." Wilder reflected on this statement for a moment, and deciding that no advantage could be gained by sacrificing his men, he announced: "I believe I will surrender."[28]

The two generals then went to see General Bragg. It was close to midnight when they entered the headquarters tent to find the commanding general busily writing out orders and reports. Bragg did not even acknowledge their presence for several minutes, and he seemed to be entranced in the paperwork he was completing. Finally, he raised his head to snappishly demand, "What do you want?" Buckner stated that a surrender could be negotiated if the Federals would be immediately paroled, allowed to keep all of their personal effects, and given four days' rations so that they could make the march to the Ohio River. In return, Wilder would surrender the position, along with all of the arms, ammunition, and government supplies. "Such terms are unheard of, and can not be considered," Bragg blustered. "We have men and guns enough in position to crush you out of existence without losing a man." When Wilder suggested that Bragg's ammunition would be better used in coping with Buell's army than wasting it in an assault on his fortifications, Bragg angrily dismissed him. Buckner and Wilder stopped to talk outside Bragg's tent. "This is willful murder," Buckner stated. Wilder replied that if it was, "he had to commit it." Seeing that Wilder was determined to hold to his demands, Buckner decided to try to convince Bragg. He excused himself, and went back into the headquarters tent, emerging a half hour later with news that Bragg had agreed to turn the whole matter over to him. They agreed on the terms that had already been offered, and arrangements were made for the official surrender to take place in the morning.[29]

Wilder returned to his command and began making out muster rolls and property lists immediately. The rolls showed that 3,546 men were to be surrendered, "600 of them without arms," but this was not entirely accurate. The actual loss to the Union army was 4,148 men, with 15 being killed and 57 wounded. The remainder were surrendered. Confederate losses amounted to 35 killed and 250 wounded. At sunrise, the Union army marched out into the open fields between the opposing lines and laid down their arms. They then drew rations from Bragg's already depleted larder and formed up to march away. Instead of making for the Ohio River, they were directed to proceed to Buell's army. Knowing that Buell faced the same supply problems that he did, Bragg hoped to burden the Union army with this large number of parolees. Through some oversight, Wilder had never been paroled, and when his command reached Buell's army, two days later, he was ordered to take command of his regiment. Buell sent 28 captured Confederate privates to Bragg in exchange for Wilder, but Bragg, in a display of temper, refused to accept. Wilder was nonetheless leading his regiment, and the regiment was leading the whole Union army toward Louisville.[30]

Brigadier General Bushrod Johnson. Before the war, Johnson had been an instructor at the Western Military Institute, and when Munfordville surrendered, he had the opportunity to visit with a few of his old pupils who were now officers in the Union army. His brigade would later see hard service at Perryville. (Courtesy of the United States Army War College.)

One of the privates in Bragg's army surely voiced the opinion of many when he breathed a sigh of relief over the way things had turned out at Munfordville.

We thought we had "struck a snag" when we were drawn up around the fort, where we could look into the muzzles of frowning guns and see the glistening bayonets of the infantry in the ditches, expecting every moment for the order to charge. We knew it would be a bloody affair if we had to take the fort by assault, although we largely outnumbered the enemy, but the afternoon passed without orders, and we slept on our arms, dreading the light of day.

We were greatly relieved when morning revealed the white flag flying, and the prisoners 4,000 or 5,000 in number, were marched out for our inspection. Besides the prisoners, we got a quantity of arms, ammunition, and other stores which we needed; the most important part of the capture, to us privates, being the hardtack and bacon, which we were in fine condition to handle satisfactorily to ourselves.[31]

The surrender of the Union forces occasioned the renewal of old acquaintances for some of the combatants. Colonel Richard Owen, of the 60th Indiana, was well known to Generals Bragg, Hardee, and Buckner, having served with them in the Mexican War. As such, he was shown every courtesy by his captors. General Bushrod Johnson also had the opportunity to talk of old times with members of the Union army. He had a pleasant visit with two of his former students when he had been an instructor at the Western Military Institute: Major I.B. Johnson and Captain Harry Flack.[32]

In reporting to his superiors, Bragg telegraphed Adjutant General Samuel Cooper that: "The garrison of this place surrendered last night without even firing a gun. We got 4,000 prisoners, 4,000 small arms, pieces of artillery, with munitions of war in large quantities. My junction with Kirby Smith complete. Buell still at Bowling Green."[33] The general's message is somewhat confusing. Though he and Kirby Smith were operating in the same general area, a "junction" of the two forces was far from being a reality.

Bragg had won a great victory. Like Kirby Smith, he had eliminated several thousand soldiers from the available Union force, and his victory had come at a substantially lower cost to his own army. Initial impressions were that the Confederates were having things their own way thus far in the campaign. They had crushed or swallowed up all of the resistance they had faced thus far. But these were merely the preliminary actions of the campaign, and while the Confederate victories at Richmond and at Munfordville were decisive, the Union army held such a numerical superiority in the region that it could afford to suffer the losses. Bragg and Buell both realized that the issue would not be decided until their two great armies faced one another on the field of battle, and both men were making preparations for that event.

If the Union military knew that they had enough men in the region to deal with the Confederate forces, the civilian population was not so well assured. The citizens of Louisville and Cincinnati were thrown into a panic by the presence of Smith's and Bragg's men, and all was a frenzy of activity, as some occupants of those cities sent property, both public and private, to safer points to the north.

41

The army in Louisville set to constructing breastworks, and as one soldier put it, they were "drilling when not digging." In Cincinnati, an active policy of civil defense was adopted that saw a resurgence of the American tradition of the Minute Man. Governor David Tod proclaimed that "the soil of Ohio must not be invaded by the enemies of our glorious government," and he made a call for all able-bodied men to take up arms. Major General Lew Wallace was assigned to the command of the defenses of Cincinnati, and in a spirit of martial law, he took control of the city. Ferryboat service on the Ohio River was cancelled, and the business of the populace was suspended so that men could be free to dig trenches under police supervision. "Citizens for labor, soldiers for battle" became the slogan. Men from the surrounding area responded to Governor Tod's appeal, and 15,000 of them arrived in the city, bringing with them muskets, powder horns, and bullet pouches. They were dubbed the "Squirrel Hunters" because of their hunting rifles and frontier appearance, and these backwoods patriots presented a colorful contrast to the citified residents of Cincinnati they had come to rescue. If the Confederates came to Cincinnati, they would find the city prepared to fight. In the end, the preparations were unnecessary, as situations in Kentucky occupied the attentions of both Rebel armies there. Cincinnati would not be suffered the appearance of a Confederate army on its doorstep.[34]

CHAPTER THREE

New Generals, New Men

On the Union side, the Kentucky campaign, and the battle of Perryville, would be a trial by fire for a large number of the men in the ranks. Thirty-five of the Federal regiments that were marching to meet Bragg's army had been mustered into the service since August 15, 1862. They had been soldiers for less than a month, had little or no training, and were completely ignorant as to the rigors of army life. For much of the Union army, this campaign would be a second Shiloh, a repeat of the experience where courage and devotion took the place of training and education. These men had been recruited in President Lincoln's latest call for volunteers, and the mere fact that they were in the army was one of the primary reasons why the invasion of Kentucky had been made in the first place. The Confederates, being aware of Lincoln's call, and of the ability of the Union to meet the latest demand for men, had determined that victories must be won on the battlefield before all of these new troops could be inducted into the army and their numbers brought to bear. It had been one of the underlying reasons why General Robert E. Lee opted to invade Maryland, and it was one of the important factors that led Bragg into Kentucky. The latest call for Federal volunteers was only partially complete, and those men who had responded were, as yet, green and untrained. Now was the time to strike, while a veteran Confederate army could possibly wreak havoc on the new recruits.

Buell would be in need of these replacements, regardless of their level of training. The march to Louisville had witnessed a huge number of desertions among the veteran troops of the Federal army. It was estimated that between 8,000 and 10,000 men had deserted, or were absent without leave, during this time. The adjutant general of the army would later testify before Congress that as many as 14,000 had dropped out of the ranks. Green though they may be, the influx of additional troops into Buell's command would be welcomed.[1]

The recruits in the ranks were not the only inexperienced soldiers who would be taking part in the Union defense of the region. A large number of the Northern officers serving with Buell were new to their positions, and would be exercising field command in positions of authority they were not accustomed to. Promotions had come in meteoric measure for some of the generals who would play key roles in the campaign. Several of their number had not even held field-grade commissions before its commencement, and their promotions would hold great consequence as events unfolded.

The greatest vacancy in the Union army had taken place when one of the ranking generals in the area had been killed. His death was not the result of a battlefield wound, and it was not even delivered at the hands of the enemy. He was shot down by a brother officer in the Union army, in the course of a private dispute. General William Nelson was the victim of this assault. He was a native Kentuckian, born in 1824. After attending Norwich University, Nelson entered the United States Navy, and served in the Mexican War with distinction as a midshipman during the landings at Vera Cruz. In 1855, he was promoted to the rank of lieutenant. He had been influential in monitoring political sentiment in his home state for the Lincoln administration. In April of 1861, he was asked to establish Camp Dick Robinson, in Garrard County, to serve as a rallying place for Kentuckians loyal to the Federal government. In September, he was appointed a brigadier general of volunteers. As such, Nelson holds the distinction of being the only naval officer, on either side to become a general in the war. A huge and imposing man, Nelson stood six feet two and weighed almost 300 pounds. His first field service came in the Shiloh campaign, where he led a division in Major General Buell's army. He then took part in the campaigns against Corinth and Chattanooga, before being detached and sent to Nashville, and thence to Kentucky to help organize resistance to Bragg's invasion of the state. It was in the midst of this preparation that his troops were defeated by the Confederates under Kirby Smith, at Richmond.[2]

Following that defeat, Nelson took active measures for the defense of Louisville. He made a public declaration that he would hold the city so long as one house remained standing, or one soldier was still alive. He also issued an order that all women, children and noncombatants should leave the city and seek shelter in Indiana. The editor of the *Louisville Journal* printed an editorial that only added to the hysteria the population was already feeling. "Your wives and children and your hearthstones are imperilled," he wrote, "and to protect them you must, if necessary, confront the foe with your bare breasts and impale yourself upon their murder-spotted bayonets." Nelson had, at that time, only raw troops and convalescent soldiers with which to oppose the Confederates and to calm local fears, but he steadfastly held to his promise to defend the city. The soldiers worked day and night, sometimes by candlelight, to construct seven forts, with connecting rifle pits, to protect the city. One of Buell's soldiers described Nelson as being "a man of courage and a strict disciplinarian ... rough and overbearing in his demeanor to inferiors." The approach of Buell's army gave Nelson the promise of support, and lessened the state of emergency in Louisville. The advance of Buell's force reached the city on September 25, and his troops marched into the city for the next three days.[3]

Brigadier General Jefferson C. Davis, whose division was a part of Buell's army en route for the city, reported for temporary duty to General Nelson, and he was assigned to command of the various home guard and convalescent units in the city. Davis was born in 1828 in Indiana, the son of Kentucky parents. He enlisted in the army during the Mexican War, and decided to make the military his life's work. The year 1861 found him a captain in the regular service, stationed at Fort Sumter, South Carolina. He endured the Confederate bombardment and capture of that place, and in December of 1861, was made a brigadier general of volunteers. He commanded a division at the battle of Elkhorn Tavern, or Pea Ridge, before being assigned to Buell's army. Davis, like Nelson, was a fiery-tempered man of action, and their similar personalities were about to come in conflict.[4]

An altercation took place when Davis was requisitioning arms for his men, but was unable to provide Nelson with an exact count. Nelson, a stickler for regulations, upbraided Davis severely for his ignorance of this information, and embellished the reprimand with a crusty, seamanlike attack on Davis himself. Nelson was so outraged by this oversight that he ordered Davis to remove himself from his department, and not to return, under penalty of imprisonment. Davis went to Cincinnati, where he waited for Buell's army, and his own division, to arrive at Louisville. When that happened, he joined the army and resumed command of his troops. Deeply insulted by Nelson's actions and the aspersions he had cast on his fitness to command, Davis insisted to Buell that Nelson make a formal apology, but Buell refused to become involved in the controversy. However, Davis did receive the support of Oliver Morton, the governor of his home state. Morton traveled to Louisville to add his weight to the demand that Nelson apologize for the slight he had made against Indiana and one of her favorite sons. He accompanied Davis to the Galt House, a hotel in the city where Nelson was staying, on September 29. Davis found Nelson in a hall in the hotel, and approached him. Reminding him of their previous exchange, he respectfully but firmly demanded that an apology be made. Nelson, never one for diplomacy, responded to the request with yet another insult. "Oh, go away, you damned coward!" he was reported as saying, as he struck Davis in the face. Nelson then

A contemporary drawing of the murder of Major General William Nelson by Brigadier General Jefferson C. Davis. Though outrage was high, both in and out of the army, for this cold-blooded act of passion, Davis was never brought up on charges, and Nelson's murder went unpunished. (Courtesy of the United States Army War College.)

turned his back to his adversary and started to walk away. Davis, outraged by this action, took a step back and announced, "I will see you again sir." He walked into a room in the hotel where he met an old friend from the Mexican War, Colonel T. Weir Gibson. Davis asked to borrow that officer's pistol, and Gibson obliged. Davis, his blood at a boil, then went in search of Nelson. He found him near the stairs that led to his room above. "General Nelson, take care of yourself," Davis called out, then leveled the revolver at his body and fired. Nelson fell to the floor with a mortal wound to the heart. He was carried up to his room, and a doctor was sent for immediately, but nothing could be done to save his life. Though he lingered for a few hours, Nelson died later that night.[5]

The sound of the shot brought Don Carlos Buell running to the hotel. Davis, who had made no attempt to flee the scene, was placed under military arrest. The shooting caused a furor in the officer corps. Some officers supported Davis, and felt that Nelson's abusive personality was to blame for the entire incident. Most, however, condemned Davis' actions and demanded that he be tried for murder.

Captain William Terrill declared that he should be hanged on the spot for "this inexcusably despicable act." Buell denounced the incident and advised that prompt and vigorous action be taken against Davis. He could not do it himself, at the present time, because of the current situation with Bragg's army. "I cannot spare officers from the army now in motion to compose a court. It can perhaps better be done from Washington," he telegraphed to Major General William Halleck, the chief of staff. But the court martial was never convened. When the Union army marched out to meet the Confederates, Davis was at the head of his division. His trial was lost in the shuffle. In the meantime, Governor Morton was pressing General Horatio G. Wright, the department commander, in Cincinnati, to waive the charges. Wright responded favorably. "The period during which an officer could be continued in arrest without charges being placed against him had expired.... I was satisfied that Davis had acted purely

Major General Horatio G. Wright. Wright was responsible for granting liberal promotions to a number of officers in the Union army, including the rank of major general to Charles Gilbert. (Courtesy of the United States Army War College.)

on the defensive in the unfortunate affair, and I presumed Buell held similar views as he took no action in the matter after placing him in arrest," Wright would later state. As this was a military matter, no civil charges could be filed, and the entire incident was allowed to pass. According to the accounts of those in attendance, even that of Davis himself, General Nelson had been murdered in a rage of passion, but there was to be no punishment for the murderer. The murder of General Nelson, and the subsequent lack of punishment for the perpetrator, was one of the most bizarre incidents in the Civil War. Davis would go on to perform good service in the Union army, but his reputation would ever after be marred by the murder.[6]

Nelson's death further exacerbated the shortage of general officers that had begun with the capture of General Manson at Richmond. When Nelson had been wounded at Richmond, Brigadier Generals Charles Cruft and James S. Jackson wrote to General Wright requesting that he promote Captain Charles Gilbert to the rank of major general, and give him the temporary command of Nelson's troops. They also requested that Captain William Terrill be promoted to brigadier general to fill the vacancy left by Manson's capture. Wright acted favorably upon both requests:

> I. Captain C.C. Gilbert, First Infantry, U.S.A., is hereby appointed a Major-General of Volunteers, subject to the approval of the President of the United States, and is assigned to the command of the Army of Kentucky during the temporary abscence [sic] of Major-General Nelson.

Major General Charles C. Gilbert. Gilbert's meteoric promotion to major general led to his being given command of a corps in the Northern army. Buell did not know until the campaign was almost over that Gilbert was operating under false pretenses. He was considered to be a martinet by his officers and men, and his leadership in the Kentucky campaign would lead to criticism and to embarrassment on the part of the government. (Courtesy of the United States Army War College.)

> II. Captain William R. Terrill, Fifth Artillery, U.S.A., is hereby appointed a Brigadier-General of Volunteers, subject to the approval of the President of the United States, and will report to Major-General Gilbert for instructions.

Thus read the general order Wright issued concerning these promotions. Now that Nelson was dead, the appointment would be more than temporary for Gilbert.[7]

Charles Gilbert was an Ohioan, born in 1822, and was a graduate of West Point in the class of 1846. He had served in the Mexican War with the 1st Infantry, and later, served as a faculty member at the academy. He was badly wounded while leading a company of regulars at Wilson's Creek, and was detailed to perform the services of inspector general for the Army of the Cumberland, and then the Army of the Ohio. He was acting in this capacity when he was called upon

48

to lead Nelson's Corps. A controversy, of sorts, arose concerning Gilbert's appointment. It was not unheard of for a commanding general to make such an emergency appointment in the field. Major General John C. Fremont had done so several times in Missouri in 1861. But even though it was not unheard of, it was still contrary to the way things were done in the military. When Abraham Lincoln was informed of the action, he overruled the rank Wright had bestowed, instead granting Gilbert the brevet rank of brigadier general. The president then submitted his name to Congress for approval at that grade. The Senate, however, refused to act on the nomination, and allowed his appointment to expire in March of 1863, at which time he reverted to his permanent rank of captain. Gilbert's performance in the Kentucky campaign was undoubtedly a prime factor in the action taken by the Senate.[8]

Though Gilbert's promotion to major general was not approved, he continued to portray himself as being one, even down to wearing the insignia of a major general on his uniform. Some of the other officers in the army questioned this, but General Wright told Gilbert that if anyone objected to his acting in that capacity, he could refer them to Wright with the threat of being detached from the service. Why Wright took such a personal interest in Gilbert's advancement is unknown, but the fact that he threatened to detach any officer who gave him grief about it smacks of some sort of conspiracy. When Buell and his army reached Louisville, he found Gilbert still parading around wearing the insignia of a major general. He had no reason to question the rank or to make an official inquiry, so, assuming that he was indeed a major general, Buell assigned him to command one of the corps in his army. Buell would later be questioned about this assignment, to which he responded: "I have no particular interest in General Gilbert at all. I assigned him to a command because I believed he was, at the time, a Major General, and when the contrary became certainly known, I relieved him from command." If Buell did not know the truth, Gilbert certainly did. He was guilty of impersonating an officer of higher rank, and when he accepted the command of a corps in Buell's army, he did so knowing that it was under false pretenses, and that he was undeserving of the position. Gilbert was not only new to the command he was about to exercise, he was unqualified by both his experience and legitimate rank. His acceptance of the position, and the responsibility it carried with it, was akin to being criminal, under the circumstances. Gilbert's appointment to corps command would have dramatic consequences in the campaign that followed.[9]

William Terrill was a Virginian, born in 1834. He was also a graduate of West Point, in the class of 1853. Upon receiving his commission, Terrill was assigned to the artillery on garrison duty in Florida. He subsequently served as an instructor of mathematics at the academy, and as a recruiting officer, and was sent to help calm the border disturbances in Kansas. When war broke out, he determined to adhere to the Union, provided he did not have to serve in Virginia, and fight in his native state. He was made captain of the 5th Regular Artillery, in Washington, and then was sent west to Kentucky. Terrill served as chief of artillery for the 2nd Division of Buell's army, taking part in the battles at Shiloh and Corinth. Like so many families, North and South, the Terrills were divided by the war. His brother, James Barbour Terrill, was a brigadier general in the Confederate army, serving in the Army of Northern Virginia. James would be killed in action in the fighting near Cold Harbor, Virginia, in 1864.[10]

A third officer who experienced meteoric rise in rank was Captain Ebenezer Gay, of the 9th Pennsylvania Cavalry. Gay was appointed chief of cavalry in Kentucky in September of 1862, and was given the brevet rank of brigadier general. Gay's rise in rank was due to Charles Gilbert, who was exercising his new authority to the fullest. The cavalry brigade Gay was to command consisted of his own 9th Pennsylvania, the 2nd Michigan, the 4th Indiana, and the 6th, 7th, 9th, and 11th Kentucky Cavalry. Gay would have his work cut out for him. The 9th

Brigadier General William Terrill. Though a Virginian, Terrill chose to stay with the old flag and fight for the Union. He would lead a brigade of newly recruited Union soldiers in the battle of Perryville. (Courtesy of the United States Army War College.)

Pennsylvania and the 2nd Michigan were the only seasoned regiments in the brigade. The rest were "perfectly raw." Gay could not even be sure of the exact number of men he commanded, because he could not receive morning reports from the green regiments. "Some of the regiments do not know what a morning report is, never having heard of such a thing, or a roll call," he reported. The only well armed regiment in the brigade was the 2nd Michigan, which was equipped with Colt repeating rifles. The 9th Pennsylvania might have been a seasoned regiment, but the men were certainly not well armed, most of them carrying only pistols and sabers. There were only 41 Sharps and 13 Maynards in the entire regiment. Gay would have to scrounge for suitable weapons for his reliable men, while he conducted on-the-job training for the majority of his troopers.[11]

Divisional and corps commanders would not be the only ones who were new to their duties. Many of the regiments in Buell's army were new to the service, and the men and officers in them were green and untrained. These soldiers were easily identified by the veterans in the ranks. Their new uniforms stood out, as did the amount of unnecessary equipment they carried with them. One Ohio veteran recalled that their bulging knapsacks "resembled freshly supplied peddler's packs." Most of this excess gear and personal baggage would be discarded during the march, as these recruits discovered the rigors of the march and endeavored to lighten their loads and keep up with the column.[12]

These new recruits endured the constant taunts and jibes of their seasoned comrades. One Union officer, Major H.B. Freeman of the 18th U.S. Infantry, recalled one of the new regiments that was added to his brigade. He remembered how it was

> nearly as large as the rest of the brigade, shod in brand-new boots and shoes, with overcoat and blanket neatly rolled on their well-filled knapsacks, took but a corporal's guard into camp that night after the march of twenty miles. They melted away like wax before the fire, and filled the fence corners, where they were greeted with cries of "What'll you take for them boots? Do you want to sell that overcoat?" Whilst another, thinking of the large bounties then being paid would shout, "Get up, you thousand-dollar warrior!" or, "You gilded patriot, come into camp; you cost too much money to be lying around loose." To these taunts they seldom replied, but their faces spoke volumes of indignation and suffering. They came out all right, though, in time; they were passing through the same experience with ourselves, only in our case there had been no yearling veterans to jeer at us.[13]

Buell would have many unknown quantities regarding the officers and men in his army, but he also had a great many that he could count on. The veteran troops in his army had been bloodied at places like Shiloh and Corinth. They

A group of men from the 21st Michigan Infantry, one of the new regiments that made up a large portion of Buell's Union army. This photograph was taken after the battle of Perryville. (Courtesy of the United States Army War College.)

had served in the army for over a year now, and in the process had become veterans. His second in command was Major General George H. Thomas, one of the most respected officers in the Union army. Born in Virginia in 1816, Thomas was yet another graduate of West Point, in the class of 1840. He had served in the artillery for the first 15 years of his military career, taking part in the operations against the Seminoles and in the Mexican War. In 1855, when the famed 2nd United States Cavalry was authorized, he became its first major, a position he held till the beginning of the war. He led a brigade at First Manassas before being transferred west, where he defeated the Confederates at Mill Springs, took part in the battle of Shiloh, and then participated in the siege of Corinth. Another son of Virginia, the general had been transferred away from scenes of war in his native state. Thomas had not yet attained the fame that would come his way in the latter years of the war, but he was a steadfast and reliable officer who could be depended upon to perform his duties.[14]

Buell's other two corps commanders had also proven their mettle in battle. Major General Alexander McCook would lead the 1st Corps. Born in Ohio in

1831, he was a member of the famed "Fighting McCooks" who boasted 14 family members in the Union army. One brother, Dan McCook, was leading a brigade in Buell's army, and another brother, General Robert McCook, had been killed by irregular Confederate cavalry during the summer, near Decherd, Tennessee. He attended West Point, graduating in the class of 1852. After a tour of service on the frontier, he became an instructor of tactics at the academy until the war broke out. McCook commanded the 1st Ohio Infantry at First Manassas, then went west to participate in the capture of Nashville, the battle of Shiloh, and the Corinth campaign.

Thomas L. Crittenden would command Buell's 2nd Corps. Crittenden was a native Kentuckian, born in 1819 to an influential family. His father was a United States senator, but that did not prevent a split in family loyalties similar to the Terrills'. His older brother, George B. Crittenden, siding with the South, became a major general in the Confederate army. Though Crittenden had no formal military training, he had served as a volunteer in the Mexican War. His influential status in Kentucky earned him a commission as a brigadier general from the Lincoln administration in September of 1861. Crittenden credibly led a division at Shiloh, and took part in the Corinth campaign. His handling of his troops had been such as to warrant his promotion to major general and corps command in July of 1862.[15]

Buell would also have the services of a number of solid division and brigade commanders who would later achieve fame for their command abilities. Among these were William B. Hazen, James B. Steedman, William P. Carlin, and Phillip H. Sheridan. He would need to do his best to balance the new with the experienced, the untried with the true, however. The Confederate army that Bragg was leading was numerically inferior to his own, but it was composed solely of veteran troops. Buell's new recruits would have to learn their duties quickly, or his advantage in numbers would be a moot point.

The War Department came very close to creating a situation where the army commander in the campaign would have been new to the job. In fact, if things had gone the way Secretary of War Edwin Stanton and General Halleck intended them to, Buell would have been replaced before the Union army could engage Bragg's forces. Pressure had been great on Buell to produce some immediate results in regard to confronting Bragg's army. General Halleck had been prodding him for over a month, going so far as to threaten to remove him. On August 18, while Buell still had his headquarters in Huntsville, Alabama, he received a telegram from the chief of staff stating: "So great is the dissatisfaction here at the apparent want of energy and activity in your district, that I was this morning notified to have you removed. I got the matter delayed till we could hear further

of your movements." To this, an insulted Buell replied that his movements were dictated by the circumstances at hand, and that there was a lack of reliable information concerning the Confederate intentions. He brought up a lack of cavalry, the need to rebuild railroad bridges, and the 400-mile supply line he needed to establish and guard. He reminded Halleck that he had requested eight additional regiments of cavalry three months before, and had never received them, and he stated that if the dissatisfaction in Washington could not cease, he wished to be relieved. Buell's defense fended off the critics for the moment, and his march to Nashville, and then to Louisville, further silenced them; but now the critics were clamoring again, clamoring for battle. Nothing short of the complete expulsion of the Confederate army from Kentucky would suffice, and in Washington it did not seem as if Buell was taking the steps necessary to make that happen.[16]

On September 30, Colonel Joseph McKibben arrived in Louisville. He had been sent there from Washington with orders from General Halleck to ascertain the situation in Buell's army. The president and the secretary of war were irritated over Buell's apparent lack of offensive action. The governors of Illinois, Indiana, and Ohio were calling for the removal of Buell, and the government felt that the time to make a change had come. The rift between the administration and Buell had already reached the media. One Cincinnati journalist fanned the flames of discontent by writing that General Buell was "the most reserved, distant and unsociable of all the generals in the army. He never has a word of cheer for his men or his officers, and in turn his subordinates care little for him." McKibben was instructed to conduct a secret interview with several of the prominent officers of the army to determine Buell's fitness for command. If, after doing so, he felt the course to be right, he was then to deliver the sealed orders he was carrying, issued by Secretary Stanton, effecting a change in command. After talking with a few of the army's leading officers, and discerning a level of discontent within the officer corps, the colonel judged the action to be necessary. He summoned Buell and George H. Thomas, and when the three men were together, he handed them the orders, and announced that Buell was relieved, and Thomas was to take his place. Thomas protested the decision. He stated that Buell's plans for the campaign were now perfected, and that it would be unfair to both of them to make the change at that time. Buell should be given the opportunity to prove his strategy to his superiors, Thomas argued. He also stated that it would be impossible for him to take over the army on the eve of an important

Opposite: **A company of Indiana recruits poses for this picture in their new uniforms. These men would undergo their trial by fire in the Kentucky Campaign. (Courtesy of the United States Army War College.)**

battle while being unfamiliar with all of the details of the campaign. Thomas sent a telegraph to Halleck at once: "Colonel McKibben handed me your dispatch placing me in command of this department. General Buell's preparations have been completed to move against the enemy, and I therefore respectfully ask that

he be retained in command. My position is very embarrassing, not being as well informed as I should be, as the commander of this army, and on the assumption of such responsibility." Thomas did not decline the position from any lack of faith in his own abilities. He did so in an effort to allow his commander to redeem himself in the eyes of his superiors, and to avoid any further delay. He realized that Buell's perceived delay in engaging the enemy was the cause of this order, and he also knew that a change in command right now would cause further delay as he familiarized himself with the plans for the upcoming battle. Buell was ready to go, and Thomas could see no reason why the offensive should be halted now for a change in command. His actions were not self-effacing, they were honorable and for the good of the army. The administration relented, and Buell was retained.[17]

Major General George H. Thomas. Though a Virginian, Thomas remained true to the Union and became one of the most capable and trusted generals in the Northern army. During the Kentucky campaign, he served as Buell's second-in-command, and was ordered to take Buell's place immediately prior to the battle at Perryville. Thomas successfully argued that Buell should retain his command, since the army was on the eve of battle, and Buell was more suited to oversee the plans he had already made. (Courtesy of the United States Army War College.)

Buell now had approximately 90,000 men under his command. About a third of these were detailed to defend Louisville and guard supply lines. The divisions of Brigadier Generals

Ebenezer Dumont and Joshua Sill were ordered to make a feint against Frankfort, in an attempt to deceive the Confederates as to the real intent to the army. Buell organized the rest into three corps, the first to be commanded by McCook, the second by Crittenden, and the third by Gilbert. He had a total of 36 batteries of artillery available to his army, and these were distributed between the various divisions and brigades. By October 1, Buell's army was in readiness, and the march was begun in the direction of Bragg's army. The three corps were to take different roads in approaching the Confederates, then in the Bardstown area. McCook was to march on the Harrodsburg Road, Crittenden on the Lebanon and Danville Road, and Gilbert on the Springfield Road. But the columns would make slow progress toward the foe. They were bogged down by wagon trains that stretched over 22 miles in length, and would average only about 10 miles a day.[18]

The march was a terrible ordeal for recruit and veteran alike. The earth had been parched by a recent drought, and the trodding of the army kicked up great clouds of dust that made it hard to see, and harder to breathe. The drought had caused a shortage of water, as creeks, streams, and wells dried up. Routes of march were sometimes altered in the hope of finding water for the men. The few houses that were to be found along the line of march would usually be left with their wells depleted of water by the time the army moved on. But there was never enough water, and the troops were more than happy to drink from any muddy hole they could find. One soldier related that he gladly drank "from a pond where men and mules drank fifteen feet apart. Across the pond soldiers washed their socks and feet. And at an end of the pond floated a dead mule." A soldier in the 80th Indiana stated that it "was very warm in daytime, and the roads remarkably dusty, so that at times while our clothing was saturated with perspiration, we were enveloped in a cloud of dust, rising high above the trees, that was almost suffocating. The season had also been dry and although there might have been sufficient water in the country to answer the ordinary purposes of travel, the quantity was entirely inadequate to supply the wants of such large bodies of troops. In consequence of this, it was sometimes necessary to prolong a day's march farther than men unaccustomed to marching were really able to travel in order to encamp convenient to a creek or pond. And sometimes even then we could only find stagnant pools, the water of which was offensive and could hardly be drank after having been made into coffee." Thirst, disease and exhaustion quickly began to decimate the ranks of the Union army.[19]

Strict orders had been issued against foraging. The North was trying to keep Kentucky in the Union and to avoid the mass enlistments in the Confederate army that Bragg was hoping for. It would not do to have the Union army conduct itself like a conquering force, placing hardships on the local populace by stripping them of their food and livestock. Despite these orders, the suffering men in Buell's army availed themselves of any opportunity to improve their lot. The heat and lack of water caused severe straggling, and the officers were hard-pressed to keep control over their men. In many instances, the column would march past a house, leaving its inhabitants untouched, only to have a band of stragglers strip the place of food and valuables afterward. General Gilbert was trying to enforce the order against pilfering, but he had already earned the disdain of the men in his command as being a tyrant. Gilbert was possessed of a sizeable ego, and his dealings with subordinate officers and men were often brash and rude. During the march, he had the colonel of the 86th Illinois arrested because his men had helped themselves to some persimmons in an orchard. He later had an altercation with the members of another regiment that came close to becoming a mutiny. The 10th Indiana had halted for the night, about midnight, along the Springfield Road. It had been a difficult day of marching, and the men were soon sound asleep by the roadside. A few of the boys had spotted an apple orchard, and had climbed a fence to fill their pockets with the fruit. General Gilbert and his staff rode up to the spot and demanded to know what regiment this was. At the same time, he ordered his escort to fire on the men who were in the orchard. Those troops within earshot of the order immediately sprang to their feet and grabbed their muskets in defiance. As charges were loaded and muskets were capped, they advised the escort against following the general's orders. "Where is the officer in charge of these miscreants?" Gilbert demanded. Captain Miller introduced himself, and the general demanded that he turn over his sword. Miller stated, "General, one word from me will call the boys out of that orchard a damned sight sooner than you can shoot them out; and should it come to that, I have the honor to assure you, General, that my boys never allow themselves to be outdone in this shooting business. I think your fellows had better put up their shooting irons, for the first flash of a carbine at one of them boys will be the death knell for every mother's son that has a hand in the business." Enraged, Gilbert demanded that the regiment turn over its colors, and placed the entire command under arrest. The color bearer cursed the general and told him if he so much as touched the flag, he would kill him. Another soldier stepped forward to tell Gilbert, "get out of here, or you are a dead man." A musket shot rang out as a member of the regiment fired a shot in the air, while still another soldier poked Gilbert's horse with a bayonet. The startled animal "reared, plunged and nearly threw Gilbert off," and finally went away at a gallop, followed by the general's escort. Gilbert had earned the hatred of the men in the 10th Indiana, many of whom promised to shoot him the first time they went into battle. But this was not an isolated incident. General James Steedman would later testify that it extended through-out his division, and throughout Gilbert's Corps. "There was a great deal of dis-satisfaction in the First Division with General Gilbert prior to the battle of Perryville, and a great deal of feeling among all of the officers of the corps that I ever heard say anything about it, after it was ascertained that he had not the right to exercise that command. There was a feeling that he was somebody's pet, and put where he had no right and for which he was not qualified. He quarreled with nearly all of the officers of the First Division about very unimportant and trifling things, and there was a general opinion that he gave his attention entirely to small things instead of attending to the important duties of his position." Such was the state of affairs with the Union corps that was leading the march toward Bragg's army, and would be the first to make contact with the Confederates. The weary, parched troops were almost in open rebellion against their commanding general, whom they considered to be a martinet.[20]

In another incident of the march, General Gilbert managed to alienate the members of the 36th Illinois. As the unit historian related

> The few springs and sparkling brooks were usually monopolized by Gen. Gilbert, who sent an aid in advance to select spots near by, in which was pitched the General's marquee, and a detachment of body guards posted to protect the sacred precincts, as well as the spring, from intrusion. Near the close of this sultry day, the 36th, soiled with dust and famished with thirst, came up to a spring of clear, cold water, near which were located the head-quarters of Gen. Gilbert. The men, acting upon the campaign maxim, "wherever and when ever you can secure a square meal or a drink of cold water, do so," eagerly crowded around the spring, with the inevitable tin cup and canteen, quaffing great draughts of the refreshing beverage, to quench a thirst of eight or ten hours duration. A dapper little staff-officer came up and ordered the boys away, to which, for awhile, they paid no more attention then to the cackling of a hen, but persisting in his impertinence, a broad-shouldered, ungainly private of Company B knocked him down with the butt of his gun — effectually silencing him for the time being. Thereupon Gen. Gilbert came out in person and reiterated the command, ordering Capt. Miller to move on with his regiment. The Captain courteously but firmly remonstrated, telling the General "that his men had marched since before mid-day without water; that the heat was oppressive; that his men were suffering from thirst, and that the refusal of water under such circumstances showed a want of common humanity." Gen. Gilbert was irate at this manly protest and ordered his body-guard to charge upon and drive the men away from the spring. Captain Miller, nothing daunted, directed his men to fix bayonets and run the first man through who should molest them, until they got the water they wanted. To be thus defied by a little, wiry Yankee captain,

A group of officers from the 36th Illinois Infantry. The men and officers of the 36th Illinois almost entered into armed conflict with General Gilbert and his staff when that officer refused to allow the men to fill their canteens from a pool of water. (Courtesy of the United States Army War College.)

was more than Kentucky dignity could stand, and addressing his body-guard (a detachment of the 2nd Kentucky Cavalry) he said, "Ye men of Kentucky; will you allow this insult to your General to go unrebuked and unpunished! If you are men, and have any regard for your honor as Kentuckians, you will instantly disperse this insolent mob, and arrest every one who refuses compliance with orders." It was then Capt. Miller's turn to talk, and turning to the men, he said, "Boys, massacre every mother's son of them that dares to lay a finger upon you until your canteens are filled," and turning to the body-guard and staff of the General, "if you, or any other Kentuckian, want to die on your own native soil, now is your chance to do so, for by the Great Eternal, my men are going to have all the water they want, before marching another foot. If you want to die, come on!" But they did not come on worth a cent, and Gen. Gilbert returned chagrined to his tent, and the 36th remained masters of the situation.[21]

Conditions were not much better in McCook's Corps. McCook was described by contemporaries as having the demeanor of a 31-year-old schoolboy, possessed of a sense of humor that antagonized many of his associates. He was boisterous, and had a swaggering manner that alienated many people. One Union soldier observed that "General McCook prides himself on being General McCook." The Union army that was about the face Bragg's Confederates was following two of its corps commanders with less than complete confidence.[22]

The Union army encountered enemy troops almost as soon as it marched out of Louisville. For the next week, as it marched over the torturous roads that led to the Bardstown area, there would be almost daily skirmishing. Joe Wheeler's Confederate troopers were doing their best to retard the Yankee movements. On October 2, one day's march from Louisville, a member of the 31st Indiana recorded in his diary, "Heard cannon about 10 AM. Crossed ground that had been fought over during the day. Crossed Salt River and camped. Heard cannon and musketry in the evening." But the Rebel cavalry could do little more than impede the Union columns. The gray troopers were an irritation to the Union infantry, but little more. Buell's men were in contact with the enemy, and though their progress was slow, they were moving forward toward a decisive engagement with the Confederates.[23]

As Buell advanced, Bragg was busy consolidating his forces and preparing his army to meet them. The great gamble was about to be decided. A Confederate victory would take Kentucky out of the Union. It would open the way for an invasion of Ohio, and would shake the Union cause to its very foundations. Failure would ensure that Kentucky, and most of Tennessee, would remain in Union hands, and the Confederacy would be denied manpower, resources, and possibly the foreign recognition it so desired. The issue would be decided in a clash of arms between tired and thirsty men on the dry and dusty ground of central Kentucky.

CHAPTER FOUR

Bragg Maneuvers for a Battle

The final days of September would find the Confederate armies in Kentucky still widely separated, and largely unaware as to the intentions of the Federal troops. Kirby Smith's army was in the vicinity of Frankfort, while Bragg's was located in the area around Bardstown and Bryantsville. Braxton Bragg was lamenting the lack of support being shown to his army by the people of Kentucky, and was actively trying to secure that support through proclamations and political displays. In his private correspondence with Adjutant General Samuel Cooper, dated September 25, he complained of the lack of support, both from Kentuckians and from his own army. "I regret to say we are sadly disappointed at the want of action by our friends in Kentucky," he wrote. "We have so far received no accession to this army. General Smith has secured about a brigade- not half our losses by casualties of different kinds. We have 15,000 stand of arms and no one to use them. Unless a change occurs soon we must abandon the garden spot of Kentucky to its cupidity." He continued by voicing his displeasure over the lack of support he was receiving from Generals Earl Van Dorn and Sterling Price. "Had the forces in North Mississippi moved as ordered, so as to have held the enemy there in check, we might have made some headway after arriving here; but we find the armies of General Grant, Rosecrans, Curtis and Buell, with many of the new levies, opposed to us. In this condition any advance is impossible. I still hope the movement of Generals Price and Van Dorn may clear away our rear and open a base for us. Otherwise we may be seriously embarrassed."[1]

In that same message, Bragg detailed the events of the campaign thus far. "I have the honor to report the occupation of this place by my forces on the 22nd. The long, arduous, and exhausting march renders it necessary for my troops to have some rest. They will therefore remain several days.

"At Munfordville I was between Buell's forces and General E.K. Smith, by

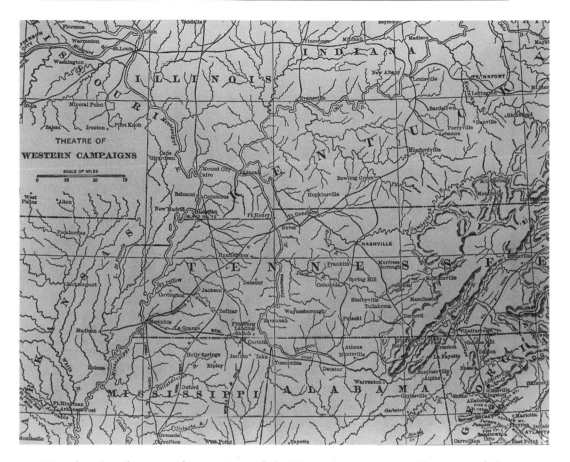

Map showing the area of operations of the Kentucky campaign. (Courtesy of the United States Army War College.)

which the latter was secured. Efforts were made to bring Buell to an engagement, but he declined, and it was reported to me he was moving by way of Brownsville to the nearest point on the Ohio. For want of provisions it was impossible for me to follow or even stay where I was, the population being nearly all hostile and the country barren and destitute, having been ravaged by the enemy. With only three days' provisions we marched on this place (59 miles), and reached here after some privation and suffering. It is a source of deep regret that this move was necessary, as it enabled Buell to reach Louisville, where a very large force is now concentrated." In this statement, Bragg explains actions that were widely criticized during the campaign. His army had been in a position to cut off Buell's forces as they marched for Louisville, but Bragg had declined to do so. His above stated reasons seem to be a valid explanation for this decision.[2]

That same day, he sent a message to General Van Dorn, at Grand Junction, Mississippi. "General: We have driven the enemy clear back to the Ohio. Push your columns to our support, and rouse the people to reenforce [sic] us. We have thousands of arms without people to handle them. Nashville is defended by only a weak garrison; Bowling Green by only a regiment. Sweep them off and push up to the Ohio. Secure the heavy guns at these places and we will secure the Tennessee and Cumberland Rivers. All depends on rapid movements. Trusting to your energy and zeal we shall confidently expect a diversion in our favor against the overwhelming force now concentrating on our front." The diversion from Van Dorn was not to come. The message was not received by him until November 28, over two months later. Van Dorn returned it to Bragg on the same day it was received, with the following endorsement: "The above dispatch was this day received and forwarded. I cannot account for the delay in transmission." The Confederate Postal Service had failed to deliver the message in a timely fashion. It seemed, for Bragg, as if anything that could go wrong, did go wrong.[3]

On September 28, Bragg determined to make an inspection tour of Lexington and Frankfort. He left Major General Leonidus Polk in command of the army while he and his staff made a sweep of the area. This was not an effort to gain firsthand knowledge of the military situation. Instead, it was a whirlwind political trip, intended to stir up enlistments and legitimize the Confederate presence in Kentucky. On September 29, Bragg issued yet another proclamation to the citizens of the state, exhorting them to rally to the Confederate cause.

> The armies of the Confederate States now within your borders were brought here more as a nucleus around which the true men of Kentucky could rally than as an invading force against the Northwest. As you value your rights of person and property and your exemption from tyranny and oppression you will now rally to the standard which protects you and has rescued your wives and mothers from insult and outrage. Troops in any number will be received by companies and armed, and will be organized into regiments as fast as practicable, company officers to be elected by their men and the field officers to be appointed by the President, on recommendation of the commanding general, after passing a proper examination. Companies should repair as soon as formed to Bryantsville and report to the officer charged with the organization and muster of recruits. Arms and ammunition are there, ready for issue to all. The usual pay and bounty will be given. Twenty companies of cavalry are wanted. After they are supplied infantry only will be received. Cavalry recruits will be received in any of the regiments now in the fields. This is the last opportunity Kentuckians will enjoy for volunteering. The conscript act will be enforced as soon as necessary arrangements can be made. For further infor-

mation as to details apply to Maj.-Gen. S.B. Buckner, who is charged with the superintendence of this duty.[4]

Bragg was attempting to rally support to the Confederate cause, but the tone and wording of this proclamation had just the opposite effect. The last few sentences were ill-advised, and they were seen by Kentuckians as a threat, not an appeal. Enlist now or be drafted later, portrayed the Confederates as conquerors, not as liberators. Bragg's final appeal to the men of Kentucky would result in bringing almost no volunteers into the ranks.

Bragg's next political act was to contact Kirby Smith and direct that he assemble his army at Frankfort on the 30th, so as to take part in the inauguration of Richard Hawes as the first Confederate governor of Kentucky. Bragg planned to stage an elaborate ceremony for the event, and to show the populace that Confederate authority was here to stay. Smith later states that he tried desperately to talk Bragg out of holding such a ceremony. He said that he tried to convince him to let political matters go, for the time being, and see to the combining of their two armies for offensive action against Buell. Union activity in the area supported Smith's views. Though Buell had not yet marched out of Louisville with his army, he had sent out strong probes to determine the location of the Confederates. The 3rd Georgia Cavalry was captured in its entirety on September 29 by one of these probes, a Union cavalry division under the command of Colonel John Kenneth. Though Smith avows that his main objective at that time was the combining of the two armies, he was not marching his own force for a concentration with Bragg's main body. Instead, Smith was conducting an independent campaign, and seemed indisposed to place himself under Bragg's authority.[5]

Bragg could not be turned from his political purpose. Hawes would be sworn in as the governor. The ceremony took place as planned on September 30. Hawes assumed the position, and was sworn in as the first Confederate governor of the state. He was in the middle of giving his inaugural address when the sounds of artillery fire interrupted the proceedings. General Sill's Union division had just reached Frankfort, and it immediately went on the offensive. The Confederates beat a hasty retreat from the city, with Governor Hawes in tow. His tenure in office had indeed been brief, and his administration was placed in exile before he could even conclude his acceptance speech.[6]

The citizens of Frankfort and Lexington had given a warm welcome to the Confederate army. Colonel George Brent, an officer on Bragg's staff, noted that "The reception of Genl. B.(ragg) in Lexington was quite enthusiastic. But it is only manifested by words and shouts. There is no action on the part of Kentuckians to take an active armed effort to sustain us." Bragg echoed those sentiments. "Enthusiasm is unbounded," he wrote, "but recruiting at a discount. Even the women are giving reasons why individuals should not go." Bragg estimated that he would need 50,000 recruits in order to be able to hold the state. By this time, a mere 5,000 seemed to be wishful thinking.[7]

Bragg was thoroughly confused by the sudden arrival of Sill's Division at Frankfort. He jumped to the conclusion that Sill's force was the main body of the Union army, and that Frankfort was Buell's objective. Polk had been instructed, upon Bragg's departure, to fall back toward Bryantsville, should he be attacked by Buell's army. All of the stores captured in the campaign had been gathered there, and it was serving as a temporary base of operations. The appearance of Sill's Division caused Bragg to change these orders. On September 30, he sent word to Polk that he was to move the army toward Louisville, occupying Taylorsville, Shepherdsville, and Elizabethtown along the way. Polk responded that his cavalry scouts were reporting that Buell was moving out from Louisville, and he worried that "It seems to me we are too much scattered." Bragg, still under the assumption that Frankfort was to be the main Union objective, then altered his orders. He directed that Polk move the army immediately to Frankfort. He was to attack what was perceived to be Buell's flank and rear, while Kirby Smith's army engaged the Federals in front. While admitting that the Federal move on Frankfort "may be a reconnaissance," Bragg stated, "should it be a real attack we have them.... With Smith in front and our gallant army on the flank I see no hope for Buell if he is rash enough to come out. I only fear it is not true." Polk's information proved to be more reliable than Bragg's He correctly assessed the situation, and determined that his army was the one that was about to be assailed by the Federal main body. He sent word to Bragg that he was being pressed so strongly that his only option was to fall back before the superior force facing him. Polk called a council of his wing and division commanders, and was unanimously supported in this belief. He then communicated to Bragg that he would not be able to obey his latest order, stating that it was "not only eminently inexpediant [sic] but impracticable."[8]

The Confederate army was indeed scattered. General Humphrey Marshall was at Mount Sterling, some 35 miles east of Lexington, with a force of 4,000 men. General Carter Stevenson had 8,000 men at Cumberland Gap, 170 miles away. Kirby Smith's main force consisted of only about 10,000 men, and it too was divided, occupying the towns of Frankfort, Lexington, and Danville. Bragg's own army was the only force that was in any way connected, in its position around Bardstown, Harrodsburg, and Bryantsville. Polk was quite right in calling for a concentration of the available Confederate forces before Buell's army could strike.

But time and distance would render that concentration an impossibility.[9]

Polk's message that he was being strongly pressed evidently caused Bragg to reassess the situation. His next message to Polk stated his new belief that the movement on Frankfort was merely a feint. He instructed Polk to position the army with "one flank at Taylorsville," unaware that Taylorsville was already within Union lines. The Union army's whereabouts and probable destination were a mystery to the Confederate commander, though Polk was convinced that the main thrust was coming his direction. Bragg was losing control of the situation. Buell was stealing a march on him, and had seized the initiative.

Bragg was now convinced that Kentuckians would only join his army once it had won an important victory on the field of battle, and he hastily made plans to give combat to the Union army with whatever forces he had at hand. On October 2, word was received that Patrick

Major General Leonidus Polk. Polk effectively served as Braxton Bragg's second-in-command during the Kentucky campaign. Though his independent actions were less than praiseworthy, he became one of Bragg's fiercest critics once the campaign was over. (Courtesy of the United States Army War College.)

Cleburne's division had been forced to evacuate Shelbyville and retire toward Frankfort. This news spurred the commanding general into an offensive mode. Kirby Smith was left to deal with Sill's column, while Polk withdrew the main army toward Harrodsburg, through Perryville. Since October 1, Joe Wheeler's cavalry had been in constant contact with the advance elements of Buell's army, and there could be little doubt about where the main Union thrust was going to come from. Smith pleaded for reinforcements with which to face Sill, but Bragg had little to spare. He would be facing the main Union army with an available force of only 18,000 men. At that strength, he would already be outnumbered three to one. Even so, he ordered the divisions of Jones Withers and Benjamin Franklin

Cheatham to march to Smith's relief. Bragg's offensive spirit seems to have come from the fact that he was still confused as to the Federal intentions. On October 7, he ordered Polk to form the cavalry, and the divisions of Cheatham, Buckner, and Patton Anderson, and attack the Union columns to their front. It was obvious to Polk that this move would be disastrous to the Confederates, as they were facing a vastly superior force, but Bragg was acting on the belief that the column under Sill was stronger than it actually was, and that the columns in front of Polk were weaker than they actually were. He was still failing to grasp the overall tactical situation on the field, and his orders exhibited the thinking of a commander who was reacting to mis-information. As such, his orders to the army were as ill-advised as was his last proclamation to the men of Kentucky. Bragg's information concerning the movements of Buell's army was not coming directly from his cavalry scouting units. Instead, through an ineffective system of command, those reports were going to his subordinate commanders: Polk, Hardee, and Smith. Those officers would then pass the information along to Bragg, according to their own individual evaluations. For some inexplicable reason, the commanding general of the army was receiving all of his military intelligence piecemeal, and through his subordinates, instead of getting it straight from his cavalry commander.[10]

Unknown to Bragg, Generals Earl Van Dorn and Sterling Price were at that moment trying to effect a diversion in favor of his invading army. On October 3, their combined forces had launched an attack against Major General William S. Rosecrans' army at Corinth. In a bloody, two-day battle, the Confederate forces were repulsed, with casualties of over 4,200 men. Rosecrans had been able to hold his own without drawing support away from Buell, who would be free to continue his own campaign. No Union troops would be diverted away from Bragg's front to guard against Confederate activities in Mississippi.[11]

Confederate cavalry had been skirmishing with Buell's columns ever since they marched out of Louisville. The 4th Tennessee Cavalry had been stationed but 12 miles southwest of Louisville, and was engaged almost immediately. Trooper L.S. Ferrell remembered that

> Our commissary sergeant had purchased a bucket full of nice yellow butter, and we were getting ready for a "good time," when the bugle sounded "You'd better saddle up, you'd better saddle up, you'd better saddle up your hor-ses!" brought every man and his "quippages" to the side of his horse. Soon there was mounting in hot haste, and a dash was made to the front.... We advanced some distance passed our picket line and to a large brick house on the left of the pike. A splendid-looking old gentleman — I understood his name was Preston — and Capt. Wharton had a lengthy conversation. I overheard this

remark distinctly: "I have just received this morning a note from my niece in Louisville saying that Buell will move early tomorrow morning with nearly a hundred thousand men."[12]

The Union army was advancing, but not with the 100,000 men that rumors were circulating. Buell had more than half that number, but of those, some 22,000 were raw recruits. Private Garrett Larew, of the 86th Indiana, was one of the soldiers new to the army. His diary entry for September 30 gives the reader some idea of the inexperience that existed among the Union ranks. "We are drawed [sic] in ranks to drill four times a day, two company drills, one review and one battalion and dress parade all at once." Thirty-five of Buell's 125 regiments were new troops. That, on the surface, would mean that 25 percent of his army was green. But most of his veteran regiments were below full strength, while the new ones were at a full complement of men. In actuality, approximately 40 percent of the Union army had spent a month or less in military service. With such a large percentage of untried troops in the Federal ranks, Bragg's veteran army could, in all reality, match itself against the superior Union numbers with at least a reasonable hope of success. Recruits were held in disdain by the veterans of both armies, and the numerical advantage was more than offset by the lack of experience.[13]

Not all of the Confederate units were in the same fighting trim as the 4th Tennessee, either. W.C. Gipson, a sergeant in the 17th Tennessee Infantry, related a scene of a different sort during the withdrawal toward Bardstown and Harrodsburg. "We started the retreat to Perryville.... I was put in charge of the rear guard. Unfortunately the Fifth Confederate, mostly Irish, had got some whiskey, and many of them were drunk, and we had a hard time in getting them forward while we were trying to keep the enemy back. We had to leave some of them, as they could not travel. We carried their guns for some time, but the enemy pressed us so hard that we hid their guns — twelve in number — under a brush pile."[14]

The lack of water and the dry, choking conditions tortured the Confederate troops as it was torturing their Union counterparts. One Confederate veteran of the campaign would later remember: "In the great draught which was burning Kentucky in the autumn of 1862 it was a most difficult matter for large armies to find a water supply." Another soldier left a more personal account: "Our Army suffers terribly for water. It's almost impossible to get any. Have seen something I never seen before, from fellows taking water out of mud hole, and drink as if it was the best water they ever tasted." Yet another stated that "some people objected to the soldiers getting water from their wells. Frequently, while we who were in the cavalry were watering our horses by companies, the infantry and artillerists would fill their canteens from under the horses with water which was wholly unfit for stock to drink. No doubt that much sickness and many deaths were attributable to the impure water. But brave men endured all this with but little murmuring."[15]

Polk was consolidating his forces in the vicinity of Perryville. It was a retrograde movement, in the face of superior forces, but it also provided the Confederates the opportunity of interposing their army between the Federals and the Southern base of supply at Bryantsville. Perryville also offered a much needed source of water, as Chaplin River and Doctor's Creek flowed by the town. Major General William J. Hardee's troops were at Perryville already. Polk's troops were marching to that place from Bardstown, and there was some doubt as to whether the junction could be made before Hardee was assailed by Buell's army. The troops in the ranks little concerned themselves with the strategic situation. They were more interested in taking care of their own comfort, and their empty bellies. A soldier in the 1st Arkansas Infantry related an amusing story that took place during the march. "On October 6th we marched through Perry ville, but on the 7th we marched back and camped in the main street of the town. Some of the boys stole a beehive and many of them got stung so their faces were swollen and eyes closed. Dr. Arnold was one of the injured ones, but he did not fail to eat his honey. As we lay on the ground that night I teased him, saying

Major General Phil Sheridan. The night before the battle, Sheridan buried an old feud with General Terrill. Before dawn of the following day, portions of his division would advance against the Confederates and bring on the battle of Perryville. (Courtesy of the United States Army War College.)

General Hardee would need no further proof; that he carried his guilt on his face. The doctor did not relish this so I turned over to go to sleep when a bee stung me on the cheek. 'Who's the guilty one now?' laughed the doctor and the joke was surely on me."[16]

Colonel Joseph Wheeler's cavalry was deployed in front of Hardee's men, and was given the daunting task of delaying Buell's advance until Polk could arrive. Wheeler performed his duty with skill and daring. He formed his cavalry in front of the Union advance, forcing them to come into line to brush the troopers away. The gray horsemen would then fall back to repeat the process, over and over again. As Wheeler stated in his report of the action: "We engaged them with artillery and small-arms, compelling them to advance very slowly, frequently deploying their infantry. We were obliged to fall back slowly when their infantry fired too heavily; but suceeded [sic] in so checking their progress that they only advanced about 4 miles from 8 A.M. until dark." By nightfall on the 7th, Wheeler was able to report, "By keeping our lines continuously skirmishing until night we prevented the enemy from making any demonstration that day upon our infantry, which had deployed in line of battle to meet the enemy on the field of Perryville."[17]

Wheeler's delaying tactics bought the Confederates the time they needed to effect a partial junction of their forces. By midnight of October 7, Polk's command had been able to join Hardee at Perryville. General Cheatham had also arrived with his command, having been called back from his mission to assail Sill's Union column at Frankfort. Withers' strong division of 8,000 men was still not on the field, however. Bragg had ordered Withers to attack the head of Sill's division at Salvisa, near Frankfort, but when Withers arrived at that place, he found that the fast-moving Union troops had already marched through. When Polk arrived at Perryville, it was with new orders from Bragg. "In view of the news from Hardee," he wrote, "you had better move with Cheatham's division to his support and give the enemy battle immediately. Rout him and then move to our support at Versailles. No time should be lost in these movements." Polk either misunderstood his orders, or deliberately disobeyed them. In any event, he was derelict in providing his commander with a clear, concise picture of the situation. At daylight on the 8th, he called a war council of his officers to discuss their proper course of action. It was determined that the army would assume a defensive-offensive posture, and await developments from Buell's army, contrary to Bragg's orders. Colonel Wheeler's troopers were back in the saddle, sent to reconnoiter the Union army, and determine its intentions. What Wheeler found was a large body of Union infantry in line of battle. This line was being steadily reinforced as new units arrived on the scene. The best Wheeler could do was to inform Polk of his findings, and then post scouts and pickets at all of the approaches to the town, to try to ensure that the enemy could not surprise the Confederate army by suddenly appearing on its flanks or rear. By ten o'clock that morning, General Bragg had finally arrived on the field to assume personal command of his army. Much to his chagrin, he found that Polk had not followed his instructions and initiated the battle. Each army seemed to be content to allow the other to make the first move. Bragg was outraged over what he perceived to be a lost opportunity. Instead of attacking Buell's army while it was strung out, and in column of march, the Federals had been allowed to concentrate a sizeable portion of their force in front of the Confederate position. From this moment on, Bragg would personally oversee the implementation of his plans, and if Buell was looking for a fight, concentrated or not, he would give him one.

The night of October 7 was a time of peacemaking, not fighting, for two officers in the Union army. General Sheridan and General Terrill had been cadets together at West Point, where they had gotten into a heated altercation that created hard feelings between them that lasted long after they left the Academy. That night, Sheridan had been called to a conference. While there, an officer inquired "General Sheridan, when you were at West Point didn't you have some trouble with a cadet named Terrill?" Sheridan replied in the affirmative, and was then informed that Terrill was commanding a brigade in McCook's Corps. "He's a brigadier general." Upon hearing Terrill's name, Sheridan's old hatreds began to surface, but as he was riding back to his own camp, the thought came to him that "We are both fighting for the Union," and he turned his horse around and went in search of Terrill's camp. When he found the man who had once been his cadet sergeant, he extended a hand and said "Sheridan. Came down to say hello." The two men made their peace with one another and talked at length of their experiences in the peacetime army. When the time came for them to part, Terrill told Sheridan "it means a lot to me that you came to bury the hatchet. I was wrong—dead wrong." Sheridan was gracious in his response. "You can't bear all the blame. I learned a lesson. My temper—I can control it now. Good luck, Bill. I'll see you after the battle." The two men parted as friends, but they were never to see one another again.[18]

CHAPTER FIVE

Opening Shots

General Gilbert's Corps was leading the march of Buell's army, and was the first to near Perryville. It was traveling on the Springfield Road, with a brigade of cavalry, under the command of acting Brigadier General Ebenezer Gay, in advance of the infantry. Gay's troopers were meeting stiff resistance, so much so that the corps was ordered to make camp before the usual hour, some four miles from the Chaplin River, and Perryville. Brigadier General Ormsby Mitchell's Division was placed across the road in line of battle, with Brigadier General Albin Schoepf's Division in support. Brigadier General Phil Sheridan's Division was placed to the right of Mitchell, on a ridge that formed almost a right-angle to the main line. Sheridan's men were also formed in line of battle, and the right of his line was the closest of any Union troops to the Confederate position. Sheridan saw to it that his artillery was all unlimbered and shotted, and made all necessary preparations to receive an attack, should the Confederates choose to launch one. Gilbert's advanced position would serve as the center of the Union line. When McCook's Corps came up, it would form to the left of Gilbert's line, and Crittenden would position his troops on Gilbert's right.[1]

At three o'clock on the morning of October 8, Brigadier General Dan McCook's Brigade was ordered to advance to its front to secure some pools of water that were supposed to be in the bed of Doctor's Creek. Gilbert's Corps had gone into camp without the benefit of having a source of water, and General Buell had sanctioned the movement of McCook's Brigade in the hope of securing water for his troops. It was a clear and moonlit night, and the advance was immediately detected by the Confederates. Skirmish fire broke out, but the Confederate pickets were driven back easily by the weight of McCook's force. The Federals advanced two miles, finding the water they sought. In order to protect the pools, McCook had his brigade occupy a ridge, known as Peter's Hill, approximately one-half mile beyond the creek. A short but fierce firefight took place as the Union troops pushed troopers from Wheeler's Confederate cavalry off of the ridge. The members of the brigade then filled their canteens, assumed defensive positions, and settled in for the night. No campfires were allowed, so as not to give away their position to the enemy, and no rations were issued. The remainder of Sheridan's Division would be moving up to join them in the morning, however, and the men hoped they would be able to brew some coffee then.[2]

Brigadier General St. John Liddell. When Union troops from Sheridan's Division advanced to secure water from Doctor's Creek they made contact with Liddell's Brigade, and the fight for control of the stagnant pools touched off a general engagement. (Courtesy of the United States Army War College.)

Opposite McCook were the five Arkansas regiments of Brigadier General St. John Richardson Liddell's Brigade, of Buckner's Division, Hardee's Corps. Liddell, a Mississippi native, had performed brilliantly at Shiloh, and Hardee had been so impressed with his capabilities that he wanted the Arkansas veterans out in front where they could cover the approaches to Perryville from the west. The brigade was positioned astride the Springfield Road, in a line that roughly conformed to that of McCook's. Liddell's Brigade would be approximately one mile outside of the town. On his left, and to his rear, would be the brigade of Brigadier General Sterling A. Wood. On his right, and to his rear, would be Brigadier General Bushrod Johnson's Brigade.[3]

The ground, at this point, was characterized by a range of ridges that ran north-south. The country around Perryville is marked by these undulating hills. Chaplin's Fork, of Salt River, is nestled between these hills, and flows in a northerly direction from the town. Approximately four or five miles north of town is Doctor's Creek, which empties into Chaplin's Fork a few more miles beyond the town. The creek beds flow in little valleys between the hills. Bull Run paralleled these hills until it flowed into Doctor's Creek, one mile north of the Springfield Road, where the Mackville Road formed an intersection. Liddell's Brigade was to defend this intersection, thereby putting itself in a position to guard against a Federal thrust from either route. Liddell placed his brigade on the high ground east of Bull Run, and reported, "As my left flank rested on the Springfield Road, all on

A photograph of Doctor's Creek looking very much as it did at the time of the battle. Note the low water level and the standing pools. (Photograph by the author.)

that side, having no support, was exposed to a flank movement of the enemy; but feeling satisfied that he must be in need of water, and that he would push for that point whence it could be obtained from pools lower down on Doctor's Fork, on my right, I seperated *[sic]* my battery, and placed one section on a high hill on my right, commanding the woods opposite and the open valley below." Directly in front of Liddell's position lay Peter's Hill, and McCook's Brigade.[4]

Liddell was quite correct in his assumptions that the Union troops would be searching for water, and the disposition of his brigade seemed to be appropriate for the situation. As he surveyed a map of the ground, Liddell decided that the only other move he needed to make was to occupy Peter's Hill, so that he would have a commanding position from which to defend the water holes. When skirmishing broke out in the early morning hours of the 8th, it was his first clue that the Federals were in such close proximity to him, and were already in possession of Peter's Hill. Still, he had no idea how many Federals were in his front, or how many more were coming.

Hardee had sent a message to Bragg, at 3:20 A.M., outlining his preparations, and admonishing the commanding general to take command of the situation. "Tomorrow morning early we may expect a fight. If the enemy does not attack us you ought unless pressed in another direction to send forward all the reinforcements necessary, take command in person, and wipe him out. I desire earnestly that you will do this. The enemy is about two miles from us; my advance of infantry, Liddell's Brigade, about one mile. If Buckner is with you send him forward. I want him. Liddell has just reported that the enemy is trying to turn his right flank."[5]

The remainder of Buell's army was rapidly approaching the town. Buell himself was only five miles away. McCook's Corps was seven to eight miles north, on the Mackville Road, and Crittenden's Corps was slightly farther away, approaching from the south, on the Lebanon Road. With the army about to be reunited, Buell named Brigadier General Speed S. Fry to be the officer of the day. Fry had been born and raised in the Perryville area, and knew the surrounding countryside well. While the majority of Schoepf's Division was held in reserve, Fry selected a regiment from his brigade of that division, the 10th Indiana, and pushed it out one and one-half miles beyond the Union position, in the direction of the town. For Fry, this was a homecoming, of sorts, and his thoughts on that moonlit night were undoubtedly of home and hearth, as he wondered what carnage and devastation the coming of daylight would promote.[6]

Buell was concerned that Gilbert's advanced corps would be attacked before the rest of his army had reached the field. He sent orders to his other two corps commanders to have their columns on the march for Perryville no later than three o'clock on the morning of October 8. Both orders were delayed in reaching the corps commanders, however. General McCook did not receive his message from Buell until 2:30 A.M., a half-hour before he was supposed to march. He made all haste to get his men on the road, after receiving the message, but even so, the corps did not move out until 5:00 A.M. Crittenden's Corps would be even more tardy in starting its march. No water was to be found along the Lebanon Road on the evening of October 7, and Crittenden had been compelled to march his corps six miles out of its way to procure it. Buell's messenger wasted valuable time in trying to locate the corps, and then, it would appear, he delivered an incorrect version of Buell's orders. According to Crittenden, the time stated by the messenger for the march to begin was 6:00 A.M. Crittenden's Corps was the farthest away from Perryville, and it would be the last to get under way, an hour after McCook took to the road, and three hours after Buell had wished for it to commence the march.[7]

Braxton Bragg was still en route to Perryville, as the forces of both sides were

Major General Alexander McCook. His corps would form the left of the Union line, and would take the full brunt of the Confederate assault, while the other two Union corps became largely spectators to the fighting. (Courtesy of the United States Army War College.)

concentrating there. At 6:00 A.M., General Polk sent him a message reporting the Federal buildup, and stating that the enemy was "disposed to press," as firing had broken out as soon as the first rays of daylight appeared. "Understanding it to be your wish to give battle, we shall do so vigorously," he stated.[8]

By 10:30 A.M., McCook's Corps was marching onto the field. Brigadier General Lovell Rousseau's Division was in the lead, followed by the division of Brigadier General James S. Jackson. Sill's Division, of McCook's Corps, was still operating in the vicinity of Frankfort, occupying the attention of Kirby Smith's forces, leaving the Corps at only two-thirds strength. One Union soldier noted that "the whole Division was put on quick time, sometimes on double-quick," as McCook's divisions plodded toward their destination. Private Joseph Glezen of the 80th Indiana Infantry, Terrell's Brigade, McCook's Corps, penned in his diary:

> The Brigade was put in marching condition about 6 o'clock in the morning, but remained in place whilst Rowson's (Rousseau's) Division and a part of

Jackson's Division passed to our advance. The day was hot and dry, the ground remarkably dusty, and what was worse than all, no water could be procured by those who had the misfortune of being placed in the rear, as every spring, well and cistern were drained by those in advance. Men were frequently detailed from the different companies, who often went out for a mile or more from the road, in search of water, and when they would return exhausted, with empty canteens, the mournful cry would run through the ranks. No water! No water! At one place I saw a poor soldier drive the hogs from a mud hole in a creek bottom and then lie down and drink where the swine had been wallowing. As we advanced on our march, the sound of artillery became louder, and the reports more frequent. Notwithstanding our fatigue and thirst, as we approached the scenes of carnage the men seemed cheerful, and appeared to move forward as if determined to do their whole duty in the approaching contest.[9]

The dry, dusty conditions were no better at Perryville. An officer in Gilbert's command later recalled that "Very early in the morning (October 8) Sheridan's division passed us, not over ten feet distant, but so dense was the dust that we could not distinguish a man. I noticed one of my men had rolled over in his sleep quite near me. I could reach him. His features were almost obliterated by dust and perspiration. Curiosity prompted me to see how much dust I could gather with a single grasp of my hand, so I reached over, securing a hand-ful. Before we were up we heard firing in our front, not over a mile from us. I was satisfied that Sheridan was engaging the enemy."[10]

Braxton Bragg arrived at Perryville at approximately ten that morning. He had passed the early morning hours at Harrodsburg, expecting to hear the sounds of Polk's attack, but no such sounds were forthcoming. Bragg had intended for the attack to be made at dawn, but Polk hesitated. Instead, he called a council of his officers to discuss the situation. Colonel Wheeler's reports indicated that the Federals were amassing a sizeable force to his front, and in view of this, Polk became indecisive. Wheeler's patrols had been sending back alarming news of large bodies of Union troops en route for Perryville, for the past two days. Trooper W.H. Davis, of the 4th Tennessee Cavalry Battalion, related one such encounter with Buell's army on the afternoon of the 7th.

Company B ... to which I belonged, was sent from our extreme right to find out General Buell's exact position. We had not proceeded more than two hundred yards over a considerable hill and had reached the foot of the western slope when we met a company of about our number, all dressed in brand new Confederate uniforms, wearing sabers and regulation brass Yankee spurs. Our respective captains saluted each other, while their horses' necks were lapped. The captain with the new uniform asked our chief, "To what command do you belong?" and he received the reply: "To Wheeler's command, Wharton's Brigade." Our captain then asked him, "To what command do you belong?" to which an evasive reply was given. During this colloquy the men of the respective companies advanced to the right and left of their respective commanders, their horses' noses touching. Their sabers and spurs gave the little game away, and as quick as thought our captain yelled out: "Boys they are damned Yankees; turn loose your six-shooters!" No quicker was this said than it was done. We emptied a volley into them, killing and wounding more than half their number. As the sham captain wheeled his horse to escape, Captain Lester shot him in the back, but it did not knock him out of the saddle. The whole troop quickly followed him, with us in hot pursuit. We got eight or ten more before running into a hornet's nest on the main line of Buell's left wing, where we received a baptism of fire and beat a hasty retreat.

Such reports of running into heavy columns of Union infantry were becoming common, and Polk seems to have lost his nerve. Bragg's orders to "Give battle immediately" were ignored, as Polk discussed the situation with his general officers. Polk would later argue that "I did not regard the letter of instructions as a peremptory order to attack at all hazards, but that ... I should carry the instructions into execution as judiciously and promptly as a willing mind and sound discretion would allow." In conference with his generals, he determined "to adopt the deffensive*[sic]*-offensive; to await the movements of the enemy and to be guided by events as they were developed."[11]

Colonel Thomas Claiborne, one of Buckner's staff officers, was present when Bragg arrived on the field, and later recorded the interview that took place between the commander and General Polk. "It was about 11 A.M. when General Bragg, at the head of his large staff, reached the point of the turnpike road where were assembled General Polk and General Buckner and General Hardee and Cheatham and their staffs ready to march to Harrodsburg. I had just ridden up as Bragg addressed General Polk. I state substantially: 'What are you doing, General Polk?' 'I am retiring, as the enemy are too many.' General Bragg quickly and on no further inquiry into conditions replied: 'Bring on the action with small arms.' General Polk and the others present seemed for a moment astonished; but recovering quickly, waved his arm and ordered that his troops, which, as I have stated above, were massed, should be deployed on the lines they had just left."[12]

To be sure, the opposing armies were already in contact. Skirmishing had taken place throughout the night, and had intensified with the coming of daybreak. The artillery of both sides joined in, as the cannon "shelled the woods" in an ineffective effort to discover the positions of the enemy. Though it was not a general engagement, Bragg should have been able to hear this firing at

Harrodsburg, but he could not. A peculiar atmospheric condition, known as an acoustic shadow, prevented the sound of the firing from reaching him. This shadow produces something similar to a bubble over an area, and alters the sound waves so that they effectively bounce over the bubble, creating a circumstance where cannon fire that could be heard 50 miles away could not be heard two miles away. The atmospheric conditions on the field that day would lead to mistakes and misperceptions for the commanders of both armies.[13]

Buell had desired to launch an attack on the Confederate position at seven that morning. The delays in his marching orders being delivered to McCook and Crittenden sabotaged this plan. Instead, Buell waited impatiently for the arrival of these two corps, hoping that the Confederates would not attack him before all of his army was on the field. Polk's hesitation had cost Bragg the chance of catching a single Union corps away from its support, and bringing its newest and most inexperienced corps commander to battle.

There was indeed already fighting taking place, even before Bragg arrived to take control of the situation. St. John Liddell's Confederate brigade had been attempting to retake Peter's Hill, and the water holes it protected, since the twilight before the dawn. The 5th and 7th Arkansas Infantry were ordered to make the charge, supported by Swett's Mississippi Battery. As the infantry formed for the attack, the cannoneers unlimbered their guns and began lobbing case shot into the woods where McCook's Brigade was taking refuge. Most of the shells exploded harmlessly in the treetops, but the 85th Illinois was hard hit by the shelling. Captain Charles Barnett's Union battery sprang into action, and responded to the Confederate artillery, forcing them to relocate their guns several times. This was accomplished even though Barnett could only use four of his guns because the gunners assigned to two of the cannon were so inexperienced that they did not know how to fire the weapons. With the opposing artillery engaged in counterbattery fire, the Confederate infantry prepared to go forward. On the hill, their arrival was awaited by the 52nd Ohio, the 125th Illinois, and the 85th Illinois. The Confederate battle flags moved forward in the early morning light, and the Union defenders had to be restrained from firing upon the advancing line too early, and giving away the position of their line. McCook ordered the men to hold their fire until the Confederates had gotten within 200 yards of them. When the gray line reached that point, the order to fire was given, and the resulting volley mowed down large numbers of the advancing Confederates.[14]

Battery I, 2nd Illinois Light Artillery claims the honor of firing the first artillery shot in the battle. It had two sections of guns posted with Sheridan's troops, two 10-pound Parrott guns, and two 10-pound James guns. This battery played a conspicuous part in the fighting on Sheridan's part of the field, even though its members had no food or water during the entire day. W.G. Putney, the battery bugler, had "gathered up the canteens of the men and started for water at a spring near by with the intention of filling them for the men so they could quench their thirst, but the 'best laid plans of men and mice aft gang aglee,' as the rebels had possession of the spring, and came near 'gobbling up' our brave bugler. Out of twenty-seven canteens, he took with him he returned with one, and that one empty."[15]

One Union soldier was amazed by the sight of so many men in Liddell's command being killed or wounded without making a sound. "An arm is shattered, a leg carried away, a bullet pierces the breast, and the soldier sinks down silently upon the ground or creeps away if he can."[16]

Liddell, in his report of the battle, would describe the assault thus: "The attempt was promptly and cheerfully made, but the force of the enemy had been increased so largely and suddenly as to force back both lines, the officers and men contesting the ground with resolute determination, unwilling to yield it to even the great odds against them."[17]

The Confederates were forced back, however, by the weight of superior numbers, and the commanding position the Federals held on Peter's Hill. Phil Sheridan was at the front by this time, and had established his headquarters at the Turpin house, a dwelling that stood on top of Peter's Hill. Sheridan had only recently won his general's star, and he was itching to prove his capabilities in division command. General William S. Rosecrans had applied for Sheridan's promotion with the endorsement that he was "worth his weight in gold." High praise, indeed, and Sheridan, never one to back down from a scrap, was now intending to prove that praise correct. General Gilbert, aware of his subordinate's aggressive nature, cautioned Sheridan against bringing on a general engagement before Buell was ready for one. Sheridan sent back word that he was not intending to make the engagement general, but that it was his opinion the Confederates were trying to do so. This was far from the truth. The two Arkansas regiments had already spent themselves in their attack on the hill, and were retiring from the field. Though skirmish fire continued, accompanied by the occasional barking from the two engaged batteries of artillery, the fighting on that part of the field was fading when Sheridan sent his message to Gilbert. The ambitious young general had plans of his own, and his impetuosity would escalate the fighting he had been ordered to contain. Not satisfied with merely repulsing the Confederate attack, Sheridan decided to drive them off their position on the opposite hill. He ordered Lieutenant Colonel Bernard Laibolt's Brigade to attack the Confederates. Laibolt sent the 2nd and 15th Missouri forward, but their attack failed to dislodge Liddell's Arkansas regiments. Laibolt then committed the 44th and 73rd Illinois to the assault. The 73rd Illinois was known in the army as the "Preachers Regiment" because 12 of its officers were Methodist preachers.[18]

Liddell's Brigade continued to hold against the increased pressure, but more Union units were entering the fray. General Gay's cavalry had been attempting to push toward the town, but was stopped by the force of Confederates in the woods. Gay dismounted his troopers, and supported by the 52nd Ohio, they advanced into the woods. The pressure became too much for Liddell's troops to stand, and his line began to give way and retreat toward Perryville.[19]

G.W. Brown, a member of the 86th Illinois, recounted the fighting in a letter to his brother, written nine days after the battle. The regiment

Major General Patton Anderson. His division would form the left of the Confederate line of battle. (Courtesy of the United States Army War College.)

was "ordered to make a charge on about 2500 of the enemy posted behind a stone wall, on a wooded hillside, and over the crest of a hill." The men advanced "with a shout on double quick. I followed the regiment. Soon a squad of sharp shooters posted on our left flank began to play on us, and the bullets plaid [sic] all around us. I expected, at least, that my horse would be killed; but not an officer was touched.... We charged up the hill and when the boys gained the crest of the hill, with a yell, they poured in a destructive volley upon the enemy. They (the Confederates) did not wait for a second, but ran precipitately from the field. As you may perhaps have seen by the papers, we lost only 1 killed and 13 wounded."[20]

Buell had intended to launch an attack as soon as all his forces were up, and he had been concerned that the Confederates might spoil his plans by mounting their own assault before he was ready. Sheridan's men had been able to push back the Confederates with apparent ease, and Buell mistakenly translated this to mean that the Southerners were not yet ready to fight. Instead of acting with haste, to seize the initiative, Buell seemed to relax after Sheridan's action, as if he already had the Confederates on the run and could take his time in formulating his own plans. The late morning and early afternoon were spent in planning the Union attack, not in making it.

Part of the reason for Buell's slowness to act could have been that he had been injured the previous day, when his horse threw him. The general was badly bruised, and had become quite stiff and sore by the morning of the 8th. Though Buell never cited his own injury as being a reason for his vacillating actions on the battlefield that day, it surely contributed to slowing him down.[21]

While Buell made his plans, Bragg prepared to bring on the battle. The ground selected for the Confederate army had been chosen by General Polk, and Bragg approved of his dispositions. Polk was given tactical control of the right portion of the line, and Hardee was assigned to oversee operations on the left. Buckner's Division, of which Liddell's Brigade was a part, would form the center of the Confederate line. To his right would be the division of Brigadier General Benjamin F. Cheatham. On his left would be the division of Brigadier General Patton Anderson. Due to the disparity in numbers, the Confederate line was approximately half the length of the Union line. The left flank,

Major General Benjamin Franklin Cheatham. In the early afternoon of October 8, Cheatham's lines of infantry swept forward to engage McCook's Corps in what would become some of the most desperate fighting to take place during the war. (Courtesy of the United States Army War College.)

under Anderson, found itself in a dangerous position, exposed and unanchored, from which it could easily be assaulted and turned by a determined Union effort. Colonel Wheeler's Cavalry was assigned to cover this portion of the line, and it was stretched very thin to accomplish that purpose. Greatly outnumbered, about all Wheeler could do was to make a presence in front of Crittenden's and Gilbert's Corps. If either Union commander decided to advance against Wheeler, the troopers would easily have been brushed aside. Once the line was formed, it was discovered that there was a large gap between the left of Cheatham's Division and the right of Buckner's. In an effort to fill this gap, Brigadier General John C. Brown's and Colonel Thomas M. Jones' Brigades, of Anderson's Division, and Brigadier General S.A.M. Wood's Brigade, of Cheatham's Division, were ordered to plug the gap. Wheeler's cavalry was further weakened, with a portion being detached to also guard the Confederate right flank. With his army thus aligned, Bragg gave the order to attack.[22]

One of Bragg's staff officers was not very impressed with the Confederate alignment. According to Colonel Brent, "The position was not so good. Genl. Polk's line was weak, his right if outflanked by the enemy would have cut us off from Harrodsburg and Genl. Smith." Another soldier observed that "On our side of the creek the bank was bluff in places, sloping by gradual descent.... The possession of the bluff ... was evidently a matter of importance, as with it, we commanded the water in our front as well as rear, and could mask our forces under the slope, concealing our strength from the enemy." From these two descriptions it can be deduced that the natural features of Bragg's line were strong, and lent themselves to the Confederate purpose. The weakness that Brent observes comes not from the features of the ground, but rather from the numerical weakness of Bragg's army. The position was a strong one, but the Confederates simply did not have enough men to cover all the ground. [23]

General Ebenezer Gay formed the troopers of the 9th Pennsylvania and the 2nd Michigan as skirmishers in front of McCook's line. The 2nd Michigan was dismounted and sent forward into the woods to ascertain the position of the enemy. When they entered the timber, they were met with a volley that killed four and wounded thirteen of their officers and men. The regiment recoiled from the unexpected fire, then regained its composure and gave the Confederates an example of the superior firepower their Colt revolving rifles gave them. One trooper wrote that "the rebels charged upon them 2 or 3 times ... they broke their charge every time and the rebels were Obliged to fall back." After this encounter with the enemy, Gay directed that the cavalry support the artillery positioned on a knoll near the Russell House. From this position, they would be able to cover the Macville Road and the ford where the road crossed Doctor's Fork.[24]

General Sheridan later stated that from his position on the line, he could see a large body of Confederates massing in McCook's front. He tried "by the use of signal flags" to alert McCook to the danger, but "my efforts failed." It would appear that the flags were the only effort Sheridan made to warn McCook. Sheridan never acknowledged that he had tried to send a messenger to the general, and McCook, in his reports, never alluded to receiving any sort of warning from Sheridan. When he could clearly see the impending danger, it is hard to understand why Sheridan allowed McCook to form his lines in ignorance, without making every possible effort to warn him.[25]

At a little after 1:00 P.M., the Confederate line surged forward. Colonel

Members of the famed Washington Artillery in camp. This Confederate battery took part in the artillery duel that preceded the infantry assault on the Union lines. (Courtesy of the United States Army War College.)

Wharton's Cavalry led the attack on the Confederate right, followed by Cheatham's infantry. "At right shoulder shift arms our troops moved in the most steady tread, despite the firing of artillery and small arms in the whole front, which inflicted much loss; but the line only in its long extent swayed as obstacles were met, steadily forming on the colors and closing the gaps made by the enemy's fire, which was so fierce that it seemed almost impossible for our troops to get at the enemy."[26]

Captain W.W. Carnes, commanding the Tennessee Battery, assigned to Cheatham's 1st Brigade, had been seriously ill the night before the battle. The regimental surgeon had advised that he be sent off in an ambulance, but Carnes refused to go. Instead, he had a bed made in the back of a caisson, persuaded the doctor to give him something to make him sleep, and stayed with his command. Carnes' Memphis Battery had been on the Confederate left in the early morning hours of the 8th, but it was shifted to the right in preparation for making the attack. The captain has left the following account of the opening of the battle on this part of the field.

> A staff officer came hurrying up with a request from Gen. Wood to send him a battery of artillery as he saw the enemy opposite him getting ready to open on his command with artillery and he had no battery at hand. General Polk

directed me to go with the officer, who directed me off to the left of the place where I had been stopped and pointed out for me a position on a high piece of wooded ground from which, across a field in my front, I could see the blue line of the enemy in the woods opposite. I went into battery here, and after carefully estimating the distance and giving proper directions as to the elevation of the sight and cutting of fuse for each gun — during which preparation no shot had been fired from the enemy — I opened fire with what was said by our people to be very good effect. The battery which General Wood had seemed so concerned about had been pointed out to me and I directed my fire at it from the start. My shot fell among them and when they opened on me they fired very high, making a great noise with bursting shells in the tree tops but really doing no harm to any of my men. Very soon, however, another battery fired on me from another point opposite, then another and another till there were four of them concentrating their fire on my one battery. Fortunately for me they all fired wildly, and before they got our range well I was aware that another battery had gone into action on my right to my support, then a little later, two more on my left, till we had Calvert's Battery (from Ark., I think), Lumsden's Battery, from Ala., and Slocum's Battery, from New Orleans, helping me to make it lively for our friends over the way. These helped to divide the fire from the enemy in time to prevent my getting the concentrated fire of the four Federal batteries after they all got down to business. This artillery duel was kept up for some time — how long I cannot remember. The enemy made a terrible row in our timber with bursting shells and limbs of trees shot off over us, but there was really not much damage done to us, but I got a few horses shot and traces cut.[27]

The Confederate batteries were occupying the attention of their Federal counterparts, and the duel that ensued allowed the gray battle line to move forward, relatively free from the barrage of canister and grapeshot that it would otherwise have had to face. Cheatham's and Buckner's men slammed into McCook's Corps. Brigadier General Rufus Terrill's Brigade, of Jackson's Division, was holding the left of McCook's line, and Brigadier General Lovell Rousseau's Division held the right. Skirmishers were sent forward, from both of these divisions, approximately 600 yards, to the Chaplin River, so that water could be obtained for the troops. McCook had given orders that the remaining two brigades of General Jackson's Division be posted on a commanding piece of ground immediately to the right of the Mackville and Perryville Road. They were to be held in column, ready to march in any direction, to reinforce any part of the line that seemed threatened. Though he had made all the necessary dispositions to receive an assault, McCook was not actually on the field when the attack began. He had been ordered to report to Buell's headquarters, and had given his assistant adjutant general, Captain J.A. Campbell, orders to oversee the final placement of the

Position of Simonson's Federal Battery facing Carnes's Confederate Battery on the ridge in the distance. From these positions, the opposing artillery roared away at one another before the infantry assault took place. (Photograph by the author.)

men. The divisional commanders would be ranking officers on the field when the attack began, and the Confederates would play havoc with that command structure.[28]

Solon Marks, a surgeon in the 9th Brigade of Rousseau's Division, remembered the "deathlike stillness" that pervaded the field before the Confederates launched their assault. The silence was broken "when all of a sudden those heights rocked and quivered beneath the discharge of twenty or thirty pieces of artillery, followed by the roar of musketry, the shrieking and explosion of shells and hissing of solid shot. It seemed to me that the very elements were in line of battle, and that old Lucifer and all his imps were dancing to the music of battle and carnage."[29]

The Confederate line first struck the skirmishers of the 33rd Ohio, as Buckner's troops surged forward. The remainder of the regiment was ordered up to the support of the skirmishers, who were giving ground. The 2nd Ohio was then ordered forward to support the 33rd Ohio, as Confederate pressure increased. The engagement became general, as the 24th Illinois and 38th Indiana were ordered up, taking positions to the left and right of the 33rd Ohio, respectively. General Rousseau personally led the 24th Illinois into position. The 94th Ohio and 10th Wisconsin were thrown into the fray, as both sides concentrated their forces at this point of attack. The 94th Ohio was one of the green regiments in the Union army. General Rousseau paid tribute to it, however, when he stated that "although new and but a few weeks in the service, it behaved most gallantly, under the steady lead of its brave Colonel Frizell." The Union troops were facing overwhelming odds, and were beginning to run low on cartridges. Rousseau praised the steadfast determination with which these men fought. "The Thirty-eighth Indiana and Second Ohio, after exhausting their ammunition and that taken from the boxes of the dead and wounded on the field, still held their positions, as did also, I believe, the Tenth Wisconsin and Thirty-third Ohio." The brigade commander, Colonel Leonard Harris, described how the 38th Indiana had "exhausted the cartridges of the dead and wounded. Colonel Scribner then directed his men to fix bayonets and hold the position, which was promptly done. The 10th Wisconsin had set the example for the 38th Indiana. Once the Wisconsin men fired every cartridge that they had, or that could be gathered from the dead and wounded on the field, they were ordered to fix bayonets. The regiment held its position by force of steel alone, until relieved by the 38th Indiana. That regiment then held till it too was out of ammunition and forced to hold with bayonets alone. Without a round of ammunition, under a heavy fire in front and an enfilading fire from the artillery, they held their position for twenty-five minutes."[30]

A private in Buckner's division recounted the action from the Confederate viewpoint:

> We were subjected to a most merciless shelling ... when we were ordered forward, and advancing within 200 or 300 yards of the enemy, spread ourselves on the ground and the following two hours had a fair, open field fight, with the exception that the enemy had some advantage of position on a hill, in scattering timber, which afforded them some protection, while we were exposed in the open field.
>
> With nothing to obstruct the view, it was a grand though horrible spectacle, when the dense smoke was lifted by a passing breeze, to witness the surging of the columns of gray and blue, which could be plainly seen a distance of more than a mile to the right.
>
> The firing was incessant, and nothing but a continuous roar could be heard. If any commands were given, they could not be distinguished above the din, so when it became necessary to move forward the Colonel had to

Position from which Jones' and Brown's brigades crossed Doctor's Creek to attack Lytle's position on the ridge above. (Photograph by the author.)

ride down the line and give the command to each Captain separately to "Fix bayonets, forward — march!"

Almost every mounted officer in the brigade was killed or disabled in the charge, and our line was perceptibly thinned before we reached the foot of the hill; but we pressed on and up until within 30 yards of the enemy.[31]

But courage and determination could not long compensate for the lack of ammunition. Harris' Brigade was forced to give way, and it retreated to the edge of a wooded piece of ground, to the rear of a cornfield, where ammunition was brought up to replenish the depleted cartridge boxes of the men. Harris then directed that his line be formed along a fence that separated the cornfield from the woods, across and at a right angle to the Mackville-Perryville road. General Rousseau was conspicuous on this part of the field, riding among the men encouraging them by his calm example to hold fast. Lieutenant Edward Ferguson, of the 16th Wisconsin, observed Rousseau. He stated that the general "with a courage that seemed almost foolhardy, in his desire to impress upon us the importance of clearing his state of invaders, rode down our line, and twirling his hat upon his sword-point, called out to our men: 'Now boys, you stand by me, and I will by you, and we will whip hell out of them!' The effect was not lost, but inspired all with an appreciation of the importance of our position and a determination to hold it if possible." The lack of ammunition with which to fight made it impossible, though, as the ever-increasing pressure of the Confederates threatened to break the line. The Union position was now being assailed by another Confederate force. Brigadier General Patrick Cleburne's Brigade was advancing in support of the main attack. While Bushrod Johnson's Brigade was engaging the Federals on the hillside, Cleburne marched the 15th Arkansas through the creek bed of Doctor's Creek, and ordered them to change front. Their position proved to be so far beneath that of the Federals that all of the shots from the enemy passed harmlessly overhead. Cleburne had observed that the left flank of the Union position was exposed, and the 15th Arkansas was now in position to exploit this advantage. His attack caught the Federals in a cross fire, threatening to break their line, but Johnson's men were at that time running out of ammunition themselves, and had to be withdrawn to replenish their supply. Cleburne's men shifted their line to fill the vacancy left by Johnson's troops. A tactical advantage was thereby lost, but Cleburne's Brigade was relatively fresh, and they kept up the pressure on the exhausted Yankees. Under orders from the division commander, the Union line was withdrawn 100 yards to the rear, where it was reinforced by the addition of the 50th Ohio. Though skirmishing and artillery fire continued on this part of the field for the remainder of the day, the fury of the battle was moving to other portions of the Union line. The hardest part of the battle for these troops was over. Rousseau's line had held, but it had done so at a frightful cost. Approximately 32.5 percent of his division were listed as killed, wounded, or missing.[32]

Lieutenant W.E. Yeatman, of the 2nd Tennessee Infantry, described the advance against Rousseau's Division as "Another battle like you see in pictures. For a mile we could see them, their splendid looking lines. Flags flying, bands playing, and cannons playing on us as we moved to attack them. They were splendidly posted in two lines, one at the foot the other on the open ridge. We had a full view of what we were expected to do. We moved up in two lines. In our front was a dry branch, on the opposite bank a breast-high rock fence, behind the fence their advance line. It was carried by our regiment and the 3rd Confederate Tennessee Regiment where we attacked jointly after an almost hand to hand fight, and in the face of their fire from both lines. As their line broke, we had them, and gave it to them in the back. It was a hot evening and the grass being dry, caught fire, the flames spreading to a barn just to our right. Rather than burn, it hustled a lot of blue coats to surrender, amonst [sic] them a negro who said he was a cook to Genl. Woolfolk (?). A great many Federals were killed here—more as they ran up the hill, than at the rock wall."[33]

W.C. Gipson, a soldier in the 17th Tennessee, of Brigadier General Bushrod Johnson's Brigade, Buckner's Division, also described the fighting:

> As our brigade was on the south end of the town, we did not strike the enemy until we got over the first range of hills. When we reached the edge of an old field we were in plain view of the enemy, and they gave us the warmest reception I ever had. Our Colonel, A.S. Marks, proposed to Gen. Bushrod Johnson, our brigade commander, to charge the stone wall, which was about four hundred yards in our front, but Gen. Johnson thought it too perilous. Col. Marks replied: "It can't be worse than this; we shall all be killed if we stay here." The charge was then ordered, and we went double-quick right for the stone wall under a heavy fire of both grapeshots and musketry. When near the wall we crossed a creek, and then bounded over the wall. The Yankees fell back through a sorghum patch, and formed behind a rail fence, some two hundred yards distant. At first we could only see their colors, but before what few of them who were not shot down left we could see them very plainly as the cane patch was mowed down. Three or four times the colors would fall, but were no sooner down then they were raised again by other hands.... After the enemy retreated, I counted thirteen of their dead in the corner of the fence, where we had seen the flag fall so often.

Gipson had been among the lucky ones, on both sides, to escape death in this charge. His luck would continue to hold as his regiment held that position amid the almost constant artillery fire from the Union batteries to the rear. "As the elements above us seemed to be on fire, we lay flat on the ground. While in this position a piece of a shell struck my gun, close to my head, and cut it in two, the front end flying over and the bayonet sticking in the ground behind the line. When I came to myself, Col. Marks was sitting on the ground resting my head against his breast. I said: 'What is the matter, boys?' He answered: 'Nothing the matter; you are all right.' 'Where is my gun then.' One of the boys pulled one piece out of the ground, while another handed me the breech." The piece of shell had buried itself in the ground, right beside Gipson's head.[34]

General Terrill's Brigade was the closest, of the Federal forces on the left, to the Chaplin River. His brigade was composed mostly of the new, green troops who had answered Lincoln's last call for volunteers. They had been in the army for only a few weeks, and had received little or no formal training. He and his men could see the stream from their position, and he was overheard by a soldier in his command to say: "That's my water." Terrill sought and received permission to secure the water from both Generals Jackson and McCook. Accordingly, he formed his brigade in line and prepared to move the men forward. Their quest for water would have to be postponed, however, as the Confederate attack drew them into the battle.[35]

On the Confederate right, General Cheatham's Division was moving up for the attack, with Brigadier General Daniel Donelson's Brigade of Tennesseans in the lead. Cheatham watched, as the battle lines swept past him. Known to be a hard-swearing man by his troops, he did not let this opportunity for an oath go by. "Give 'em hell, boys!" he shouted in encouragement, waving the men forward. General Polk happened to be with Cheatham at the time, and he was equally caught up in urging the men forward. Being an Episcopal bishop, however, he was not inclined to using harsh language. "Give it to 'em, boys!" he shouted. "Give 'em what General Cheatham says!"[36]

It was past 1:30 P.M. when Cheatham's men moved forward to the attack. By 1:00 P.M., Bragg had become highly agitated over what he saw as a failure on

Brigadier General Daniel Donelson. Donelson's Confederate brigade delivered the knockout punch to Terrill's raw recruits, and it was during the assault of this brigade that General Terrill was mortally wounded. (Courtesy of the United States Army War College.)

the part of his subordinates to carry out his orders. Bragg had ordered that the attack be made as soon as he had reached the field, and it was now three hours after his arrival, and the issuing of those orders. He rode over to the left of his line, where he found General Polk in consultation with Colonel Gabriel Wharton. Wharton's cavalry was protecting the right flank of the army, and he had reported a large column of Union troops moving toward the battlefield, on the New Mackville Pike. This information had prompted Polk to delay his assault until the Federal column had taken its place in the line. As Polk explained to an impatient Bragg, if he launched the attack while this column was still on the road, it would be in a position to slam into his assaulting line in the flank. The commanding general could see the logic in Polk's decision, but he was still agitated over what he saw as a lack of enthusiasm in taking the offensive. Ordering Polk to get the attack under way at the earliest possible moment, Bragg then rode back to the rear of the line to await the results. The column that Wharton had observed should not have even been approaching the battlefield, if Confederate strategy had gone as planned. General Withers' Division had been ordered to intercept the Federal rear guard, and prevent it from reaching the battlefield. This column was part of Crittenden's Corps. Withers was marching toward where he expected the enemy to be when he came upon the advance elements of Kirby Smith's army, about 12 miles north of Harrodsburg, near the Louisville Pike. Smith's men were bound for Perryville to support Bragg's forces. They were all dressed in brand new Union uniforms, having traded in their own tattered rags for the new clothing they had captured at Richmond. When Withers' men spotted the new blue uniforms, they assumed that it was the Union column they had been sent to detain, and immediately opened fire. Both sides deployed skirmishers, and the fighting continued for some time before some of Smith's men realized that they were fighting friends, not foes. A flag of truce was sent forward, and the mistake was discovered by both sides, but not before Crittenden's rear guard had been allowed the time to unite with Buell's main body and cause the attack Cheatham was now making to be delayed.[37]

A second military column was approaching Perryville that did not arrive on the field in time to partake in the battle. General Humphry Marshall's Brigade was not having very much luck in fighting any Yankees during this campaign. The brigade had tried to be part of Stevenson's trap for Morgan's Federals at Cumberland Gap, but the Yankees had escaped without being brought to battle. Now, Marshall was marching his men for Perryville to take part in the general engagement. His troops were at Hickman Bridge, still some miles away when the battle was joined. His troops reported that they were "close enough to hear the gunfire, even the shouting of the men in charge" but not close enough to lend their numbers to the attack.[38]

It was nearing two o'clock when Cheatham finally gave the order to send in his infantry. As his battle lines advanced, they were hidden from the view of the Yankees by the rolling terrain until they suddenly appeared right in front of Rousseau's and Jackson's lines. The Federals were still in the process of preparing their defenses when the Confederates were first spotted, and it created a flurry of activity as soldiers hurriedly scampered to take their place in the line. A soldier in the 2nd Ohio Infantry, George W. Landrum, had been the first to spot the Confederates and sound the alarm. He had been scanning the countryside with a telescope when he noticed that there were a number of mounted Confederate officers, who were obviously scouting the area, in the woods, some distance in front of the Union line. This assemblage of officers caught Landrum's attention, and even after the officers had departed, "I kept my glass on the point they had left.... Suddenly there emerged from the wood the head of a column of men, and as they came out, their bayonets glistened in the sun, and then I knew they were coming for us."[39]

W.H. Davis described the assault of Wharton's Cavalry on the Confederate right, in conjunction with Cheatham's attack: "Our bugler sounded 'Mount!' and in quick succession 'Charge!' At them we went full speed against the battery double-shotted with grape and canister. We had reached to within twenty yards of the guns when the line of infantry arose and poured a volley into us, shattering our line, killing a number of our horses, and emptying numerous saddles. We retired quickly to our original position, reformed, and made a second assault, again being repulsed." Wharton's troopers re-formed for a third charge, and their commander issued them a challenge: "Boys, never let it be said that our flag went down in defeat. We are going to take that battery this time and run roughshod over that line of infantry and shatter it to pieces. Soldiers do your duty." This third attack was successful, and Wharton's mounted men swept through the line of Jackson's infantry.[40]

Thomas L. Crawford, a reporter for the Louisville Courier Journal, describes the advance of Cheatham's men. "Cheatham moved his division, stationed at a cave, down Chaplin Creek, to a dug road in the bluff at Walker's Bend. There they ascended by the roadway to an open woodland, which they crossed through to a rail fence overgrown with bushes and grapevines; behind that they formed their line of battle. On the hill above them was located Parson's Battery (Federal), firing at Ledbetter's Battery, supposed to be nearly a mile and a half across Chaplin. Cheatham's Division charged over the fence, waving their hats and yelling. This unexpected attack so excited Parson's men they forgot to lower their guns and were routed. From then until dark the battle raged furiously."[41]

William Johnson, who "joined the Southern army at Harper's Ferry at the beginning of the war," was duly impressed with the savagery of the fighting, later stating that "the hottest fight I was in during the war was at Perryville." Johnson would remember: "When orders were given to fire, it looked as if it were a solid sheet of flames." Johnson never knew what regiment of Yankees had been in front of him, but they melted away after the destructive volley was fired. "I never knew what became of the opposing regiment except thirty men who crawled to us," he remembered.[42]

Not all of Cheatham's veterans took such a serious view of the struggle that lay before them. Davis Biggs, a member of the 38th Tennessee, Donelson's Brigade, recounted how "Some of the boys began to crack walnuts while the shells and long range Minies were dropping around and whistling overhead." Donelson's Tennesseans made the most of their time of respite, until they were ordered forward. "Soon we advanced through a field where the grapeshot and shrapnel

The ground over which Donelson's Confederates and Terrill's Federals fought. (Photograph by the author.)

were rattling against the cornstalks, which had been cut and shocked up, also thinning our ranks. Here Colonel Carter's (commander of the 38th Tennessee) horse was killed and he himself being wounded in the leg; but he continued to advance on foot until a loose horse, which had been ridden by a Federal colonel (general), Jackson, who had been killed in our front, was caught by a member of the regiment, and the Colonel was assisted to mount." The 38th Tennessee became intermingled with the men of the 16th Tennessee, during the advance, but the commander of the latter regiment, Colonel John Savage, kept pressing the attack forward, not taking time to realign the commands. Savage was a veteran of the Mexican War, and a dependable officer, but he had a slight problem with diction. In rallying the men forward, and imploring them to charge with bayonets, his voice could be heard along the line to be calling "Bagonets, bagonets!" The Federals were already beginning to fall back from their positions by the time the Confederates reached a rock fence in front of the Union line. Biggs described the clatter that was added to the sound of musketry when the regiment reached the

The monument to Donelson's Brigade is one of only a handful to dot the Perryville battlefield. (Photograph by the author.)

fence with "each (man) pushing off a few rocks to make climbing easier." The Union line was being assailed in front and flank, and the infantry took flight, leaving the Union batteries unsupported. Many prisoners were taken during the fighting, and this led to accusations of wrong-doing by their Confederate captors. "Some of the prisoners we captured looked very like part of the 5,000 we had previously captured at Mumfordsville, and we accused them of violating their paroles."[43]

One Confederate trooper, L.S. Ferrell, belonging to Wharton's command, was detailed to take a prisoner back to headquarters. The trooper was not enthused about his assignment, and felt that at any minute he would find himself being the prisoner instead, as Federal infantry was all over the field. On his way to

The position held by Parsons's Union artillery, looking toward the ground over which Cheatham's Division advanced. (Photograph by the author.)

headquarters he happened upon another Confederate with a prisoner in hand, who asked what he intended to do with his charge. "Take him to headquarters," was the reply. "Yes, and we will both be captured," the second soldier responded. "I am going to kill mine right here." Ferrell persuaded his comrade not to do such a cowardly thing, and stated that he would take both prisoners. The second soldier readily agreed, before spurring his horse and fleeing the area.[44]

Terrill's Brigade, of Jackson's Division, was holding the extreme left of the Union line when the Confederate attack was launched. Colonel George Webster's Brigade held the line between Terrell and the left of Rousseau's line. Colonel John C. Starkweather's Brigade, of Rousseau's Division, was held in reserve, to the rear of Jackson's main line. Lieutenant Charles C. Parsons' Improvised Battery was on the left, and Captain Samuel J. Harris' 19th Indiana Battery was located on the right portion of the line. Artillery fire opened the engagement, and a brisk duel developed between the opposing batteries, while the Union commanders were still endeavoring to get all their men in battle line. While General

This bronze tablet marks the spot where General Jackson received his mortal wound during the battle. (Photograph by the author.)

Jackson was thus employed, arranging infantry support for Parsons Battery, a 12-pounder shot came within a foot of striking him. Parsons' guns were opening huge holes in the lines of the advancing Confederates. From his position on the left of the line, he was able to fire his guns obliquely into the Rebel ranks. The Confederates, seeing this, changed their front to face the battery, and charged directly upon the guns. Parsons' artillery was now using grapeshot and canister at a range of 90 yards, but Cheatham's adjusted line now overlapped the left flank of the Federal position, and the Confederates were closing the gaps caused by the Union artillery and pushing their attack forward. General Terrill observed that his left flank was in danger, and he ordered Colonel James Monroe of the 123rd Illinois to make a bayonet charge and throw the enemy back. Monroe's Illinois men moved out gallantly, but their charge was retarded by the presence of a rail fence that stood between them and the Confederates. The attack faltered, due to this obstruction, and the regiment fired one volley before retreating back to their

Loomis Heights, the position of Lytle's Brigade, looking toward the Confederate lines. (Photograph by the author.)

own lines, closely followed by the Confederates. General Jackson, still with the guns, was struck in the breast by two bullets, at about this same time. Major James Connelly was next to Jackson when he was shot "a few feet from me." "He was on foot and had just advised me to dismount when he fell. Most of the bullets went over our heads and sounded like a swarm of bees running away in the hot summer air overhead."[45]

Terrill assumed command of the division, upon the death of Jackson, and tried desperately to hold his men in their lines. Most of his troops were raw levies, however, part of the recent wave of volunteers who had answered President Lincoln's latest call. This was the first battle most of them had ever seen, and the veteran Confederate regiments that were advancing toward them seemed impossible to stop. His command started to melt away, as the frightened recruits scampered for the rear. The entire line seemed to be collapsing, as Jackson's and

Site of Webster's Brigade, facing the Confederate lines. It was here that Colonel Webster received his mortal wound while trying to rally his fleeing troops. (Photograph by the author.)

Rousseau's first lines were pierced. General William Lytle, whose brigade of Rousseau's Division, was posted to the right of Jackson's line, was wounded and captured. Bushrod Johnson's Brigade and Daniel W. Adams' Brigade had converged on the position, and swept Lytle's Brigade from the field. The 37th Tennessee drove in the Union skirmishers, and the 25th and 44th Tennessee advanced up the slope to where Lytle's men were in line of battle, and closed on the position. Johnson ordered these two regiments to fix bayonets, and the final charge was made with cold steel, as Johnson and Adams drove everything before them. While trying to rally his men, Lytle received a creasing wound in the head, which knocked him out of the saddle. Before he could remount his horse, he was surrounded and captured by the attacking Confederates. Command then was passed to Colonel Curran Pope, of the 15th Kentucky, but that officer was soon carried to the rear with a mortal wound. Lytle's Brigade was melting away. Bushrod Johnson emerged from the attack unscathed, but he had five horses shot out from under him as he pressed his men forward.[46]

Colonel Webster, Jackson's other brigade commander, was killed trying to rally his men, as Buckner's and Cheatham's lines swarmed over the Union position, carrying with them all in their path. His brigade had been heavily assailed in front, and the sight of a Confederate battle flag bearing a black ball on a white field advancing through a corn field on his right indicated that his flank was about to be attacked. Webster moved his command to the right face to counter this new threat, and formed a new line that was at a right angle to the one he previously held. The line, which had been on exposed ground, withdrew to a patch of woods to the rear, where it opened a heavy fire on the Confederates. The arrival of a fresh brigade from the right would stabilize the situation before the line evaporated, but not before Webster fell from his horse, mortally wounded while trying to rally his men. Webster reportedly received his mortal wound at 5:30 P.M., just as darkness was beginning to settle on the battlefield.[47]

Terrill had become the ranking

Brigadier General George Maney. His Tennesseans and Georgians were responsible for capturing Parsons's Artillery Battery, and for exhibiting gallantry in allowing Lieutenant Parsons to walk off the field, in recognition of his personal bravery. (Courtesy of the United States Army War College.)

officer on his part of the Federal battle line with the death of General Jackson. His line had been sorely pressed since early on in the engagement, but they were trying to hold on. General George Maney's Brigade of Tennesseans and Georgians was making straight for Parsons' guns. Almost all of the battery's horses had been shot down, along with half of its officers and men, and those that had survived were abandoning their guns. Lieutenant Parsons continued to fight on, single-handedly keeping one of his guns in action. As the Confederate infantry swarmed in around him, Parsons showed his mettle by drawing his sword and standing at "parade rest" while he awaited the fire from the enemy that was sure to come. Parsons' courage had been noted by the Confederates, however, and the officers ordered that their men not fire upon this courageous soldier. Honor would not permit his act of courage and devotion to be rewarded with a volley of muskets. Instead, Parsons was allowed to walk away from his guns and rejoin his Federal comrades in the rear.[48]

John Euclid Magee, one of Cheatham's men involved in the charge, said that the "infantry now went in — the right wing — our division soon drove the enemy from his position. The center where we were, went slower than the right wing. We changed position to the right and front upon a high hill and took a new position. The enemy were behind a stone fence firing at our men. We threw a few read shells into them, which soon made them leave and our men engaged them.... The battle now raged with unabated fury all along the line. The roar of musketry was terrific while the booming of cannon was unceasing. Our men on the right drove them for over a mile. Losses on both sides were extremely heavy ... a beautiful but bloody day."[49]

It was now approximately 4:00 P.M. While trying to exhort his men to hold, Terrill was struck by an artillery shell. Major Connelly, who had also been beside Jackson when he was struck, said that Terrill was hit "within 5 feet of me, and while he was giving me directions for rallying the men. I was the only one with him; I raised him to a sitting position, and saw that nearly his entire breast was torn away by the shell. He recognized me and his first words were: 'Major do you think it is fatal?' I knew it must be, but to encourage him I answered: "Oh I hope not General.' He then said: 'My poor wife, my poor wife.'" Terrill languished in pain until two o'clock the next morning, before death finally ended his suffering.[50]

It was a good thing that Connelly had been close by when General Terrill was struck down. Otherwise there may have been reason to doubt if his wound had been the result of enemy fire, or of fire from his own men. Terrill was not well liked by his own troops, and many had allegedly pledged to shoot him themselves. Stanley Lockwood, a soldier in the 105th Ohio, wrote a letter in which he detailed how Terrill had struck a soldier of the regiment in the head with his sword for dropping out of the ranks on a particularly hot day. Lockwood talked about the bad feeling toward Terrill that was rampant in the regiment, and stated that the general "is a drunken old tyrant and deserves to be shot by his own men and if he don't come to that fate it will be because the oaths of hundreds of men in the 105th Regiment is good for nothing." Had Connelly not been on hand to testify as to the cause of Terrill's death, historians might have had to speculate whether he had been killed by the Confederates or by his own men.[51]

The Union line was breaking, and it was not just the men who were running away. Colonel Jonah Taylor, commander of the 50th Ohio Infantry, in Webster's Brigade, was also swept up in the panic. He ran to the rear, leaving his regiment without a commander. The colonel would resign his commission the next morning, rather than face a court martial and be dismissed from the army

The portion of Terrill's line that was attacked by Maney's Brigade. Picture is taken from the Union line looking toward the ground over which Maney advanced. (Photograph by the author.)

in disgrace. The capture of Lytle, and the deaths of Jackson, Webster, and Terrill created a lack of command control on that part of the field that further demoralized the Union troops, already facing what appeared to be an irresistible assault from Cheatham's men. Colonel Albert Hall, of the 105th Ohio Infantry, assumed command of Terrill's Brigade when the general was hit, but the situation was already beyond his ability to control. In less than an hour, his own command had already suffered casualties of 29 dead and 130 wounded. The rest of the brigade had suffered similar carnage. Webster's Brigade was faring little better. The five regiments in his brigade reported losses in killed, wounded, and missing of 579 men. The Union left was folding up, and it seemed as if there was nothing that could stop the Confederates from crushing McCook's entire corps, and possibly putting the whole Federal army to flight.[52]

Bragg's great gamble appeared to be working. He had taken a terrible risk in facing Buell's army with a force that was less than half its size, and had truly thrown caution to the wind in assuming the role of the aggressor in the battle, but his veterans were thus far proving his judgment to be correct. One final effort should push McCook's men off the field, leaving Cheatham's Division free to make a left wheel and assault Gilbert's line on its left flank. With pressure from front and flank, this next Federal corps should then be driven from the field, and the day would be won. At this critical time in the battle the possibility of Union victory seemed to have dried up as much as the creeks and streams in the surrounding countryside.

The sun was hanging low in the sky and was partially obscured by the smoke of the battlefield. A soldier of McCook's Corps spoke for many when he said: "I believe those men on the left of that field could have appreciated the feelings of Wellington when his troops were hard pressed at Waterloo, when he said, 'Would to God, the sun would set or Blucher come.' Our men could have said, 'Would to God the sun would set or Buell move the right.'"[53]

CHAPTER SIX

The Fire and the Fury

The lack of a viable command structure was posing a serious problem on the Union left, due to the loss of Jackson, Terrill, Webster, and Lytle. But that command breakdown had begun before the first Union commander had been killed or wounded. The commanding general had been conspicuous by his absence in any control over the events that were transpiring. As has been previously stated, Buell was suffering the effects of having been thrown from his horse on October 7, but that was not the reason for his lack of command control while the battle was being fought. The elements themselves had conspired to relegate Buell to a non-facto position with his own army. What took place on the field of Perryville that day was a curious atmospheric phenomenon known scientifically as an acoustic shadow. When this phenomenon takes place, it is as if a dome was placed over an area where sound is occurring. Sound waves bounce over the area of this dome, and are inaudible to those who happen to be within it, even though they can be heard at great distances from the site where the noise was made. People in Louisville over 70 miles away, could clearly hear the thumps and thuds of the artillery at Perryville, while Buell, only a few miles from the scene of the actual fighting, did not even know that his army was being attacked, as he was within the dome, and the sound waves bounced over his position.

This peculiar atmospheric condition was responsible for Bragg not being able to hear the sounds of battle when he was at Harrodsburg that morning. It also made it impossible for Buell to hear the raging battle a few miles behind his own lines. Occasional thuds of artillery were noticed at the Union headquarters, but they were passed off as being merely probing efforts of both sides to develop the position of the other. It was not until 4:00 P.M., with the Union left flank in retreat and the critical point of the battle already at hand, that Buell was first able to hear the roar of battle. General Gilbert was at headquarters, and when the sounds first fell upon Buell's ears, he turned to Gilbert and said: "That is something more than 'shelling the woods!' It sounds like a fight." He immediately dispatched Gilbert to the front to find out the condition of affairs. Along the route, Gilbert happened upon one of McCook's aides, who was making his way to headquarters with a belated report of the fighting and an appeal for aid from the rest of the army. The receipt of this information was the first time Buell had been made aware that there was a full-scale battle being fought by his army. McCook had taken for granted that his commanding general was able to hear the sounds of the fighting, and had assumed that relief would soon be on the way. He had no idea that almost two hours of fighting had gone completely unnoticed at headquarters. Buell and Gilbert both sprang into action, but as reports of the disaster on the Federal left began to come in, it was doubtful if their efforts would be in time to save the day from defeat. Buell ordered Colonel Michael Goodling's Brigade, of Mitchell's Division, to march to the relief of the left flank, and he began to organize his forces to resist the onslaught that he now knew existed.[1]

McCook's presence was conspicuous on the battlefield. Numerous officers recounted receiving instructions from him in their reports of the battle, and from all indications, he was everywhere on his line, ordering battery fire, exhorting the troops, and directing his officers. But McCook was so involved in fighting the battle that he had no time to oversee it. He was forced to run from one threatened point to another, and was never able to perform any service other than crisis management. Effectively, he was reduced from performing the responsibilities of a corps commander to acting as a division commander on the field. He was so hard pressed to defend his lines that he did not even have time to personally seek reinforcements. But McCook was doing exactly what he should have been doing. He was confident that the rest of the army must surely be coming to his assistance. After all, how could they not know that his troops were being assaulted by the entire Confederate army? Why would they not come to his aid? McCook would be sorely disappointed in his assumption, partly because of the acoustic shadow that had kept the battle a secret from his commander, and partly due to the inaction of his fellow corps commander, Charles Gilbert.

A Minnesota soldier in Gilbert's Corps spoke for a number of Federal troops on the field that day when he wrote in his diary: "Time passed on & still we lay under arms, talking and laughing as if all was well. Little did we know that such a conflict was raging & many of our fellow Americans were laying bleeding upon the battlefield. Not till afternoon did we learn that a battle was actually being fought." Even then, the news of the battle only reached the members of this regiment because they had observed the messages being sent by flag by the Signal

A contemporary artist's depiction of the battle of Perryville. (Courtesy of the United States Army War College.)

Corps." This soldier places the time that he learned of the battle at 3:00 P.M., one hour before the commanding general was made aware of it.[2]

The left of the Union line was seemingly melting away, but portions of the line were holding. Webster's 34th Brigade was making a desperate fight of it, despite the fact that the brigade was made up of raw recruits, and their brigade commander had already been killed. They were holding tight to Gilbert's Corps, on their right, and providing an anchor for the rest of Jackson's Division to try to hold on to. Private Joseph Glezen described the valiant stand on this part of the field:

> We were ordered to "rise and fire." Now came the "tug of war," for at this time the bullets were whistling over us with such fury that it appeared that no man could stand erect and live. But at the word of command we bounced to our feet like so many parched peas, determined to pour our muskets into the ranks of the rebels. Before firing it was necessary to advance about two rods to the top of the hill, in order to bring our arms to bear against the enemy. And even then they kept so well concealed behind trees that only a few could be seen. Notwithstanding this, our bullets, though blind, found their hiding places, and strewd the ground with their mangled corpses, the legitimate fruits of their diabolical treason and folly.

Glezen was truly a raw recruit. Like most of the new inductees into the army, he had had only the scantest of training, and this included firing his musket. He remembered the difficulty he had had in firing at the Confederates. "I found that I had two loads in my musket. I reprimed however and thought I would double the dose by firing two balls at once, but my gun refused to fire. I again retired down the hill, took off the tube, picked powder into the touch hole, primed, advanced and made the 3rd effort to fire, but this time there was not sufficient powder in the lock to burst the cap. I stood and snapped four times but in vain." Glezen was not alone in his inexperience. "I then threw down my gun in disgust, picked up another and found it in the same condition as my own, containing two loads. I picked up the second and it was in the same condition, the third was the same way, the fourth had a load just about 1 foot from the muzzle." Glezen hid on the back side of the hill for a few minutes, not willing to allow himself to be a target when he could not fire back at his attackers. After this brief respite, he determined to find another musket and get back into the fight. He selected two more fouled pieces from the field before finding one that was empty and would fire. Once more in the battle, he proclaimed that "The firing between the 80th and the enemy in front, was incessant and terrific for nearly four hours, we maintaining our ground against a whole Brigade." By the end of the fighting, Glezen "found that I had only discharged 15 rounds ... far below the average in the Regiment." The majority of the men in the 80th had expended all of their forty rounds, and had "replenished from the cartridge boxes of the killed and wounded."[3]

The 34th Brigade had held. It was the baptism of fire for the members of its four regiments, and they had met the test with courage and determination. This was not a new revelation for green Civil War regiments. It had already happened many times in the war, and would happen many more times before the conflict was ended. It was true, in most cases, that new regiments were apt to flee at the first volley from the enemy, but sometimes the exact opposite occurred, as it had in this instance. Pride and patriotic ardor motivated most of the volunteers in the ranks, and often compensated for a lack of experience and training. There were many instances in the war where a green regiment held a position for no other reason than the fact that the men in it were too unschooled as soldiers to know that they were beaten. They would remain in their position long after veterans would have abandoned it because they did not know any better. This appears to be the case in the stand of the 34th Brigade. Although a large number of the men in the ranks did not even know how to load and fire their weapons, as attested to by Glezen's search to find a musket that was not fouled, they remained on the field, defiantly holding the Confederates back. Force of will made up for the training they lacked, and pride compensated for a lack of experience. Five hundred seventy-nine men had fallen as casualties, but they still held their assigned ground.

While Webster's Brigade was holding, efforts were being made to prevent the crisis on the far left of the Federal line from turning into a complete rout, and thus compromising the entire Union position. General Rousseau stated that "If our left was turned, our position was lost and a total rout of the army corps would follow." As Terrill's demoralized regiments broke for the rear, they passed through the ranks of the brigade of John Converse Starkweather. The brigade, belonging to Rousseau's Division, had been posted on high ground behind Terrill's position to act in a reserve capacity. The fact is, the brigade never should have been in the position it now held. It had become separated from the rest of Rousseau's Division during the march to the battlefield, and had been positioned where it was because the rest of the line had been formed by the time it rejoined the division. They were now the only cohesive unit remaining on that part of the field. If Cheatham's attack was to be foiled, it would be up to them.[4]

Starkweather's Brigade was composed of far different troops than that of Terrill's. The men in his battle line were veterans of the many hard-fought campaigns of the western army, and they had shown their mettle in battle on numerous occasions. Even as they made way for their fleeing comrades to pass through, they could see the gray battle line advancing toward them. "On swept the enemy," wrote one Union veteran, "over the field they had just won, scattering the fragments of Terrill's recruits like snowflakes before the wind, crushing the dead and wounded beneath their horses' hoofs and cannon wheels, and with terrific yells rushing into the deadly embrace of Starkweather's veterans." Behind the brigade was the Benton Road, upon which were the ammunition train, supply train, and ambulances for the whole division. If Starkweather was unable to hold, all of the wagons in the road would cause another traffic jam like the one that had been witnessed at First Manassas, and a similar panic could have overtaken the army. Starkweather's regiments — the 24th Illinois, 79th Pennsylvania, 1st Wisconsin, and 21st Wisconsin — braced themselves to receive the thus-far victorious Confederates. A Union soldier recalled: "From their well dressed lines rang out the sharp crash of musketry, before which many in the front rank of assailants went down. Fresh troops step up and close the gaps, and in solid masses once more advance to again be mowed down by a whirlwind of fire. The survivors paused not for an instant, but rushed forward to within a few yards of the Federal line, and then halting, delivered a close fire that sent many a patriot reeling to the ground."[5]

The Confederates making this charge belonged to Brigadier General George Maney's Brigade. Major John Knight of the 41st Georgia stated that when Terrill's Brigade retreated, his men "seemed to vie with one another in seeing who could do the most to drive the enemy from the field. Never perhaps did troops

Starkweather Hill, as the Confederates at the foot of the ridge saw it. The stand made by General Starkweather's troops on this high ground was crucial in preventing the left wing of the Union army from crumbling. (Photograph by the author.)

fight more desperately than did these on this occasion." The fact that the regiment had six color bearers shot down during the assault adds credence to Knight's assertion.[6] Colonel H.R. Field of the 1st Tennessee testified to the deadly effect of the volley fire being poured into the Confederate ranks by Starkweather's men. "The regiments on our left then opened their fire upon us, killing and wounding a dozen officers and men at each discharge."[7] Colonel George Porter described the desperate advance of his 6th Tennessee, as the men tried to follow their battle flag to the Yankee lines. "The color-bearer, John Andrews, was here too badly wounded to proceed farther and had to be carried to the rear. They were then seized by John Ayeres, one of the color guard, who carried them gallantly for a short distance and was killed. A.M. Pegues then carried them to the summit ... where he was badly wounded, being shot in three places. They were then seized by Ed Quinn, private, Company H, who bore them in advance of the regiment across the field into the wood, where he was killed."[8] Major George Kelsoe of the 9th Tennessee observed that for his men, "the command forward was entirely unnecessary, as at all times the men in the line repeated the command without orders. It was an exception to see any of the men taking advantage of trees or other kind of shelter; the majority never lying down, but erect, advanced with determination to carry the field or never leave it." It was well that the men in the command were advancing without orders. Every company commander in the regiment had been shot down while making the charge.[9]

When it received the Confederate volley, Starkweather's Brigade "wavered a little, but McCook was there watching the progress of the fight, cheering and encouraging the men. Pride and discipline at length asserted its way over the troops, every man moved forward to his former position and inflexibility held the line.... For half an hour wave after wave of Southern valor dashed against Starkweather's Brigade, to be again hurled back, their ranks bleeding and discomfitted [sic], followed by wild, irregular cheers. Under such circumstances it does men good to shout. It infuses a sort of inspiration, tones up their waning courage, and is equal in value and practical results to a reinforcement of fresh men." Starkweather's men were standing fast, but they were taking losses at the same rate they were delivering them upon Maney's Brigade. The brigade would suffer 756 casualties during this fight. Lytle's crushed brigade would be the only Federal unit in the fight that day that would suffer more. Much of the fighting took place at such close quarters that 109 of the brigade's casualties would be those who were captured by the enemy. The 79th Pennsylvania and the 1st Wisconsin bore the largest share of the losses, suffering casualties of 216 and 204, respectively.[10]

Charge after charge was made by the Confederate attackers. General A.P. Stewart's Brigade had been ordered to support Maney's assault, and the added weight of this additional brigade threatened to sway the balance of power on the ridge. Stewart's all Tennessee brigade formed on the left of Maney's and advanced with Maney's men in a double line of battle, right into the hell of Union artillery and small-arms fire. The artillery was proving to be especially deadly to the Confederates. Bush's Indiana Battery, located on the left of the Union line, was punishing the gray-clad soldiers with every step they made toward Starkweather's position. Private Sam Watkins, whose 1st Tennessee Regiment was the closest to these cannon, noted that: "The guns were discharged so rapidly that it seemed the earth itself was in a volcanic uproar. The iron storm passed through our ranks, mangling and tearing men to pieces. The very air seemed full of stiffling smoke [sic] and fire, which seemed the very pit of hell, peopled by contending demons." A Confederate veteran of Shiloh proclaimed that "Such fighting I never witnessed and in fact never had been witnessed on the battlefields of America." Stewart's

Maney's assault was stopped at the top of this ridge (Photograph by the author.)

Brigade was forced to retire, exposing Maney's left flank, and compelling that general to also order a withdrawal. Starkweather's men had suffered severely in defending their position, losing one-third of the men in the command. But they had had the opportunity of fighting on the defensive, from a strong position on the top of the hill. Maney's men had done the attacking, up the slope and against that strong position. The valor and courage of the Confederates making the repeated charges against Starkweather's Brigade can be validated by the fact that they left nearly half their number lying dead and wounded in front of the Federal position.[11]

The 21st Wisconsin, of Starkweather's Brigade, had been badly shaken, and was driven from the field. It was one of the new regiments with the army, and this was its baptism of fire. Another member of the brigade noted: "It is due to the 21st Wisconsin to say here, as everyone familar [sic] with the facts said at the time, that no discredit could be attached to their conduct in that engagement. It was a new regiment, almost entirely unaquainted [sic] with the simplest battal-

The position of the 21st Wisconsin, as seen from the Confederate lines. During the battle, the fields were planted in corn, with the dried stalks being 10 feet high. (Photograph by the author.)

ion movements, and when they had fought as well as they could in such a position, there was nothing left for them but to get into the position in their own way that they would have been taken to more deliberately had they been familiar with battalion movements. Many of them rallied on our line and fought well."[12]

General Cheatham took an opportunity to get personally involved in the fighting during the assault on Starkweather's Brigade. His artillery had been shelling the enemy with canister and case shot, at a distance of 250 to 300 yards. Cheatham was with the artillery, and at one point he shouted, "Let me have my hand at them." Cheatham took over the operation of one of the guns and "fired several rounds, pointing the gun and directing the fire apparently with as much pleasure as a boy shooting rabbits."[13]

As the fighting subsided in Starkweather's front, both sides pulled back and

Adams's and Cleburne's brigades formed at the bottom of this hill, around the Widow Bottom House, to make their attacks on the Union line. (Photograph by the author.)

tried to catch their breaths. General Rousseau had been present for most of the fighting that had taken place on the flank, but he was not there when it reached its final conclusion. Messages had arrived that the division's right was being sorely pressed, and he went to see what he could do to aid Harris' and Lytle's Brigades to stave off defeat.

Rousseau arrived at his right to find the flank collapsed and falling back. Harris' and Lytle's Brigades had been cut to pieces, and were retiring to the rear. The remnants were forming another line in the vicinity of a house owned by a family named Russell. Rousseau's appearance on the field heartened the men, and the 15th Kentucky rose to its feet to cheer his arrival. The advancing Confederates could be plainly seen, and Rousseau scrambled to form some sort of a defense with which to stop them. He ordered his men to lie down, and not to expose themselves to the murderous fire, while he tried to find help in holding the position. Rousseau's most natural source of support should have been from Gilbert's Corps. Gilbert's left flank was only 400 yards away, and his troops could see the

The Widow Bottom House. Though inhabited as a private dwelling, the house still looks much the same as it did at the time of the battle. (Photograph by the author.)

advancing Confederates as well as Rousseau's men could, but they were taking no part in the battle. Gilbert had issued no orders for his men to aid the faltering left, and they were holding their position, reduced to becoming spectators to the fighting that was taking place. Rousseau noticed that Loomis' Michigan Light Artillery was posted on commanding ground behind the Russell House, in a strong position from which to repel an attack. The guns were strangely quiet, however, and when the general rode up to inquire as to the reason for their silence, he was informed that Loomis was acting under the orders of General McCook to reserve his fire "for close work." Rousseau pointed to the attacking Confederates and announced to Loomis that the enemy was "close enough, and would be even closer in a moment." Loomis decided that the general was right. The enemy was indeed close enough. His battery roared into action, tearing gaping holes in the line of the advancing Rebels.[14]

The surging Confederate line was made up of the brigades of Brigadier

Generals Samuel Adams, Patrick Cleburne, and S.A.M. Wood, from left to right. General Hardee, who had seen the retreating Federals re-forming at the Russell House, directed that Wood's Brigade be added to the assault, in an effort to deliver a knockout blow.

Cleburne's advance against the Union line had been hampered by his own artillery. The majority of his men were wearing captured blue Union trousers, and the Confederate gunners mistook them for Yankees and opened fire on them. Several men of the command were killed or wounded before the mistake could be made known to the artillerists, and the fire properly directed against the Union position. Moving forward, once again, the gray wave swept passed the position where the first Union line had been. Colonel Lytle had been trying to rally a portion of his fleeing men, and had managed to gather approximately 100 together, but they were promptly brushed aside by the Southern attack, which had resulted in Lytle being wounded and captured. Cleburne re-formed his line, with the left resting on the Mackville Road, before pushing forward toward the new line the Federals were creating, approximately one mile to the rear. The Southern infantry outran its artillery support, and it also outdistanced the rest of the Confederate battle line. Cleburne's men were advancing with both flanks exposed, and they were being raked by Union artillery at every step. Cleburne was able to push his troops to within seventy-five yards of the new Federal line, but his brigade could go no farther. They were running out of ammunition, exposed, and exhausted. Being one of the smaller brigades in the army, with no more than 800 men in the ranks, not as many as a full-sized regiment, they had done all that dutiful soldiers could do. Cleburne ordered their withdrawal, and the brigade made a retrograde movement back to the location of the first Union line of the day.[15]

Cleburne received his second wound of the campaign during this assault. His horse had been killed by a cannon shot, as the general was pressing his men forward, and the same ball had wounded Cleburne in the leg. Lieutenant Seay, of his staff, was killed beside him, and his aide, Lieutenant Magnum, was wounded seven times by a Union volley.[16]

General Adams was advancing his brigade to the left of Cleburne's. When the latter brigade withdrew, Adams found his troops to be isolated and unsupported. His men then received the full attention of the Union artillery. Adams reported that "I halted my command under a very heavy and rapid fire from this point, when I was soon opened upon from the left and rather to the rear by a well-directed battery of artillery. Using my glass, I discerned the enemy moving their forces and forming line of battle at a distance of 600 to 800 yards to my left. Deeming the position to be untenable I ordered the brigade to fall back." Without support, under heavy artillery fire, and with the prospect of being assailed

The open fields over which Cleburne's Division advanced to assault the Union lines. (Photograph by the author.)

on his left flank by a heavy body of infantry, Adams felt a further advance to be foolhardy.[17]

General Wood's brigade was having more success on the extreme right of the Confederate line, where Webster's Union Brigade had been driven from the field. The Confederate attack could still have the desired results if a penetration could be made at this point. Jackson's Division, on the extreme left, was badly shaken and cut up. Starkweather's stand was all that was preventing the Union left from melting away. If Wood could drive a wedge in between Rousseau's and Jackson's Divisions it was probable that the latter would quit the field, while the former would then face the prospect of being attacked on front and flank. McCook's Corps could yet be pried from the field if the Confederates could drive off the battered remnants of Webster's Brigade before fresh units could shore up the position. Wood's men rushed to exploit their success, but they were not the only ones rushing to this critical point. Colonel Michael Goodling's Union Brigade was finally on the scene.

General Gay had noticed a 400-yard gap in the Union line between the right of McCook's Corps and the left of Gilbert's Without orders, he led his cavalry brigade to the spot and positioned it to hold the line. A few Hotchkiss guns were brought up, and they began to shell the Confederate line. Gay was called upon to repel several attempts to break his line, but the main thrusts of the Confederate attackers were to his left, against McCook. Late in the day, the troopers watched as Rousseau's right began to crumble under the weight of the assault. Seeing the danger, General Gay got his command in the saddle and rode to the support of Rousseau. Before they reached the spot, Goodling's Brigade of infantry had arrived, and the troopers were not called upon to seal the breach.[18]

General Buell had ordered Goodling to support McCook's Corps as soon as he received word that the left flank was being hard pressed. Goodling received his orders to advance at 3:30 P.M., and once the brigade was formed, he double-quick marched it to the intersection of the Mackville and Benton Roads where he found Webster's forces "badly cut up and retreating ... hotly pressed by the enemy." Captain Oscar Pinney's Wisconsin Light Artillery was placed on high ground, bordered by trees, to the rear of the brigade. Goodling then formed his line of battle with the 59th Illinois, 75th Illinois, and 22nd Indiana, from left to right. The line being hastily formed, it was immediately pushed forward amid the retreating remnants of Rousseau's shocked command. Goodling's Brigade crashed into Wood's line. "The battle now raged furiously," Goodling wrote, "one after another of my men were cut down, but still, with unyielding hearts, they severely pressed the enemy, and in many instances forced them to give way. Here we fought alone and unsupported for two hours and twenty minutes, opposed to the rebel General Woods entire division, composed of fifteen regiments and a battery of ten guns." Wood was, of course, not in command of a division, but the savagery with which his men attacked induced Goodling to reason that he was facing a force many times the size of his own. "Fiercer and fiercer grew the contest and more and more dreadful became the onslaught. Almost hand-to-hand they fought at least five times their own number, often charging upon them with such fiercelessness [sic] and impetuosity as would force them to reel and give way, but as fast as they were cut down their ranks were filled with fresh ones. At one time the Twenty-second Indiana charged on them with fixed bayonets and succeeded in completely routing and throwing them from their position on our right, but at the same time they brought in a reserve force on our left."[19]

Wood's men were fighting with a determination that seemed impossible to stop, but Goodling's men were giving as good as they got. They were outnumbered, to be sure, but not nearly by the ratio that Goodling had thought. The odds against them were about to increase, however, and Pinney's Battery was doing deadly service in helping to even out the odds. General Polk, seeing an opportunity, ordered General Liddell's Brigade to support Wood's attack. It was now close to 5:00 P.M., and darkness would soon fill the Kentucky sky. The Union line must be broken before nightfall brought an end to the hostilities and gave the Union army a chance to reorganize and strengthen its position. The men of Liddell's Brigade had been bloodied from their fight with Sheridan's Division, earlier that morning, but they went forward with a cheer, taking Goodling's line in the flank. Goodling described the fighting as Liddell's men entered the fray. "The impetuosity of the firing now ceased for a moment, and I advanced to ascertain if possible the position of the enemy. As I advanced down the line we were greeted with a heavy volley of musketry, which plainly enough told me the direction of the enemy. With shouts and exclamations my men again rallied to the onset." The addition of Liddell's men was having the desired effect. Goodling's men were finally being forced to give ground. Goodling would not be available to rally his men against this latest threat. "At this time my horse was shot from under me, and before I could escape through the darkness I was taken prisoner and conveyed from the field." The final Confederate thrust had cleared Goodling's Brigade from the field, but time had run out. The landscape was beginning to become cloaked in darkness, making it hard to distinguish friend from foe. Goodling's Brigade fell back and formed a new line, under the cover of a hill. They soon learned, however, that the closest Union support was almost a mile away. Given that information, the brigade was withdrawn from the field and fell back to Gilbert's lines. The Union line had been broken, but the Confederates could not exploit it in the darkness. The Federals would be given the time they needed to regroup, and the opportunity for victory had passed. As darkness was falling on the field, General James Steedman's Brigade appeared on the Union left. General McCook directed that they be posted on ground to the right, and in front of, Pinney's Battery, to the right and rear of the Russell House. But Steedman's men would not be called upon to stem the Confederate tide. General Polk had ordered the attack to be halted. The men were to "cease fire and to bivouac for the night."[20]

Steedman's presence on the battlefield was releasing him temporarily from the ire of his corps commander. The general had been placed under arrest by Gilbert for some minor infraction, and the day before the battle Steedman had been forced during the march to ride with 50 other officers of Gilbert's Corps who were in like circumstances, behind Gilbert's staff. Those under arrest included Colonel John T. Croxton of the 4th Kentucky, and Colonel Ferdinand Van Deveer of the 35th Ohio.[21]

General Hardee pronounced the fighting to be the most severe that he had

The ridge in the distance, just in front of the tree line, is the position occupied by the left wing of the Union army at the close of the battle. Though it had been roughly handled, pushed back, and had several times threatened to break, McCook's Corps had managed to hang on and avert the disaster that might have befallen the Union army if it had been routed. (Photograph by the author.)

ever seen, and turning to a staff officer he said "that it was Nip & Tuck" for a while and "he once thought Nip had it." The Confederates had pushed the Union line back, but the issue had been in doubt the entire day.[22]

An officer with Steedman noted the acoustic shadow that had had such an effect on the lack of Union response that day. He was amazed that he could not hear the battle raging until he came over the crest of a hill, when all could suddenly be heard with distinct clarity. "There was not the warning of an instant. At one bound, my horse carried me from the stillness into the uproar of battle."[23]

Another one of Steedman's men remembered being called to the aid of the left.

> We were ordered to march with three days rations. Marched a short distance & halted. Stragglers came back telling us that our force was victorious having

driven the enemy in all directions, that they was retreating in disaster but shortly the peels of cannon & musketry opened louder than ever which proved the reports a mistake.... Forward again and marched about a mile. Passed troops standing in line of battle. Filed to the left just before reaching 'Chaplin Hill' & passed through a low piece of land that was filled with the smoke of the battlefield. The enemies batteries was playing upon us. Bolts & shells were continually passing over our heads. The hill to our right protected us from them. We took position on the top of the hill behind Smith's Battery which opened a deadly fire on the enemy. A Rise of ground to our front was lined with the enemies batteries.... They charged upon the battery at our left but Smith put in such a fire that they had to pull back. A battery at our left did great execution. We could hear the enemy yell as they charged. The balls fell thick around us.... A heavy fire was kept up until dark when firing ceased & we moved to the right & was in plain sight and hearing of the enemies batteries.... After all was still on our side I went out in front and sat down by a stump & listened.... I could hear their ambulances moving and men talking ... while our side was perfectly still.[24]

But all was quiet now. Solon Marks, a surgeon with the 9th Brigade, prepared for an onslaught of another kind: an onslaught of wounded men needing medical attention. "The sun set, and one by one the guns ceased their thunderings, and all was still except the rumblings of ambulances as they moved over the field collecting the dead and wounded."[25]

In the gathering twilight, General Polk nearly became the only Confederate general officer to become a casualty in the day's fighting. Polk was attempting to stop what he felt to be two Confederate units from firing on one another when he inadvertently found himself to be within the Federal lines. A Union colonel approached him and demanded to know his identity. Polk decided to "brazen it out." He wore a dark blouse, and in the darkness it was hard to distinguish it from the Federal blue that was all around him. Polk identified himself to be a Federal officer, and in an authoritative tone he yelled at the Yankee colonel. "I'll soon show you who I am, sir; cease firing, sir, at once!" Then, turning from the Federals, he rode slowly away, in the direction of his own lines. Once out of musket range, he put spurs to his steed and made all possible haste to reach Liddell's position. He informed Liddell that there was no mistaking the fact that Yankees were in front of him, stating "I have reconnoitered those fellows pretty closely." Liddell formed his men in line and "closed the operations of the day in that part of the field with a succession of the most deadly volleys I have witnessed. The enemy's command in their immediate front was well-nigh annihilated."[26]

Another Confederate soldier was confused by the darkness. Colonel Thomas Claiborne was trying to find Cheatham's headquarters when he rode in among a large number of soldiers who were excitedly talking about the day's fighting. They were clustered together in a patch of woods, and as the leaves had not yet fallen from the trees, the moonlight did not illuminate the colonel's Confederate uniform clearly. "What soldiers are you?" Claiborne demanded, and he was answered by "Buell's." "All right! Please let my horse move forward," he said, and the group of Union soldiers parted and allowed him to pass. Once clear of the danger, Claiborne made a wide turn to the left, and at length found General Polk's headquarters.[27]

The salient between McCook's right flank and Gilbert's left was going to hold, though little of the credit belonged to either of those generals. Gilbert's Corps was still out of the fight, watching as their comrades fought for their lives. Many of his officers had begged for permission to advance their men in support of McCook's beleaguered line, but Gilbert refused to grant it. It was as if he had become paralyzed by the battle. He was in over his head. The command that he now held demanded more than this staff officer was able give. He would hold his line, and let the rest of the army fend for itself. His men would continue to be spectators to one of the most sanguinary struggles of the war. One Union soldier noted that "there was no great amount of generalship displayed on that field," other than that of General Rousseau. He noted how Rousseau had been seen all along the line, "with his hat on his sword high up above his head, waving it and cheering the men on, perfectly fearless, his countinance [sic] all aglow." Starkweather had saved the left of McCook's line, and Rousseau had saved the right. On October 22, 1862, Rousseau would receive the thanks of the government in the form of his promotion to major general, dated October 8, the date of the battle.[28]

Gilbert had failed to aid McCook's Corps because of a fear of being attacked himself. The lowliest private in the ranks could clearly see that their proper place was on the left, at the scene of conflict, but Gilbert would not issue the orders. A soldier in the 36th Illinois, Gilbert's Corps, who was watching the destruction of the Federal left, spoke for many of his comrades when he said: "When Rousseau's line was broken, and the enemy's hosts were surging over the field, their advanced line fringed with fire, every glass was directed thitherward, and when our lines went down before the irresistable [sic] charge, many a prayer went up to heaven, 'God help our poor boys now!'"[29]

Many of the officers in Gilbert's Corps could see their proper duty even more clearly than the privates in the ranks. Colonel Nicholas Greusel was watching the battle while standing near Captain Henry Hescock's Missouri Light Artillery Battery. "Captain Hescock," Gruesel said, "those fellows over yonder are using McCook's boys rather roughly. Can't you reach them with your shot?"

Hescock replied that he would try to get the range, and elevated his cannon to attempt it. From its position on the line, the fire from this battery was enfilading the Confederate line, and each shell burst was opening gaping holes in the ranks. The men on Gilbert's line cheered each shell burst. It was the closest they could come to actually helping their hard-pressed comrades. Hescock's fire was so deadly that it caused the attacking Southerners to waver, and small bodies of troops could be seen retreating to the rear. Without orders from the corps commander, this small part of Gilbert's command had gotten itself into the fight, and was contributing appreciably to the left flank's ability to hold. Surgeons who later canvassed the field for wounded reported to have found 430 dead and wounded Confederates in the area into which Hescock's guns were firing.[30]

One possible explanation for Gilbert's reluctance to order his men into the fight can be found in the pages of the regimental history for the 6th Ohio Infantry. The regimental historian wrote that "The writer once had the following statement from a general officer whose high character, no less than the command which he held at the period under consideration, entitles it to credence: Generals Thomas and Crittenden, both of whom were on the ground and in the same state of expectancy as the men, at one time during the afternoon were about taking the responsibility of attacking without orders, when they were dissuaded from it by the representations of a "Union citizen," just arrived by a circuitous route from Perryville, who informed them that Bragg had concentrated 30,000 men and several batteries of artillery to receive the threatened attack on the Lebanon road. This story was ingeniously elaborated, but although containing some particles of truth, was in the main a fabrication, and there can scarcely be a doubt that the worthy farmer (as he appeared to be) was a spy of General Bragg's."[31]

It is true that neither Buell nor his subordinate officers had any real idea concerning the size of the Confederate force they were facing. Buell had originally thought it to be only a division. The fact that Bragg was willing to offer battle on this ground changed the thinking in the Union army and promoted caution. Obviously, there was a considerable force in their front, but how large was it. Had Kirby Smith been able to join Bragg? Had Withers returned to the main body? Without reliable information to the contrary, the Union commanders had seemed perfectly willing to concede the possibility that Bragg had been able to concentrate all of the Confederate forces then in Kentucky in front of Buell's army. A charitable explanation of Gilbert's actions would be to give the benefit of the doubt that he was acting cautiously, not willing to commit his forces to the left, fearing that Bragg really did have the resources the spy had stated, and that by doing so he would be playing right into Bragg's hands by weakening his own line. Gilbert made reference to his fears over the strength of the enemy in an article on the battle that he wrote for *Southern Bivouac Magazine* in February of 1886. Twenty-four years after the battle, after numerous articles had been written by its participants, North and South, Gilbert appeared to have little knowledge as to the actual numbers in the Confederate army that day. He wrote: "Crittenden's corps and Gilbert's corps were intact, but together they could have shown only about thirty-six thousand men in line. Allowing to McCook's corps, in the absence of Sill, six thousand men, the Confederates would have in numbers a superiority of fully fifteen thousand, all seasoned troops. It is true that the Army of the Ohio had better arms, and was better supplied also, advantages which go far to compensate for inferiority of numbers; but then from a quarter to a third of its force was of raw troops."[32] According to this statement, Bragg's army was being credited with having in excess of 50,000 men on the field of Perryville. In reality, it had less than one-third of that number. In any event, Gilbert was either duped by misinformation or was exercising a command position he was unsuited for. The latter assertion is probably closest to the truth. Even if Gilbert had feared that Bragg had reserves that he was waiting to throw into the fight, his actions were contrary to sound military judgment. If McCook's Corps had been driven from the field it wouldn't have mattered if Bragg had more troops or not. The battle would have been lost, and the Union army would have been driven from the field. It was incumbent upon Gilbert to support the left, regardless of any fears he might have entertained regarding his own line. If the left was defeated, his position would hold no military value, as his line would be vulnerable from front and flank. No matter how one examines it, Gilbert was derelict in not forwarding all the support he could muster to McCook. With the exception of Sheridan's 11th Division, and Goodling's Brigade, which Buell had ordered sent to McCook, he had effectively kept his corps out of the fight.

Colonel William Carlin, commanding a brigade in Gilbert's Corps, would later write a scathing rebuke of Gilbert's conduct during the battle, and of Gilbert's reluctance to send aid to McCook. "The morning of the 8th of October was marked by a bright sun and hazy atmosphere. Away off to our left we could see the head of McCook's column approaching near Chaplin Creek. My position was so commanding that from it we could see over the lower ground in that direction two miles, and I knew that McCook was approaching Perryville on a road somewhat southeasterly to Perryville. Some artillery firing began, perhaps as early as 9 o'clock, near Chaplin's Creek. No orders had come to me to be prepared to move into battle.... It was about 10 o'clock A.M. when the cannonading became quite heavy; soon afterward musketry-firing began, and from that time on, for several hours, each minute seemed to increase the uproar. Up to that time I had not heard such continued firing of artillery, or such incessant volleys of musketry.

We could see the smoke of the battle in and through the woods, but could not see the lines of troops actually engaged. But all the signs and proofs of terrific fighting were visable *[sic]* to us on that high ridge, where both sight and hearing were unobstructed by other ridges, or obstacles to the passage of sound and light. Yet no orders came for us to go in."[33]

An officer in Gilbert's Eleventh Division was even more critical. He told of how the men were outraged, forced to watch as their comrades-in-arms were being pushed off the field. "How those men cursed! What little they could see and hear from those who came back to us of how our left was hammered and broken, while thousands stood within supporting distance and were not ordered up, enraged them. They were intelligent enough to see that a real opportunity was lost. There was bitter blasphemy coming from many parched lips that I had never heard blaspheme before or afterward, for they knew that the wasted opportunity would compel them to face the foe again with probably less advantage to us, thus prolonging the war."[34]

Sheridan's Division had borne the brunt of the fighting on Gilbert's line. His division had precipitated the battle that morning in its search for water, against Buell's orders not to bring on a general engagement before the army was all up and ready to fight. Phil Sheridan's star was in its ascendancy, and he received a great deal of credit for saving the Union army at Perryville. His friend and biographer, Captain H.C. Greiner, stated in his book *General Phil Sheridan, As I Knew Him* that "From what I was able to learn, it was only Sheridan's fierce fighting that saved McCook."[35] In his book *Battle Cry of Freedom*, James M. McPherson states: "The green troops broke, sweeping the other Union division back with them a mile or more before reinforcements halted the rout. Meanwhile in the center, Sheridan attacked the remaining southern division and drove it back through the streets of Perryville."[36] In reality, Sheridan was hardly to be considered the savior of the battlefield, and had not swept the Confederates he faced off the field and driven them the distance of two miles or more that separated them from the town of Perryville. In fact, after his foray against Liddell's troops that morning, he and his division experienced a lull in the fighting that lasted through much of the late morning and early afternoon. There was continual skirmishing and sharpshooting, to be sure, but probing and skirmishing were the order of the hour as the Confederates readied their right flank for the assault, and McCook's Corps filed into its position on the Federal left.

Sheridan's Division had been ordered to fall back from its most advanced position, and make its line along the position it had carried opposite Peter's Hill earlier that morning, about one-half mile to the rear. General Rousseau's Division was still forming on Sheridan's left, and was already attracting the attention of the Confederates. Eleventh Division brigade commander Colonel Dan McCook stated in his official report that their withdrawal offered the Confederates an opportunity "leaving General Rousseau without support on the right, exposing his flank. The enemy was not disturbed any longer by the batteries of our division."[37] The withdrawal of Sheridan's Division to the rear created a salient on the right of Rousseau's line. His flank was in the air and exposed, and as Colonel McCook stated, Sheridan's Division had pulled back to such an extent that it could not even receive the benefit of the Eleventh Division's artillery.

In his front, Sheridan was opposed mostly by the Confederate division of Patton Anderson. The right of Anderson's line joined with the left of Buckner's just short of the left flank of the Eleventh Division line, so Sheridan would have members of two Southern divisions in the front, but they were predominantly the members of Anderson's Division. Anderson's troops were emboldened by Sheridan's withdrawal. As Colonel McCook observed, "The enemy, assured by our retrograde movement, began to show themselves upon out right." Anderson's Confederates attempted to turn Sheridan's flank, and threw themselves upon the brigades of McCook and Greusel. The Rebels made two determined assaults on the Union line, and the fighting was done at close quarters, with the second assault being thrown back by a bayonet charge made by the 85th and 125th Illinois. Dan McCook's Brigade was shifting to the right, in support of Barnett's Illinois Light Artillery Battery, further extending the distance between it and the right flank of Alexander McCook's Corps. Men of the 36th Illinois, supporting this battery, stood their ground against the Confederates until all of their ammunition had been expended. They were replaced in the line by the 52nd Ohio, which took up the fight as soon as the soldiers assumed their place at the front. Charlie Common, the drummer boy of the regiment, lost his drum during the advance, but he picked up a musket and took a place in the line, where he "fought manfully." It was now 5:00 P.M., and the sun was already beginning to sink into the horizon. The regiment kept up a steady fire for 30 minutes, until darkness settled over the field and the Confederate forces retired.[38]

Captain Greiner observed several vignettes of the fighting along Sheridan's line. At one point in the battle, "I saw on a slight eminence about twenty steps to my right, a mule standing broadside to us, head up, ears pointing back, with a cannon ball hole through his neck and such a look of interest in his steadfast gaze upon the battle that one might have supposed he was enjoying the fight. I could distinctly see through the neck. I said to my first sergeant, who was walking by my side, 'Garrett, look at that mule!' He stared for some time, as though fearing his eyes were deceiving him, and I shall not forget his quaint saying, so characteristic of him: 'That would be a damned good place for a winder (window).'" On another part of the line, Greiner came across a scene of pitiful heartbreak. "On descending a little hill we found two soldiers digging a grave under the shade of a tree." Greiner asked a few questions, and was told that "they belonged to Sheridan; to one of the new regiments; that the pick and shovel they were using to bury their dead brother, pointing to a small soldier who lay near another a few feet away, belonged to their company." They went on to explain that this was their youngest brother, and when they thought of how heartbroken their poor mother would be when she received the news, both men wept openly. "I asked of the brother if he would accept our services to carry out the remainder of the sad duties, and they were glad to accept."[39]

General William Hardee described the attack his part of the Confederate line made on Sheridan's Division. "Simultaneously the brigades of (Brigadier General D.W.) Adams and (Colonel Samuel) Powell, on the left of Cleburne and Johnson, assailed the enemy in front, while Adams,' diverging to the right, united with Buckner's left. The whole force thus united then advanced, aided by a crushing fire from the artillery, which partially enfiladed their lines. This combined attack was irresistable [sic], and drove the enemy in wild disorder from the position nearly a mile to the rear." Hardee was speaking of McCook's Corps in observing that they had been pushed a mile from their lines. Sheridan's Division was not forced to relinquish nearly that much ground in holding its line against Anderson's men. With darkness falling, Hardee ordered a cease to the fighting and directed that the men make camp. "Night closing in our camp fires were lighted upon the ground so obstinately contested by the enemy, so bravely won by the valor of our troops."[40]

The 52nd Ohio had been the regiment that first made contact with the Confederates when it was pushed forward to secure the pools of water so many hours before. The regiment was on the front line when darkness ended the conflict, furiously firing at Anderson's attacking line. The 52nd Ohio had truly fought from dawn to dusk. They had the dubious honor of being part of the beginning and the conclusion of the fight.

An examination of the statistical record will easily show that Sheridan's Division was not nearly as pivotal, or heavily engaged in the fighting as to make Sheridan the savior of the Union army in this battle. Casualties in his entire division were 44 killed, 287 wounded, and 14 captured, for a total of 345. This was a fraction of any brigade in the First Corps, or of Goodling's Brigade, of the Second Corps. In terms of total casualties, the First Corps brigades suffered as follows: Harris' 591, Lytle's 823, Starkweather's 756, Jackson's 527, Webster's 579. Goodling's Brigade suffered total casualties of 499. Sheridan's brigades were engaged in the fighting, and heavily so, but they were not witness to the savagery with which the battle on the Federal left was being conducted. The Confederates were making a maximum effort to crush the exposed First Corps, and the desperate struggle that took place there is attested to by the aforementioned statistics.[41]

At 2:30 P.M., General McCook had sent his aide, Lieutenant L.M. Hosea, to Sheridan to request his assistance in fending off the attack that was then being made against his line. Sheridan declined, and forwarded the request to Gilbert. McCook repeated the entreaty at 3:00 P.M., when he sent another aide, Captain Fisher. This second request met with the same fate as the first. It was not until Fisher, on his own responsibility, went to Beull's headquarters that satisfaction was finally obtained. This was the first time that Buell had been informed of the danger to his left, and it was at this time that the commanding general had directed that Goodling's Brigade be sent to McCook's support. For one and one-half hours, Gilbert and Sheridan had allowed the pleas from the left to go unanswered. It is indeed a mystery why an officer with the fighting reputation that Sheridan already possessed, would allow the requests of McCook to go unanswered. Sheridan had exceeded his orders that morning in escalating the engagement and helping to bring about a full-scale battle. Why then was he so hesitant to lend assistance to the Federal left when it was in danger of being overrun?[42]

Crittenden's Corps was virtually unengaged in the fighting. It had seen even less action than had Gilbert's. Crittenden had marched to Perryville on the Lebanon Road, arriving there about 11:00 A.M., with Brigadier General William Smith's Division in the lead. Smith's men were immediately formed in line of battle across the Lebanon Road. This created a large gap between the left of Crittenden's Corps and the right of Gilbert's. Crittenden filled that gap by placing the divisions of Brigadier Generals Horatio Van Cleve and Thomas J. Wood in line to Smith's left, extending the front and connecting to the right of Gilbert's Corps. Colonel William Grose's 10th Brigade held the extreme right flank of the Union army, near the Lebanon Pike. From that point on, the members of Crittenden's Corps were like spectators at a sporting event who had been given obstructed seats. The battle raged to the left of them, but they could not follow its progress. "For hours the troops lay in the sun, momentarily expecting to be ordered forward, for the purpose of a diversion, if nothing more ... the day declined, the shadows lengthened, and still no orders for the Fourth Division. There was fitful skirmishing all the afternoon, with some artillery firing, and once or twice a brilliant cavalry charge, but not a regiment of Crittenden's infantry got into action until late in the day when Wood had the good fortune to be enabled to lend a helping hand in repelling a flank attack upon General R.B. Mitchell's division, holding the right of Gilbert's corps."[43]

Despite some light skirmishing with Wheeler's Cavalry, Crittenden's entire corps had been permitted to pass the day lying idly in the sun. They effectively played no part in the battle. In fact, their presence on the battlefield had no impact on the fighting in any way. If Crittenden had not gotten his men to the field that day, the battle most probably would have progressed exactly as it had. Crittenden bears no blame for the inactivity of his corps on the field of Perryville. He reported for action, as ordered, took his assigned position, and awaited further orders that never came. While McCook had made appeals for help to Gilbert, none were received by Crittenden. Though he commanded the troops that could have swung the balance of power on the battlefield firmly in favor of the Federals, it was not his fault that the opportunity was missed. Blame for the blunder in not committing his men to battle seems to belong to no one. McCook had appealed for reinforcements to his closest source for them—Gilbert—and Buell had not even learned that a battle was being fought till four o'clock. There had

Major General Thomas Crittenden. His Union corps was virtually unengaged in the battle, serving as spectators to the action on the Federal left. (Courtesy of the United States Army War College.)

been no reason for McCook to contact Crittenden, with Gilbert's men close at hand, and by the time Buell got into the fight his proper response was to commit reserves who were closest to the place where they were needed—once again, Gilbert's men. True, Buell could have ordered Crittenden's line to advance, in an effort to take the heat off of the embattled left, but his attentions seem to have been focused on getting more men into the breach the Confederates were creating on McCook's line. Whatever the causes, Crittenden's entire corps was allowed to remain inactive during the battle, and a golden opportunity was lost. The introduction of these men into the contest would surely have resulted in the battle being a crushing defeat for the Confederates, and might have made possible the elimination of Bragg's entire army. Crittenden's line overlapped that of the

Confederates by a huge margin, and an advance on his part would have taken the Rebel army in the flank and rear, and possibly cut it off from its routes of retreat. But it was not to be. The Union army had literally fought the Confederates with one hand tied behind its back. The total casualty list for Crittenden's entire corps amounted to only two men wounded.

Though the general engagement had been ceased by both sides with the coming of darkness, sporadic firing from artillery and small arms continued for several hours. There was a full moon, but the smoke from the battle still clung to the field, casting an eerie haze over the landscape. As it grew darker, one could not even see the smoke, only the flash of the flames from the mouths of the cannon and the muzzles of the muskets. "Gradually the fire slackened, the moon rose high and lit up the ghastly faces of the dead, until at 8 o'clock, all was the stillness of death." The battle was over. The fighting had been brought on largely as a result of trying to obtain water. The next night after the battle rain began falling freely, as if the firmaments were mocking the discomfiture of the men on the field.[44]

CHAPTER SEVEN

The Retreat

Though it had been confined to only a portion of the Union army, the fighting at Perryville had been as desperate as any that was ever seen on the American continent. Sam Watkins, of the 1st Tennessee, had felt it to be the fiercest fight he had been in during the war. His statement, "When the accounts of the hard battles fought during the war are rendered by the true historians, it will be found that the battle of Perryville was one of the hardest contested and one of the most sanguinary during the war. It was like two huge monsters together in one death-grasp, and each trying to drink the last drop of the other's blood. It was the only battle in which bayonets and butts of guns were used with death-dealing effect," was echoed by many who struggled in the rolling hills of Kentucky that day.[1]

This was a battle that was primarily fought by subordinate commanders, or by the men themselves, a "soldier's fight." On the Confederate side, Braxton Bragg had been instrumental in bringing on the engagement. In fact, had it not been for his arrival on the field that morning, it is doubtful if an attack would have been made at all. Bragg provided the catalyst, but from that point on, he largely allowed his subordinates to control the situation. He approved the line selected by General Polk, divided the army into two wings, to be commanded by Polk and Hardee, and then allowed them to fight the battle. The mode of attack, frontal assaults against the enemy flank, was reminiscent of the fighting at Shiloh, and would become a trademark of Bragg's military style. It was Napoleonic tactics in its simplest form, and was to be seen from Bragg on many other battlefields. In some cases, Confederate regiments were committed to the battle in a piecemeal manner, and the Confederates were never able to mount a cohesive, combined assault by all of their attacking force that would certainly have guaranteed them the victory. It was all the Union line could do to resist the individual attacks that were being made upon it. Had the Rebels been able to coordinate their efforts into one grand assault, McCook's Corps would certainly have been eliminated as a fighting force, and Bragg's army would have been free to concentrate on the then exposed flank of Gilbert's Corps before Buell would have had time to respond to the emergency.

For the Union side, almost the entire battle was fought without the benefit of the army commander. Buell was widely criticized for his absence of control over his army, but he seems to have been largely the victim of circumstance. Because of the acoustic shadow, he did not even learn that a battle was being fought until around four o'clock, and at that time, with only a little more than an hour of daylight available, there was little influence that he could assert over the outcome. In his own defense, Buell stated in his official report that "I was not early enough apprised of the condition of affairs on my left. This must be admitted to have been a grave error. I ascribe it to the too great confidence of General McCook, which made him believe that he could manage the difficulty without the aid or control of his commander."[2] To be sure, McCook was remiss in not notifying Buell immediately when he encountered such a strong force of Confederates in his front. It is true that he sent several requests for aid to General Gilbert, but it was not until one of these messengers took it upon himself to go to army headquarters that Buell was informed of the situation. Without the decision of this officer to go beyond his orders, the battle could have been fought in its entirety without Buell knowing anything about it. In McCook's defense, it is sure that he felt such a message was unnecessary. The roar of artillery and musketry should have been plainly audible to Buell, four miles away, and McCook must have wondered why his corps was being sacrificed, and why no support was forthcoming from the rest of the army. He had no idea that nature was at that time an ally of the Confederates, and that he was isolated not only by position, but by sound as well. Still, McCook was guilty of assuming, and it was his responsibility to keep Buell informed of the situation in his front. A messenger should have been dispatched to army headquarters as soon as the action became general, with information about the size and composition of the enemy force he was facing. Though McCook certainly had extenuating circumstances, his communication with his superior was lacking.

Both armies settled in for the night. The soldiers, weary, hungry, and most of them thirsty, had no idea what the coming day would bring. Hostilities might be resumed. It was sure that reinforcements would be marching toward both armies, and, as at Shiloh, the day's fighting might merely be a prelude to the decisive action. The 15th Ohio was one of the Union units with Sill that was marching for Perryville with all possible haste. The regiment was far removed from

Perryville when the battle was fought, but it had been making every effort to get there, having marched 27 miles on October 8. During that night orders were received to be up early and to be on the road once more by 7:00 A.M. The regiment was formed and just "getting ready to move when we heard cannonading behind us. We formed line of battle and the 32nd Indiana, 1st Ohio, and the 15th and 19th Regulars were sent out as skirmishers and met the enemy's forces coming up in our rear. A severe skirmish ensued." The skirmish, which this soldier termed to be "severe," resulted in five killed and eight wounded. A supply train that had strayed from the column, in order to allow the animals to drink from a stream, was captured. The animals were taken, the wagons were burned, and the officers and men were paroled. Among the property captured and destroyed was the regimental and company records.[3]

The action the 15th Ohio was involved in took place near Salvisa, and was known as the battle of Dog Walk. Kirby Smith had tried to capture or destroy Sill's Division and prevent it from joining with Buell. A spirited little fight of a few hours ensued, but Sill was able to escape the trap and continue on toward Perryville with only minor casualties.[4]

Daybreak on the battlefield found the opposing armies still facing one another. Johnson Culp of the 87th Illinois reported that there was "some considerable shooting yet this morning." He and two others had been detailed to look after 17 "sick" men, and Culp noted that it was raining "and our sick men have no shelter. We tore down a rye stack and built a rail pen and covered it with rye and got all 17 fellows in it but there was no room for us and as we had been on short rations for a while we went to a farmhouse to get something to eat." The owner of the house was hesitant to offer them anything. In fact, he would not even talk to them at first, and when he did, it was to curse the Yankees. The soldiers were not making a social call, and when the farmer spotted the revolvers in their hands he stepped out into the yard and allowed them to go inside, where they had a "tolerably fair supper of corn bread and mutton." As it turned out, the farmer had reason to object to the presence of Union soldiers in his home. His son had been part of Bragg's army and had been wounded in the fighting of the previous day. He had been brought to the house and was suffering in another room. Culp had to admit "I suppose that made the old man contrary with us." When the three soldiers returned to the temporary shelter they had built, it was to find that the soldiers inside had been "gobbled" up by Confederate "guerrillas."[5]

While some men, like Culp, looked to matters of comfort and necessity such as food and shelter, others were impressed by the scene of carnage that confronted them. One Confederate described the battlefield as being "A ghastly scene of dead and dying ... the blue and the grey mingled together in sickening confusion."[6] Sergeant Sam Shepardson of the 30th Indiana wrote to his sister about the horrible sights of the battlefield. He told her that, in addition to the Union dead, there were about 1,000 dead Confederates on the field. "They did not ask permission to bury them, and we hadn't time to bury them, so they were left to the mercy of the buzzards. I know it is rather horrible to think of, but we must get through the world the best way we can."[7]

Shepardson's assessment about the dead Confederates being left to the forces of nature proved quite correct. Union soldiers began to be picked up by ambulances and burial details as soon as medical aid or burial detachments could reach them, but the army only had the time or resources to tend to its own men. Eight days after the battle was over, another Union soldier would write his wife that the battlefield was "the most horrible sight that ever man beheld. Today, there are hundreds of men being eaten up by the buzzards and hogs."[8]

Virtually every house and building in and around Perryville was converted into a hospital for the wounded. One Confederate who had been wounded in the fighting said that "the moaning and sighing of the wounded and dying that night was heartrending and enough to make any man oppose war." In later years he would remember "the dead were laying thick on both sides. That was sixty years ago, but the terrible slaughter there yet haunts me in my dreams." A Union soldier related that "The enemy's wounded lay in every fence corner. Our boys behaved themselves, and treated them kindly, bringing water whenever they desired it. They were mostly Tennessee troops. Some of them deserved no compassion for they spoke impudently and disdainfully. Nevertheless, on account of their wounds, no notice was taken of it." The surgeon's attendants "were continually passing by leading and carrying and hauling the wounded who were crying and screaming with pain. But the most horrible sight I witnessed was in passing over the battlefield, where were to be seen men lying one on another and for rods one might have walked on the dead bodies."[9]

A soldier from the 1st Wisconsin who was wounded in the battle left an account of what it was like to spend the night in one of these improvised hospitals:

> The memory of the almost intolerable thirst and pain that followed (the wounding, the being gathered up in a blanket by sympathizing comrades and friends, and transported as tenderly as possible in an ambulance to the deserted house taken as a field hospital), is much clearer than the more important events that followed. So also was impressed upon my mind the picture of the examining surgeon's cot in front of the house, with its flaming torch to aid him in his examination of the wounds that determined the assignment; the being placed upon a large bed already occupied by a one-

armed comrade, while the floor was literally covered with improvised beds containing other specimens of shattered humanity. One thing I am glad to remember is that of all that number of wounded men not one was bemoaning his lot, but each appeared to be trying to outdo the other in absurd remarks that would call out a burst of laughter. Occasionally a careless attendant would stumble in the half darkness over some recumbent form and call forth a volley of remonstrances, but it would so soon be followed by the ready laugh at some new suggestion of the advantage in having a limited number of sound members."[10]

G.W. Brown was equally horrified by the battlefield and the hospitals. In a letter to his brother, he described the scenes of both.

The battlefield, as I looked upon it the next day and for days following, was enough to satisfy me for a life time. Friends and foe lay together, scattered over a wide extent of country; but especially the destruction was fearful upon the left wing. How many perished I know not and I think none but God will know. The battlefield was awful, but, I think the hospital was more awful still. Here were living mutilated in every possible shape, that could be done and still live. They were generally patient and very brave, though some moaned and complained bitterly.[11]

A Union officer left a record of the disrespect shown to the dead on the field. When he examined the ground the next morning,

I found on this field, as on others, that as soon as night spread its black veil over the horrors of the day, the soldier robber goes out to search the dead for their valuables. I found the pockets of the slain turned inside out, and their rings taken from their fingers. I saw a Confederate officer whose hand was covered with dried blood, except where a wide ring had left the skin white, in striking contrast to the remainder of the crimson member. In their search for valuables, letters would be thrown out. I felt curious to read one that lay beside a fine-looking man. I intended to return it to the writer, explaining my possession of it. It was a well-written, patriotic love letter from a girl to her betrothed, but she did not appear to realize the uncertainties of war, as she concluded by painting a picture of the most perfect happiness for them after his return, which she thought would not be delayed longer than a year. How terribly her bright anticipations were shattered only a few days afterward! The letter had not been written more than two weeks before he was killed. It was probably the first time he had heard from her, as he was a member of one of the new Illinois regiments that had joined us a few days before. I carried the letter several days, as we were pursuing the enemy and no mail was received or sent, so there was no opportunity to return it to the girl. When a chance came I found it so badly faded from rain and perspiration that it was illegible.[12]

The Confederate Cemetery at Perryville battlefield. Constructed with funds raised through private donations, the stone walls of this cemetery encircle some 400 Confederate dead who were buried there shortly after the battle, near the spot where Cheatham's men had entered the fight. (Photograph by the author.)

When the Union army got around to burying the dead, it began with its own men. Union troops were placed in temporary graves along the Springfield road. This was merely to get them off the field, and was only a short-term solution. They were later exhumed and moved to permanent national cemeteries elsewhere in Kentucky. As for the Confederate dead, a local citizen, Squire Henry P. Bottom, gathered some 400 of them together, and had them buried on ground near the place where Cheatham's men had entered the battle. Much of the fighting had taken place around his house, as the Confederates had pushed back the first Union line that extended on either side of it. A number of other Confederates were buried beside the Chaplin River, near a house belonging to the Goodnight family. In 1895, S.W. Peoples launched a subscription campaign on behalf of the Confederates buried by Bottom. Eight men donated $25 apiece to have the cemetery enclosed by a stone wall, and a monument was placed there. Mr.

Monument to the fallen soldiers that stands guard inside the Confederate cemetery. (Photograph by the author.)

Bottom donated the stone for the wall, as well as the land that the cemetery was on, deeding it to the Confederate Veteran Association of Kentucky. The cemetery remains there today, near the site of the present-day visitor center.[13]

Samuel Starling, an officer in Jackson's command, ventured out onto the battlefield at sunrise of October 9. He and a companion sought to recover Jackson's body, which they had been unable to bring off the field during the fight. He observed that there were a great number of Union and Confederate soldiers mingling about the field, ministering to the needs of the wounded and looking at the battlefield. To Starling it seemed that "all animosity had ceased and they were mixing like friends." Jackson's body was found right where he had been left, but his boots and hat were gone, and the buttons had been removed from his coat.[14]

Neither the armies nor the small town of Perryville was prepared to care for the huge number of wounded men. Both armies had with them an insufficient amount of medicine and medical stores. There were few ambulances or tents, and no hospital furniture. The armies had been on short rations to begin with, and the population of the surrounding countryside had already been stripped of any spare larder by the contending troops, so even food was in short supply for the wounded. Everything that was needed would have to be brought to the town, and the wagon transport would take time. The wounded would endure many agonizing days before those who were caring for them had the adequate supplies to do so.

Many on both sides felt sure that the battle would be resumed on October 9. Buell was certain that the fighting would be renewed and made every preparation to attack the Confederates in the morning. Most of the officers and men in the Southern army also felt certain that the battle would be continued. They had thus far been victorious, and were in possession of the battlefield when night put an end to the fighting. They expected to finish the job they had started with first light, but Bragg had other plans. By this time, the Confederate commander was finally convinced that he was facing Buell's whole army, and he knew that he was heavily outnumbered. At midnight, Bragg ordered his main lines to be pulled back to the town of Perryville, and plans were made to retreat in the direction of Harrodsburg at dawn. The Confederates had captured 15 pieces of Union artillery during the battle. When the army retreated, 13 cannon were left on the battlefield. Though they only took two additional big guns with them, many of the cannon that were left on the field had been traded for better Union ordnance. Bragg sent a message to Kirby Smith, who was then at Lawrenceburg, ordering him to march his command to Harrodsburg, where the two armies would finally be consolidated. If there was to be another battle fought, Bragg wanted to make sure he had all of the Confederate troops in the region at his disposal. Joe Wheeler was given the task of screening the Confederate movements. Though his troopers had taken little part in the actual battle, Wheeler and his command would shine in performing the rear-guard assignment. To Wheeler would go much of the credit for staving off a disaster to Bragg's army and allowing it to safely reach Tennessee.[15]

Once Buell learned that Bragg was retreating, he sent word to General Sill to join the army with all possible haste. Both commanders wanted to have all their men accounted for if another battle took place. Buell then decided to assume a defensive posture and wait for Sill to arrive. He formed his army facing in a northerly direction, facing toward Bragg's army. His right was four miles from Danville, his center on the Harrodsburg and Perryville Road, and his left was near Dicksville. The Union army was held in this position for three days while it waited for Sill to arrive. Finally, on October 11, the army was consolidated, and Buell made his preparations to advance. On the morning of October 12, the Union army marched out to give battle to the Confederates, known to be at Camp Dick Robinson, dubbed Camp Breckinridge by the Southerners. When they arrived at that place, Buell found that the Rebels had vacated the position and were moving south, leaving Kentucky.[16]

"A few days after the battle Bragg had collected his army at Camp Dick Robinson, about fifteen miles from the battle ground," wrote one Confederate soldier. "The natural strength of this camp for a large army acting on the defensive was very great. To the north was the long line of the Kentucky River cliffs, higher than the Hudson Pallisades [sic] and reaching from the mountains to below Frankfort, effectually blocking any attacking army from the north. To the west and southwest frowned the Dick's River cliffs, only a little lower than those of the Kentucky and furnishing a secure defense in those quarters. Dick's River pours into the Kentucky a few miles northwest of Camp Dick Robinson ... thus the camp was in an acute angle of the two rivers and unassailable save from the southeast."[17]

Buell was severely criticized for not attacking Bragg while he was at Camp Dick Robinson. He tried to counter the criticism by stating that the nature of the stronghold made it almost impregnable to an attack from his army. Even if he had ventured to make such an assault, he would have been compelled to march his army far to the south, in order to pass the head of Dick's River, a maneuver that would have left Louisville and all of northern Kentucky open to the Confederates while he was getting into position. Buell was obviously heartened to find out that Bragg had abandoned the place on his own. Many of the men in the Confederate army were mystified over the decision. They could not understand "why did Bragg abandon Dick Robinson? In that strong camp, with several of the richest counties of Kentucky behind him and able to feed his whole army during the coming winter; with the roads and the mountain passes toward Tennessee open, undisputed, and ready for his retreat if it should become necessary; with the seat of war suddenly transferred two hundred miles to the north; with one of the richest regions of the South in his grasp and able to feed his army; with the chances for large accessions to his army from the Kentucky seccessionists [sic], who were not likely to enlist with the certainty that they must leave their homes in the enemy's hands and with no prospects of return — under all these conditions, why did General Bragg evacuate Kentucky?"[18]

Kirby Smith's army finally reached the vicinity of Harrodsburg and Camp Dick Robinson on October 10, and the two Confederate armies were at last united. Smith was impressed with the natural strength of the position, and urged Bragg to make a stand against Buell. It was Smith's opinion that the campaign could yet be won with such a stronghold to defend, and that the Union army could be destroyed in trying to take it. Bragg initially agreed, and plans were made to fight the decisive battle of the campaign. When Buell showed no signs of being willing to accommodate the Confederates by attacking them in the position of their choosing, Bragg changed his mind and determined to abandon Kentucky and return to Tennessee.[19]

Bragg's reasons for quitting the state were sound. He had received information that another Union army was marching to Buell's assistance from Cincinnati. For his own part, he could expect to receive no reinforcements from any quarter. The men of Kentucky had failed to rally to his banner, and on October 12, he received word of the defeat of Van Dorn and Price at Corinth. Up to this point, Bragg had still entertained the notion that these forces would be forwarded to Kentucky to join his own, but the news of the defeat that had taken place on October 4 caused him to immediately make up his mind to return to Tennessee. In addition to the concerns over manpower, apprehension over transport and logistics played a large part in his decision. Bragg feared that the rain that had begun after the battle might signal the start of the autumn rainy season in the region. If so, it could make the roads south impassable to his army, and trap him in the mud. There was also a problem with the supplies that had been gathered at Bryantsville. Bragg had ordered on September 27 that all food rations from Danville and Lexington be sent to Bryantsville, but when his army arrived there, he found that only four days' rations were on hand.[20]

Bragg's decision caused the first serious rift between Kirby Smith and himself. Smith was firmly opposed to leaving the state, and he later asserted that Bragg had exaggerated the supply problem at Bryantsville, that there were plenty of supplies there for the army. The evidence, however, seems to support Bragg.

An inventory of supplies, taken just before the Confederate army reached that point, shows that there were 33,000 pounds of hardtack, 10,000 pounds of bacon, 500 pounds of lard, 3,000 barrels of pork, 250 barrels of flour, 130 barrels of sugar, 702 cattle, 75 sacks of coffee, 5 sacks of salt, and 1sack of rice at the Bryantsville depot. While this may sound like a mountain of food, one must consider that it was intended to feed 45,000 men. Bragg's estimation that there were only four days of rations there would be correct.[21]

On October 13, the Confederate army started its march for Cumberland Gap. The progress was necessarily slow. The army had nearly 4,000 wagons in its train, loaded with food, uniforms, blankets, weapons, and other spoils of war that had been collected during the campaign. The majority of the wagons themselves had been captured from the Federal army. The Confederates would need these supplies, but the conveyance of them to Tennessee would mean that the army would be forced to march at a slow rate, making it possible for Buell to catch them and bring them to battle before they could reach safety.[22]

The route of the march was to be from Camp Dick Robinson to Crab Orchard. From there, the army would march to Mount Vernon, Wild-Cat Bend, Cumberland Gap, and then to Knoxville. On October 13, the retreat to Tennessee began. Colonel Joe Wheeler received an order from Bragg before the sun was up that day.

> Special Orders,
>   No. 14
>   I. Colonel Wheeler is hereby appointed chief of cavalry and is authorized to give orders in the name of the commanding general. He is charged, under Major-General Smith, with covering the rear of the army and holding the enemy in check. All cavalry will report to him and receive his orders.

Later that day, Wheeler received a message from Kirby Smith's chief of staff: "Maj. Gen. E. Kirby Smith directs me to say to you that you are hereby placed in command of all the cavalry of the whole army." Wheeler's orders continued: "The condition of that army, with its large train, &c., being now considerably in the rear, will require that you should send your largest cavalry force for covering well its rear.... The officer commanding the force for covering the rear of the column on this road must keep his position well, and not fall back on the infantry unless driven back by the enemy."[23]

Wheeler took to his assignment with enthusiasm. He began at once to drive the Union commanders crazy with his innovative rear-guard action by obstructing their line of march with felled trees. Judging by the reports of the Federal officers, this was evidently a new and unexpected approach to warfare. General

William S. Smith, in command of the Union advance, voiced sentiments repeated by many of his officers. "We are pressing the rebel cavalry back, skirmishing with them at every turn of the road. They have so obstructed the road by felling trees that our progress is very slow.... They fell trees until we come up to them, then fall back rapidly and chop away again." Wheeler's combination of engaging the head of the Union column, forcing the Yankees to come on line, combined with the natural obstructions he was placing in their path, had the desired result. Bragg's army was moving at a slow rate, but the Union army was forced to advance at a crawl. Wheeler reported that at times "our cavalry dismounted and fought behind stone fences and hastily erected rail breastworks, and when opportunity offered charged the advancing enemy. Each expedient was adopted several times a day, and when practicable the road was obstructed by felling timber."[24]

The rift between Bragg and Smith came to a head during the retreat. When the army reached Lancaster it was divided, to march by separate, parallel roads that would reunite at Barbourville, north of Cumberland Gap. Bragg's forces marched on the road to Crab Orchard, while Smith's took a route a little farther to the east, toward Big Hill. The majority of the supply and baggage wagons were entrusted to Smith, and he complained bitterly about the slow progress he was making, thus encumbered by the wagon train. In a message to Bragg dated October 14, Smith states "I have no hope of saving the whole of my train." The next day, he repeated his alarm and sent Bragg word that "I have little hope of saving any of the trains, and fear much of the artillery will be lost." While issuing these pessimistic statements to Bragg, Smith was openly complaining to Polk about the state of affairs. He voiced his opinion that Bragg had selected the easier route for himself, and had placed Smith's men in a position where they could be gobbled up by the Federal army. "He gives up Wild Cat Pass, exposes my flank, and leaves the enemy only 9 miles to march to meet my front.... I have marched by a circuitous route, while he has taken the direct one.... My train is now turned off by a circuitous route and one that is almost impassable, and on which ... (the wagons) must be delayed a long time, if not abandoned."[25]

It was Wheeler who calmed Smith's fears. When news of Smith's apprehension reached "Fighting Joe" he sent a short but reassuring message to ease Smith's concerns: "Tell General Smith to abandon nothing; we will save all." It was a bold statement for the colonel of a cavalry brigade that could boast only six regiments to make when he was facing the massed forces of the entire Union army, but Wheeler's troopers were performing Herculean efforts in preventing the Federals from overtaking the rear of the Confederate army. Smith pushed forward, and Wheeler made good his boast. Nothing was lost.[26]

The roads and the wagon train was not the only problem for Kirby Smith or the Confederate army. Both wings of the army were suffering terribly for want of food during the march. A soldier in the 2nd Tennessee remembered the hardship: "On that march we suffered hunger. My rations from Perryville to Knoxville were 8 small, very small biscuits and four onions ... no meat. I don't believe anyone who went through the rest of the war can give a perfectly accurate account of it (the march)."[27]

Though he would later assert that there had been an ample supply of food at Bryantsville when Bragg decided to retreat, even Kirby Smith commented on the scarcity of food: "My men have suffered on this march everything excepting actual starvation. Not less than 10,000 of them are scattered through the country trying to find something upon which to live.... There can not now be more than 6,000 effective men left in my whole force." Conditions were no better in Bragg's wing. Straggling and the search for food led General Polk to write that "Many of the regiments of the Army of the Mississippi are reduced to 100 men."[28]

The pursuing Union army was experiencing little better conditions on the march. A soldier in Buell's Army wrote to his wife "I don't care to fight any more battles, but we are pushing on after the flying rebels and will fight them again if we can catch them.... My health is good, but I am pretty tired of this campaign. I have not had a change of clothing for two weeks, and for many nights have slept with no cover but my saddle blanket."[29]

Joe Wheeler continued to hamper and harass the Federal pursuit. Major Albert Hart of the 41st Ohio told of a brush with the Confederate rear guard when

> just at dark we reached a point called Pitman's Cross Roads. As we halted, a native came up, and said that the rebels had two pieces of what our men called "Jackass Artillery" planted on the road a little ahead of us. This light gun could be unlimbered, mounted on a couple of mules, and trotted off almost instantly. The regiment was strung along the road, and we were sitting on both sides of it. We all knew how inconsiderate the rebels were in the use of these guns, and that at any moment they were liable to make a ten-strike along our line; but the major commanding did not see it that way and that the sooner he got us off that road the better. The delay was brief. There was a murderous shreik [sic], and that villainous shell passed just over our heads straight down the whole length of our line. Before we had time to move, the second shot came. It seemed the first cousin to the other, and a great deal too familiar for comfort.[30]

Buell's pursuit was never able to make contact with the rear of the Confederate forces. The most that the Union army was able to do was to collect the Rebel stragglers it happened upon during the march. Lancelot Ewbank of the 31st Indiana made an entry in his diary for October 15 that they had "tried to intercept rebels on Lancaster Pike. All had passed except 15 who were caught in a house of ill fame."[31]

Federal pursuit continued for 12 days, but the results were the same. "Oct. 19 ... In camp all day except those who were gathering up stragglers.... Oct. 20 ... Followed rebels 14 miles, took a few stragglers." Buell finally called off the pursuit by the time his army reached the vicinity of Crab Orchard. The Union army turned about and retraced its steps. The weather was turning colder, and Buell did not fancy campaigning over the harsh Kentucky roads in the autumn snow and rain. As the Northern army plodded back through the towns and hamlets it had passed in chasing the Confederates, Private Ewbank noted a fitting end to the campaign. In his diary entry for October 25, he wrote simply: "Marched to within 3½ miles of Mt. Vernon. Snowed."[32]

The end of the game of chase with Bragg also signaled the end of a game of bluff. During the pursuit, Buell received official confirmation that Charles Gilbert was not a real major general, and he summarily relieved him of command when the army was in the vicinity of Crab Orchard. No officer was assigned to replace him. Instead, the divisions of his corps were distributed between McCook and Crittenden.[33]

Buell had decided to give up the pursuit on October 16, and he advised General Halleck, in Washington, of the decision stating that he thought it would be useless to continue further. He also announced his intentions to retire his main body to Nashville. Halleck telegraphed his strong opposition to Buell's proposal on October 18, stating that the Federal army must drive the Confederates out of Kentucky and Tennessee while they had the army there to do it. Halleck felt that a retrograde movement to Nashville would only invite Bragg's army to once more enter Kentucky or east Tennessee. He suggested that Buell march on Knoxville, or Chattanooga, instead, citing that Knoxville and Chattanooga were both approximately the same distance as Nashville from where Buell then was. Halleck reasoned that if Buell marched on either of those two places the Confederates would be compelled to retreat into Virginia or Georgia. Buell's mind was unchanged by the advice, so the following day, Halleck sent another, stronger telegram. He stated that he had discussed the matter with President Lincoln, and the president concurred with his opinions. He told Buell that the president directed him to say that Buell's army "must enter (east) Tennessee this fall and that it ought to move there while the roads are passable." He added that the president "does not understand why we cannot march as the enemy marches, live as he lives and fight as he fights, unless we admit the inferiority of our troops and of our generals."[34]

Buell remained adamant in his decision, despite the obvious insult, and the insinuation of the chief of staff's last telegraph. He telegraphed Halleck, restating his previous objections, and adding that it was his estimation that it would take a force of 80,000 men to take and hold east Tennessee. His objections fell upon deaf ears. On October 20, Halleck issued Buell a direct order to march his army directly to east Tennessee, and to do so with all possible dispatch. In the end, it was Braxton Bragg who settled the squabbling between the two Union generals. He had gotten his army safely back into middle Tennessee, and was marching toward Nashville. The Union army now was to be making forced marches to reach the destination Buell had selected all along. Though Buell had been proven correct in his decision, it did not end the harassing tone of the correspondence from Washington.[35]

Braxton Bragg's army was allowed to reach east Tennessee, and safety, but his command had suffered further losses during the march. As Kirby Smith had stated, many troops were forced to leave the march to forage for something to eat, and a number of these men had not yet rejoined their commands. To be sure, a number of those absent in the search of provisions would not be returning, as they had been captured by Buell's army. In addition to these, fully one-half of the 3,000 Kentuckians who had joined his army deserted during the retreat. When a misguided report reached the army that 32 regiments had been raised in Kentucky, Captain E. John Ellis took the opportunity to quip: "We found indeed 32 men who were willing to be Colonels. 32 willing to serve as Lieut Cols and Majors, any quantity ready to tack on their collars the bars of a captain or Lieut. but few, very few willing to serve in the ranks."[36]

Bragg's arrival in east Tennessee marked the official end of the Kentucky campaign. "This terminates the Kentucky campaign," wrote Colonel Brent of his staff. "It failed owing to several causes. The failure of Ky to co-operate actively and efficiently, the scarcity of subsustence [sic] stores &c., the overwhelming superiority of the enemy's force, the failure of Van Dorn at Corinth which exposed our left, clearly indicated the propriety and wisdom of the retreat at the very moment the General decided upon it."[37]

The Confederate army had marched over 1,000 miles during the campaign, and the footsore veterans of Bragg's army were glad to be back on what they deemed to be friendly soil, back at Murfreesboro, near the spot where the campaign had begun two months before. This campaign had extended over more territory than any other during the war, but that was its only claim to fame.

Chapter Eight

Back in Tennessee

Both armies were destined to return to Tennessee, where each had been when the Kentucky Campaign began. Nashville was once again threatened, and the principal armies were once more doing hard marching to gain an advantage, but Don Carlos Buell was to have only a week to direct the actions of his army. His lack of success on the field of Perryville, combined with his refusal to follow the Rebels into east Tennessee, finally served to cement the opinion of his superiors against him. On October 23, General Halleck telegraphed General William S. Rosecrans, who was then at Corinth, Mississippi, to proceed with all possible haste to Cincinnati, where he would receive further orders placing him in command of Buell's army. Buell was informed of the change of command when he received a telegram from Halleck dated October 24. But Rosecrans was delayed in reporting, and was not able to assume command until October 30.[1]

Buell was relieved and accused of dilatory tactics. He would have to refight the battle of Perryville a year later, in 1863, when he was called before the Congressional Committee on the Conduct of the War to defend his actions during the campaign. The committee reviewed the testimony of every leading officer who had been with the army, and concluded that Buell was guilty of poor judgment in the conduct of his campaign. The committee's official opinion was that Buell could have prevented the invasion of Kentucky if he had offered Bragg's army battle instead of marching for Louisville. The report stated:

> This he could have done, in our opinion, by an early concentration of his army at Sparta, McMinnville or Murfreesboro, with a view to active offensive operations against Bragg the moment he debouched from the Sequatchie Valley. Instead of that he waited until the 5th of September before concentrating at Murfreesboro, from which he retired to Nashville, thereby allowing Bragg to cross the Cumberland river without interruption. The Commission

146

cannot justify the falling back from Murfreesboro to Nashville, but is of the opinion that it was General Buell's duty from that point to have attacked the rebel army before it crossed the Cumberland, and it is the belief that had that course been pursued Bragg would have been defeated.[2]

Buell also suffered from the exasperation of his own army. It had failed to defeat the Confederates again, and the soldiers in the ranks could clearly see that generalship, not their own fighting ability, was the reason for the failure. As Buell was the commanding officer, he stood to receive the lion's share of the complaints. His failure to administer a solid defeat to Bragg was a point of contention with his own soldiers, and the rumor was even spread throughout the army that he and Bragg were brothers-in-law.[3]

But it would seem that the evidence was stacked against Buell. The War Department had been receiving misrepresentations about the general and his campaign for some time from sources placed high in political power. The chief assailant had been Andrew Johnson, the governor of Tennessee, who was particularly vocal in his animosity toward Buell. Johnson had gone so far as to urge the governors of Illinois, Indiana, and Ohio to submit their concerns about Buell's leadership to Washington, and these petitions had been instrumental in effecting Buell's removal from command.[4]

The findings of the committee besmirched Buell's reputation, and he was not again assigned to active duty. He lingered in the army, without a command, until May of 1864, when he was mustered out of the volunteer service. In June of that same year, he resigned his commission in the regular army. Ulysses S. Grant would later recommend his reinstatement to duty, but Grant's request was not acted upon by the War Department despite that officer's high stature with the administration. Grant was well aware of Buell's abilities, and wished to have him take some important role in the final phases of the war, but the administration would not hear of it. Buell entered civilian life, where he worked as the supervisor of an ironworks and a coal mine before becoming a government pension agent.[5]

Buell was known throughout the old army as a good organizer and disciplinarian, and his performance up to the battle of Perryville had earned him the thanks of the administration. General William Farrar Smith, a well-respected Union officer, described Buell as "a capital soldier and a student in his profession. He fought a battle with courage, coolness, and intelligence, saving us from utter rout at Shiloh, into which false position Halleck's ambition and Grant's density had begotten us."

Another officer who received the rebuke of the committee was Charles Gilbert. Though Gilbert's testimony was filled with information that was intended to justify his actions and lay blame on others, the strategy did not work. The committee saw through Gilbert's efforts to allay blame, and the testimony of other officers completely refuted his words. When the committee issued its findings in the matter, the portion that dealt with Gilbert's actions was particularly stern. "There can be no question about its being the duty of somebody to assist McCook. As his right had been posted not exceeding three hundred yards from Gilbert's left, and as the severest fighting was on McCook's right, we can not see why Gilbert did not re-enforce him when so requested. He should have done so, if for no other reason than that McCook's discomfiture exposed his own flank. Nothing but positive orders, fixing and holding him in position, can justify his failure. If such there were, they have not been heard of in this testimony." The judge advocate of the commission was brief but scathing in his treatment of Gilbert in his summary of the findings. "All the while Gilbert's Corps remained idle spectators of the unequal contest, and not only failed to tender reinforcements, but when such aid was solicited, positively refused."[6]

Buell had been effectively kicked out of the army, but Gilbert was allowed to return to his prior assignment as a staff officer in the Inspector General's Department. In the postwar years, he would become a prolific writer on the subject of Perryville, contributing material on the battle to *Century Magazine*, and a multipart series to *Southern Bivouac Magazine*. His material continues to be read by students of the war in the pages of Battles and Leaders of the Civil War, which was a compilation of the *Century Magazine* articles. In his writings, Gilbert slanted the facts and provided a great deal of mis-information in an effort to present his service in a positive light. Much of what he wrote was imperfect, at best, and fabrication, at worst, but being the most active writer on the subject, he was often quoted by historians of the battle. The ultimate irony dealing with Gilbert is that not only was he reinstated to his previous assignment following the battle, but he received a brevet in the regular army, to the rank of colonel, for "gallant and meritorious services at the battle of Perryville." This promotion was an insult to every soldier who took an active part in the fighting.[7]

The committee never formally addressed the fact that Gilbert had misrepresented himself to be a major general, impersonating an officer of a higher rank. Though this situation was brought up in the hearings, it was allowed to pass with no formal proceeding being launched. This was surely an offense that deserved to be tried before a court-martial, and Gilbert should have been brought up on charges. He had knowingly and willingly committed a military crime of unspeakable proportions. Through his intentional misrepresentations he had secured a post that he was unqualified for that endangered the lives of thousands of men under his control. The part he played in the defeat of the left wing at Perryville should have been considered a criminal act, both civil and military. Why this crime was allowed to pass unpunished is an unsolved mystery of the war. But then the Union military seemed to be granting a blanket amnesty for military crimes committed during this campaign. General Jefferson Davis was never brought up on charges, civil or military, for the murder of General Nelson, either. He would continue in his command position until the end of the war.

Though George H. Thomas received no such public rebukes from the War Department or the Committee on the Conduct of the War, he did feel the displeasure of his superiors. He had been offered command of the army immediately prior to Buell's forces marching out of Louisville in pursuit of Bragg, but declined the position on the grounds that on the eve of an active campaign he was ill-prepared to assume that command. Thomas should have been the natural choice to replace Buell, when that officer was relieved, but Rosecrans was selected instead. Part of the reason for this is that Thomas' superiors felt that he bore some responsibility for the failures at Perryville. Thomas was second in command of the army, and was with the right wing during the battle. It was within his authority to have ordered assistance to the left flank, and his lack of aggression on that field was a factor in the army command not being offered to him. He would eventually be given command of the army, and he would prove himself to be one of the best generals in the Union army when he crushed the Army of Tennessee at the battles of Franklin and Nashville, but it would be almost two years before the post was offered to him again.

The majority of the officers in Buell's army would go on to serve in the Army of the Cumberland, under General Rosecrans. Approximately two months after the Kentucky campaign had ended, they would meet their old foes in the sanguinary two-day struggle that was Murfreesboro, or Stones River. The army would finally accomplish Halleck's desire of capturing Chattanooga in the summer of 1863, but would then almost be destroyed at Chickamauga. Retreating to Chattanooga, the army would withstand a siege that threatened to destroy it as a military force. When Grant took command and broke the siege at the battles of Missionary Ridge and Lookout Mountain, the Army of the Cumberland began a march through the South that did not end until the surrender of General Joseph E. Johnston's army had been accomplished in April of 1865.

Phil Sheridan would continue to rise in stature until he became one of the leading generals in the Union army, and was second only to Sherman as a lieutenant to General Grant. Perryville had been his first test at divisional command, and he had passed the test with high marks. His handling of his division provided a bright star for Gilbert's Corps, which was otherwise largely inactive, and brought Sheridan to the forefront as a top-notch commander. Though Sheridan received unwarranted credit for saving the Union army at Perryville, and though he failed to aid McCook when asked to do so, he seems to have conducted his own affairs with skillful intelligence.

Captain Ebenezer Gay seems to have been caught up in the conspiracy regarding Gilbert and his pretended rank. Gay performed admirably in the campaign, and the Union cavalry did a credible job despite its inexperience and lack of weaponry. Regardless of this, Gay was returned to his permanent rank of captain, and the brevet position of general and chief of cavalry that Gilbert had bestowed on him was taken away. If any officer deserved the promotion that Gilbert was given, it was Gay. His conduct in the campaign was steady and reliable, and his decisions on the battlefield showed fighting spirit and a firm grasp of his responsibilities. As such, he deserved better treatment than that afforded him by the committee.

For Braxton Bragg, the return to Tennessee brought with it a trip to Richmond for a private interview with Jefferson Davis. Public sentiment was running strongly against Bragg for his failure in the campaign, and Davis wished to give the general an opportunity to defend himself. It was not only the public that was denouncing Bragg. Generals Polk, Hardee, and Kirby Smith openly criticized him. Smith went so far as to state that Bragg had lost his mind, and he made reference to it in his personal report of the campaign to President Davis. Senator G.A. Henry wrote to his colleague Louis T. Wigfall that "...never have I heard so much dissaticfaction [sic] as this army expresses at the result of Bragg's campaign into Ky. Even common soldiers say he ought to have whipped Buell at Mumfordville.... The army is clamoring for Joe Johnston to lead them, or for Beauregard." A private citizen voiced the opinion of many when he said: "I do not doubt Gen. Bragg's loyalty as some have done, nor question his sanity, as others have done; but, believing him to be both sane and loyal, I concur in the judgement [sic] already rendered by the people and the army ... that as a military commander he is utterly incompetent."[8]

Bragg received orders to report to Richmond on October 23. Upon his arrival there, he wrote his wife that he was one of the most unpopular people in the city. "At once the dogs of detraction were let loose upon me, and the venal press ... decided I was removed from my command." In President Davis, Bragg found a friendly and open-minded ally. Bragg met the president and the secretary of war in closed-door conferences that lasted from 10 A.M. until 4 P.M. for several days, as he explained the details of the campaign and answered the questions of his superiors. In the end, Davis was satisfied that Bragg's conduct in the campaign was appropriate, and he expressed his delight that the general had been able to safely return the army to Tennessee. Davis discounted most of the complaints against Bragg as being the result of political posturing. Those in Congress who were screaming loudest for Bragg's removal were the very same people who were openly hostile toward Davis and his administration. Publicly attacking Bragg was just another way of criticizing Davis. The president had come to expect a certain amount of this sort of grumbling, and once he had the opportunity to talk to Bragg, he was convinced that most of the accusations against him were the result of politics, not the result of genuine concern for the army.[9]

One thing did bother Davis in regard to the allegations, and that was that the army had lost confidence in Bragg. In an effort to curb such talk, Davis summoned Bragg's chief detractors, Leonidus Polk and Kirby Smith, to Richmond for a private briefing. Both men continued to blame Bragg for the failure of the Kentucky campaign and lobbied for his replacement by Joe Johnston. Polk was gracious enough to acknowledge that Bragg displayed talent as an organizer and disciplinarian, but lacked "the higher elements of generalship." Smith made no concessions to Bragg's abilities whatsoever, and requested to never again be asked to cooperate with him in a campaign.[10]

Davis continued to support Bragg, and in a letter to Kirby Smith he tried to explain his reasons and gain that general's endorsement.

> I have held long and free conversations with Genl. Bragg ... he uniformly spoke of you in the most complimentary terms, and does not seem to imagine your dissatisfaction. He has explained in a direct and frank manner the circumstances of his campaign and has envinced [sic] the most self denying temper in relation to his future position.... That another Genl. might excite more enthusiasm is probable, but as all have their defects I have not seen how to make a change with advantage to the public service. His administrative capacity has been felt by the Army of Mississippi, his knowlege [sic] of the troops is intimate and a new man would not probably for a time with even greater ability be equally useful.... Of the Generals, Cooper is at the head of the Bureau, Lee is in command of the army in Va., Johnston still disabled by the wound received at Seven Pines, Beauregard was tried as Commander of the army of the West and left it without leave, when the troops were demoralized and the country he was sent to protect was threatened with conquest. Bragg succeeded to the command and organized the army and marched to your support with efficient troops.

The president's words seem to have had the desired effect, so far as Smith was concerned. Smith claimed that after he left Richmond he never "uttered a recorded word of criticism of Bragg's Kentucky campaign for the duration of the war."[11]

Polk was another matter. He continued to attack Bragg publicly and privately. He also seems to have been a ring leader in several attempts to have Bragg removed from command. Relations between Bragg and Polk would continue to be adversarial for as long as the two men were joined together.

Regardless of the controversy concerning him personally, once Bragg returned from Richmond, he took the opportunity of congratulating the troops for their efforts in Kentucky. From his old headquarters at Tullahoma, Tennessee, he issued the following order:

> 1. The several regiments, battalions, and independent companies engaged in the ever-memorable battle at Perryville, Ky., on October 8, in which they achieved a signal victory over the enemy, numbering three to their one, and drove him from the field with terrible slaughter and the loss of his artillery, will inscribe the name of that field on their colors. The corps of Cheatham's division which made the gallant and desperate charge resulting in the capture of three of the enemy's batteries will, in addition to the name, place the cross cannon inverted.[12]

Bragg's greatest detractors, Polk and Smith, were also those men who seem to have materially damaged the outcome of the campaign. Smith seemed hesitant to fully cooperate in a joint operation from the start. He valued his semi-independent position and did little to foster combined effort. After the battle of Richmond, he became hesitant and indecisive at a time when aggressive action would have kept the Federals off balance and brought success to the Confederate cause. Polk failed to follow Bragg's direct orders, or to give his commander full and comprehensive reasons for those failures. Bragg was informed that Polk felt his orders of concentration and attack to be inexpedient, but the general never fully informed Bragg of the reasons why he felt so. The commanding general was not provided pertinent information that Polk had on hand concerning the size and composition of the Federal army that was facing him, even when Polk was made aware that his commander mistakenly felt the main thrust to be Sill's force near Frankfort. It was as if Polk became agitated that his counsel was not being adopted, and felt that he should not have to explain his reasons once he had stated his opinion.

While Bragg was attacked by his own officers and people, some of his highest praise came from his counterpart in the campaign. Shortly after the battle, General Buell would say of the Confederate army: "It was composed of veteran troops, well armed and thoroughly inured to hardships. Every circumstance of its march and the concurrent testimony of all who came within reach of its line attest that it was under perfect discipline."[13]

The officer corps of the Army of Tennessee had performed admirably in the campaign, and there were none of the replacements that were evident in the Union army after its conclusion. President Davis, always a supporter of his fighting men, saw to it that many of the officers who had taken a prominent part were rewarded for their efforts by promotion, including Leonidus Polk and Kirby

Smith. Joe Wheeler received his general's stars, and was catapulted into a position of responsibility with the army that would earn him fame and glory. His conduct during the campaign had been exemplary. Wheeler's style of fighting was an innovation in military tactics for the cavalry. The primary school of thought in the military had been to utilize cavalry along the lines of European armies, as heavy cavalry or dragoons, advancing and fighting in massed formations. The increased efficiency of Civil War era firearms made such tactics suicide for the mounted men. The idea of using the cavalry as mounted infantry had been previously experimented with, but Wheeler was the first person in the war to adopt it as his primary tactic of fighting, and to use it on such a large scale. His troopers could still make a mounted charge with pistol and saber, but they were more apt to fight dismounted, using their carbines to full effect. When doing so, they were little inferior to infantry, and he proved the advantages of this style of fighting in his execution of the rear-guard action during the retreat. A small body of men armed with rifles could seriously retard the movements of a much larger body when fighting in this manner. Wheeler would go on to write a manual on cavalry tactics that was predicated on this usage of the cavalry arm.[14]

The fruits of the Kentucky campaign were far less than had been expected by either side. For the Confederates, it amounted only to the material spoils they had captured in their victories at Richmond, Munfordville, and Perryville. The value of these captures is not to be underestimated, however. For an army that was short on everything, the acquisition of war materials, by any means, was imperative. The Confederate army was much improved by these acquisitions, particularly in respect to weaponry. It is estimated that as many as 15,000 Southern troops were able to trade in their outdated muskets for new ones captured from the Federals. When next they fought, it would not be with the old buck and ball antique smoothbores that they had carried since Shiloh. They would be equipped with the most modern rifled muskets. The rest of the campaign was a failure. The Confederate army was unable to move the seat of war to Kentucky, and what was more discouraging, it was unable to induce any appreciable numbers of Kentuckians to enlist in the army. John Hunt Morgan and Simon B. Buckner had assured the military that their native state would rise up to support a Confederate army of liberation, but that simply did not happen. The flood of expected enlistments proved to be only a trickle, and did not justify the undertaking of the campaign.

According to their official reports, in the course of the campaign the Confederates had captured 25 pieces of artillery, 15,000 muskets, 330 wagons, and 1,750 mules, and had inflicted casualties on the enemy of approximately 2,400 killed, 9,500 wounded, and 14,200 captured. The numbers they estimated for killed and wounded were overstated, as Confederate officials thought that 2,000 of the enemy had been killed and 8,000 had been wounded at Perryville. The actual number was a little less than half of that. The remainder of the statistics seem to be accurate. In addition to the above stated numbers, Bragg's army had captured in excess of two million cartridges. The Confederacy had inflicted great damage on the Union forces operating in Kentucky, and had escaped with large amounts of military plunder, but it had not materially affected the Northern ability to wage war. All of the Union losses in materials and manpower could be easily replaced. The only way Bragg's army could have retarded the Union war effort was to have defeated Buell's army on the field, crippling or destroying it so that the Union forces in the area were forced to assume a defensive posture while they re-formed their army. This might have given Bragg time to consolidate his position in Kentucky, which would probably have led to his receiving some of the enlistments that he so sorely needed.[15]

For the Federals, the campaign proved to be an example of opportunities lost. True, Buell had expelled the Confederate army from the environs of Kentucky, and had kept the state firmly in the Union, and that was a victory in its own right, but he had failed to destroy the threat when it was within his power to have done so. The expectations of the administration were that he eliminate Bragg's army as a threat, and thus free both Kentucky and Tennessee from the menace of Southern arms. The government in Washington was too used to seeing its military suffer reverses at the hands of the Rebels, and it was demanding victories. By this point in the war, a half victory was deemed to be little better than a defeat.

Buell was not well served by some of his subordinate officers, and much of the blame for the results of the battle do not rest with him. However, the administration was already dissatisfied with his generalship, as evidenced by the order to remove him from command on September 30, before his march against Bragg began. To his superiors, Perryville proved to be just another example of why a change in top command needed to be made. Thomas had bought Buell some time in declining to assume the command of the army on September 30, but only a decisive victory over the Confederates would have allowed him to retain his position.

Epilogue

The battle of Perryville witnessed some of the most terrible fighting that was ever seen on the American continent. A glance at the casualty figures does not seem to support this assertion until one considers the relatively small number of men engaged and the short duration of the battle. The combined casualties, for both sides, amounted to approximately 7,600 men. When one takes into account that the battle did not start in earnest till some time just before 2:00 P.M., and that it ended with darkness at about 5:30, it can be seen that almost 2,000 men an hour were being added to the casualty rolls. The numbers of men engaged were about equal, and totaled something over 30,000 men, meaning that approximately 25 percent of those engaged became casualties. In terms of percentages of those engaged, the casualties suffered by the Union army at Perryville were higher than those suffered at Gettysburg.

Though the Confederates pushed back the Union left flank and occupied the ground they had won at the close of the fighting, the battle has to be considered a drawn contest. The Southerners were facing overwhelming odds, and were forced to retreat from their position the following day, before they could be brought to battle by Buell's superior numbers and crushed. Though Bragg claimed a tactical victory at Perryville, the truth is that the battle cost him the campaign and ended any hopes of an extended Confederate presence in Kentucky. With the host of Federal forces arrayed against him in the region, the only hope Bragg had of being able to stay in the state rested with his ability to cripple or destroy Buell's army at Perryville. This he failed to do. To be sure, he had roughly handled McCook's Corps, but his own army had suffered terribly in the process. Buell still had two reasonably fresh corps to throw into the contest, while Bragg could receive no further reinforcements other than Smith's men and Withers' Division, units already taking part in the campaign trying to prevent additional

155

Federal forces from joining Buell's army. Anything short of a complete victory over Buell's army, at this point, was the equivalent of a strategic loss, and Bragg had accomplished only a partial victory, at best. To have remained on the field on October 9 would have been inviting the defeat and possible destruction of his army.

The battle had been largely fought without the supervision of the army commanders of either side. Once Bragg had set the attack in motion, he largely relied on Generals Polk and Hardee to carry it out. In this, he was ably served. Polk and Hardee handled the army well, and the Confederate command structure on the battlefield excelled that of the Federals. One can point out that even though they were the attacking body, the Confederates suffered almost 25 percent fewer casualties than did the Federals. Still, the Confederates failed to mass an overwhelming assault against the Federal line. Union regiments were in some cases permitted time to regroup and to re-form in the time between assaults.

Buell's lack of participation in the battle was attributable to a freak of nature that was beyond his control. He did not even learn that a battle was being fought until it was over two hours into the contest. Once he was made aware of the fact, he reacted to the situations and endeavored to send aid to his left to bolster the line. Buell cannot be held accountable for his lack of knowledge concerning the fighting. He can, however, be held accountable for his lack of knowledge concerning the enemy. Buell knew that there was a sizable force of the enemy in his front, so much so that he wanted to wait until all three of his corps were on the field before attacking it. Even if he was unaware that Bragg had concentrated his whole army at Perryville, Buell knew that the force before him was worthy of his attention. His actions on October 8 would seem to show a lack of vigilance, on his part, and a neglectful approach to gathering intelligence. He also failed to grasp the entire situation once he did become involved in the battle. His only focus seemed to be on the Federal left, and his only orders were for a few brigades to march to that point. No orders were given to Crittenden's Corps whatsoever. Crittenden's Corps could have been ordered to McCook's support, or it could have been given directions to advance and relieve the pressure on the left. If the latter had been adopted, it would have placed the Confederate army between that corps and the rest of the Union army, and possibly would have cut off the Rebel line of retreat. In that event, Bragg's army would surely have been decimated.

The battle of Perryville might have been touched off by circumstances that were not planned by either side, but it was sure that once Buell's army took up the march in pursuit of Bragg, a battle would have to be fought, or the state would have to be abandoned to the Federals. The objectives of the campaign had been to transfer the seat of war out of Tennessee and Mississippi, and to make it possible to bring Kentucky into the Confederacy. Bragg had accomplished the first objective, but the second one eluded him. A purely military man, Bragg was unsuited to the political ramifications he faced in his dealings with the people of Kentucky. The general expected the men of the state to rise up and follow as soon as they saw a Confederate army in their state. Bragg was a man of duty and of conviction, and he could not comprehend the reluctance the men of Kentucky showed in joining his banner. His proclamations to the populace exhibited an increasing level of exasperation, and those issued immediately prior to the battle were couched in threatening tones that evinced the words of a conqueror, not a liberator. The men of Kentucky were simply not willing to leave their homes and follow a Confederate banner that, in all likelihood, was headed back to Tennessee and Mississippi. The plight of the Orphan Brigade was known to all, and men were not anxious to exile themselves from their homes and loved ones. In the end, Bragg was caught in a dilemma to which there was no solution: the men of Kentucky would not enlist unless the army was there to stay, and the army could not remain in the state unless the men of Kentucky enlisted.

The campaign saw the rise and fall of numerous officers on both sides. The murder of General Nelson cast a pall over the Union army, though it did little to effect the career of his assailant, Jeff Davis. The deaths of Jackson and Terrill, and the capture of Lytle created command holes in McCook's Corps. Gilbert and Buell were both relieved of command, and McCook's actions were questioned. The Army of the Ohio was no more, and William S. Rosecrans was assigned to command of the consolidated Army of the Cumberland. On the other side, this was Phil Sheridan's first experience at division command, and he seems to have done a credible job in that capacity. Though he was hardly the hero of the battle that some contemporaries tried to make him out to be, he handled his division in a professional manner, and did good service where he was called upon to do so. For Sheridan, Perryville was another step in attaining the rank and recognition that would eventually make him one of the leading Union generals of the war. General Rousseau would also receive commendation for his services at Perryville. His efforts in saving the Union left would be rewarded when he received a second star. The promotion was made some weeks after the battle, but it was predated to October 8, to mark the date when he had won the honor through his valor. Starkweather and Goodling are both worthy of commendation for their services in the battle. Had it not been for the determined stand made by the members of their brigades it might have been possible for the Confederates to accomplish their goal of routing the Union left wing and stampeding the Federal forces before darkness brought an end to the fighting.

Captain Ebenezer Gay appears to be the Union officer who received the least of the credit that was due him. Gay's handling of the cavalry brigade during the campaign was efficient and professional, and he seems to have performed his duties in a manner deserving of reward. But with the conclusion of the campaign, Gay was returned to his permanent rank, and no thanks were forthcoming from the army. It is probable that this was largely due to his connection with General Gilbert and to the fact that it was Gilbert, operating in a false capacity, who had conferred the brevet rank of general upon him. If so, this officer was punished for military indiscretions he did not commit. His occupying of the gap between McCook and Gilbert, without orders to do so, and his similar actions in riding to the support of Rousseau's right when it began to crumble showed a capacity for quick thinking and action that deserved to be rewarded. At a time when the military was looking for fighting generals, Gay seemed to fill the bill.

For the Confederates, Kirby Smith seems to have been reluctant to subordinate himself to Bragg's command, and the semiautonomous actions of his army hurt Confederate efforts at a time when they needed to present a united front. To be sure, Bragg had allowed Smith an unusually large amount of discretion in his movements, but Smith seemed to relish his independent command to the detriment of the common cause. In his book *Their Tattered Flags*, historian Frank Vandiver asks: "Who was really in charge? Bragg thought he was, but was not certain. Smith feared Bragg was, and guarded his prerogatives. Result: Bragg could request Smith's aid but could not order it; Smith was free to follow pride's dictates."[1] His failure to damage or destroy General George Morgan's force at Cumberland Gap was a missed opportunity. Morgan was allowed to escape to his own lines with relatively little damage, and the opportunity to repeat a second victory like Smith had won at Richmond was gone. Such a victory could have heartened Southern Kentuckians and deepened the consternation of Union forces operating in the area, but it was not to be. Braxton Bragg had devised a sound plan of campaign for the invasion of Kentucky. It would be one of his best campaigns of the war ... on paper. Once the campaign began, however, Bragg seems to have become indecisive. He allowed Buell's army to reach Louisville, where it received large reinforcements, without offering it battle. Once Buell did march out from Louisville, Bragg allowed himself to be deluded as to Buell's intentions, as well as the composition of his forces. He spent wasted time at Frankfort installing a provisional governor who could not hope to take over the reins of government unless the Confederate army was victorious, while Buell was able to steal a march on him. Bragg continued to believe that Sill's Division was the main thrust of the Union army long after Polk first alerted him to the possibility that he was facing Buell's main force. In Bragg's defense, he was trying to make the best of a bad situation. Union forces in other sectors were not being held in place as they were supposed to have been, and Kentucky was drawing reinforcements from all over the region. Bragg himself was getting none of the support that he was to have received. The forces of Earl Van Dorn and Sterling Price would never join his army, and the cooperation he received from Kirby Smith left something to be desired. In many ways, Bragg was the leader of a combined operation in which his forces were the only ones that were doing what they were supposed to do.

The campaign also demonstrated the need for rapid movements for an army that was numerically weaker when moving within the territory of enemy occupation. Bragg's initial movements into Kentucky had been swift and sure, but the Confederates lost the rapidity of their initial thrust. Kirby Smith bogged down after the battle of Richmond, and Bragg lost precious time in eliminating Wilder's forces at Munfordville. Once these events transpired, the impetus seems to have gone out of the Confederate movements, and indecision replaced audacity. The Union forces were given time to reorganize, refit, and take the offensive, and the Confederates were forced to react to changing situations instead of dictating the progress of their own campaign.

In Bragg's subordinate officer corps, Polk and Hardee seem to have performed credibly, their actions in the battle and on the march adding to an already good reputation. Cheatham and Cleburne both distinguished themselves, giving view to the fame and glory that was still in the future for both men. The real standout on the Confederate side was Joe Wheeler. He had seen precious little service in the actual battle, but the conduct of his command on the march, and particularly during the retreat, elevated him to a status as one of the top cavalry commanders in the Confederate army. His services earned him the post of chief of cavalry during the campaign, and they would win him a general's star at its conclusion.

On the surface, the battle of Perryville, and the Kentucky campaign, did little to affect the outcome of the war, one way or another, but that is just on the surface. The great thing about history is the ability to examine the "what ifs" and the "might have beens," the ability, with perfect hindsight, to speculate on the outcome of events if they had transpired differently. With that in mind, it can easily be seen that the results of the Kentucky campaign were immensely important to the eventual victory of the Union cause. Had Bragg's army been successful in making Kentucky the seat of war, instead of Tennessee, it would have changed the perception of the conflict, at home and abroad. War weariness was already taking hold in the North. McClellan's perceived victory at Antietam, coupled with Lincoln's Emancipation Proclamation, were all that prevented a Democratic sweep of the Congressional elections that fall. A tragic Union defeat in

Kentucky could have undermined the restoration of confidence the Northern people felt after those two events, and allowed the Democrats to gain a majority in Congress. If this had happened, it would surely have meant an end of the war. The Democrats had conducted their election campaign on a "peace platform" vowing to stop the fighting as soon as they gained a majority in the Washington government.

Besides the effect that a Confederate victory in Kentucky might have had on the people at home, it would most certainly have had positive repercussions in Europe. The governments of France and England stood poised to officially recognize the Confederacy. The Emancipation Proclamation had made it difficult for the leaders of those two nations to tender that recognition, but that difficulty was intensified by the fact that military operations seemed to be going against the South. Lee had been driven out of Maryland, and Bragg had been forced to abandon Kentucky. The Confederate army was not looking as invincible as it had in the summer of 1862, and neither France nor England was willing to openly back a loser. The governments of both countries decided to take a wait-and-see attitude, and another opportunity was lost to the Confederacy.

A transfer of the war to Kentucky would also have given the South an opportunity to replenish its overtaxed resources. Just as Lee's invasion of Maryland was, in part, intended to give the state of Virginia a breather, Bragg's invasion of Kentucky was to give Tennessee and Mississippi the same sort of respite from the demands that had been made on the limited assets those states had to support its own army, and that of an invader. A successful campaign could have also visited the ravages of war upon the North. Cincinnati, as well as other Northern cities, could have been made to feel the sting and hardship that had thus far been reserved for the cities of the South, further fueling the antiwar sentiments and war weariness that was growing in the North.

As already stated, a Confederate army that was able to maintain its position in Kentucky would have undoubtedly realized the enlistments that Bragg had sought all along. Southern sentiments were strong in the state, and if the people could have been convinced that they would be fighting for their homes and families, and not just for the Confederacy, it is probable that large numbers of troops would have been added to Bragg's army.

The results of the battle of Perryville, and the Kentucky campaign, when viewed by themselves, do not appear to be terribly significant to the fortunes of either side. When one examines how they affected other aspects of the war and how they fit into the overall picture, another conclusion can be drawn. Combined with Antietam, the results of Perryville served as a halt to Confederate military fortunes, which had been riding high throughout the year. It provided the people of the North with rare instances that the Confederate armies really could be beaten, and restored confidence in Lincoln and his administration. Though Perryville was not a decisive battle, the ability of the Union army to stave off defeat on that field contributed greatly toward giving the government the time and opportunity to pursue the conflict to a victorious end.

The conclusion of the campaign witnessed the end for the Army of the Ohio. The men who served in it would face their Confederate adversaries in the Army of Tennessee on many more hard-fought battlefields: Murfreesboro, Chickamauga, and Atlanta, but they would do so under the name of the Army of the Cumberland. The autumn of 1862 would also see a reorganization of Union army command, east and west. In the east, General McClellan was dismissed, and supporters like Fitz John Porter and William B. Franklin were either dismissed or reassigned. Buell was felt by many to be McClellan's counterpart in the west, was known to be a friend to both McClellan and his policies, and was likewise dismissed. The end of the Kentucky campaign was also the end of Buell's military career. Although no less an officer than U.S. Grant later recommended his reinstatement to command, he was never reassigned, and resigned his commission in disgrace.

Perryville was the most important battle to be fought in Kentucky during the war, and its effects were felt throughout the nation. It was especially felt by those residents of states that had regiments taking part in the fighting; and many homes, North and South, grieved the loss of loved ones on that bloody field. It was best remembered by those who took part in the struggle. The contemporary press, and later historians, concentrated on larger, more famous fields of conflict, but to the men who fought and sacrificed on the fields of Perryville, it was the equal of them all.

Mrs. J.G. McMynn eloquently captured the essence of the struggle with her diary entry dated October 12, 1862. News of the battle at Perryville was just reaching the general public, and Mrs. McMynn thoughtfully wrote: "The price that is being paid for the maintenance of the Union is beyond computation — beyond comprehension. Every patriot soldier is a hero inspired by a nobler sentiment than ambition, and when the smoke of battle rolls away, may a grateful nation honor both her dead and her living heroes."[2]

APPENDIX I

The Opposing Forces —
Cumberland Gap

THE UNION ARMY

Army of the Ohio

Seventh Division — Brigadier General George W. Morgan

24th Brigade — Brigadier General Samuel P. Carter
49th Indiana
3rd Kentucky
2nd Tennessee

25th Brigade — Brigadier General James G. Spears
3rd Tennessee
4th Tennessee
5th Tennessee
6th Tennessee

26th Brigade — Colonel John F. De Courcy
22nd Kentucky
16th Ohio
42nd Ohio

27th Brigade — Brigadier General Absalom Baird
33rd Indiana
14th Kentucky
19th Kentucky

Artillery

Foster's 7th Michigan Light Artillery
Barrows's 9th Ohio Light Artillery
Anderson's 1st Wisconsin Light Artillery
Webster's Siege Battery

Cavalry

Kentucky Battalion

THE CONFEDERATE ARMY

Department of Tennessee

First Division — Brigadier General Carter Stevenson

2nd Brigade — Colonel James E. Rains

4th Tennessee
11th Tennessee
42nd Georgia
3rd Georgia Battalion
29th North Carolina
Vance's Georgia Light Artillery

3rd Brigade — Brigadier General S.M. Barton

30th Alabama
31st Alabama
40th Georgia
52nd Georgia
9th Georgia Battalion
Anderson's Virginia Light Artillery

4th Brigade — Colonel A.W. Reynolds

20th Alabama
36th Georgia
39th Georgia
43rd Georgia
39th North Carolina
Latrobe's Maryland Light Artillery

5th Brigade—Colonel T.H. Taylor
    23rd Alabama
    46th Alabama
    3rd Tennessee
    31st Tennessee
    59th Tennessee
    Cooke's Tennessee Light Artillery

APPENDIX II

The Opposing Forces — Perryville

THE UNION ARMY

Army of the Ohio

Major General Don Carlos Buell

Major General George H. Thomas, second in command

Headquarters Escort: Anderson Troop (Pennsylvania), 4th U.S. Cavalry, 7th
Pennsylvania Cavalry

First Army Corps — Major General Alexander McD. McCook

Third Division — Brigadier General Lovell H. Rousseau

9th Brigade — Colonel Leonard A. Harris

38th Indiana
2nd Ohio
38th Ohio
94th Ohio
10th Wisconsin
5th Indiana Light Artillery

17th Brigade — Colonel William H. Lytle

42nd Indiana
88th Indiana
15th Kentucky
3rd Ohio
10th Ohio
1st Michigan Light Artillery

166

28th Brigade— Colonel John C. Starkweather
24th Illinois
79th Pennsylvania
1st Wisconsin
21st Wisconsin
4th Indiana Light Artillery
1st Kentucky Light Artillery

Unattached
2nd Kentucky Cavalry
1st Michigan Engineers

Tenth Division— Brigadier General James S. Jackson

33rd Brigade— Brigadier General William R. Terrill
80th Illinois
123rd Illinois
7th Kentucky
32nd Kentucky
105th Ohio
3rd Tennessee
Parsons' Battery

34th Brigade— Colonel George Webster
80th Indiana
50th Ohio
98th Ohio
121st Ohio
19th Indiana Light Artillery

Second Army Corps— Major General Thomas L. Crittenden.

Fourth Division— Brigadier General William S. Smith.

10th Brigade— Colonel William Grose
84th Illinois
36th Indiana
23rd Kentucky
6th Ohio
24th Ohio
4th U.S. Light Artillery

19th Brigade— Colonel William B. Hazen
110th Illinois
9th Indiana
6th Kentucky
27th Kentucky
41st Ohio
1st Ohio Light Artillery

22nd Brigade— Brigadier General Charles Cruft
31st Indiana
1st Kentucky
2nd Kentucky
20th Kentucky
90th Ohio
1st Ohio Light Artillery

Fifth Division— Brigadier General Horatio P. Van Cleve

11th Brigade— Colonel Samuel Beatty
79th Indiana
9th Kentucky
13th Kentucky
19th Ohio
59th Ohio

14th Brigade— Colonel Pierce B. Hawkins
44th Indiana
86th Indiana
11th Kentucky
26th Kentucky
13th Ohio

23rd Brigade— Colonel Stanley Matthews
35th Indiana
8th Kentucky
21st Kentucky
51st Ohio
99th Ohio
7th Indiana Light Artillery
3rd Wisconsin Light Artillery

Sixth Division — Brigadier General Thomas J. Wood

15th Brigade — Brigadier General Milo S. Hascall
100th Illinois
17th Indiana
58th Indiana
3rd Kentucky
26th Ohio
8th Indiana Light Artillery

20th Brigade — Colonel Charles G. Harker
51st Indiana
73rd Indiana
13th Michigan
64th Ohio
65th Ohio
6th Ohio Light Artillery

21st Brigade — Colonel George D. Wagner
15th Indiana
40th Indiana
57th Indiana
24th Kentucky
97th Ohio
10th Indiana Light Artillery

Unattached
1st Ohio Cavalry

Third Army Corps — Major General Charles C. Gilbert

First Division — Brigadier General Alvin Schoepf

1st Brigade — Colonel Moses B. Walker
82nd Indiana
12th Kentucky
17th Ohio
31st Ohio
38th Ohio

2nd Brigade — Brigadier General Speed S. Fry
10th Indiana

74th Indiana
4th Kentucky
10th Kentucky
14th Ohio

3rd Brigade— Brigadier General James B. Steedman

87th Indiana
2nd Minnesota
9th Ohio
35th Ohio
18th U.S. Regulars

Artillery

4th Michigan Light Artillery
1st Ohio Light Artillery
4th U.S. Light Artillery

Cavalry

1st Ohio Cavalry (detachment)

Ninth Division— Brigadier General Robert B. Mitchell

30th Brigade— Colonel Michael Goodling

59th Illinois
74th Illinois
75th Illinois
22nd Indiana
5th Wisconsin Light Artillery

31st Brigade— Colonel William P. Carlin

21st Illinois
38th Illinois
101st Ohio
15th Wisconsin
2nd Minnesota Light Artillery

32nd Brigade— Lieutenant Colonel James S. McClelland

35th Illinois, 81st Indiana, 8th Kansas, 8th Wisconsin Light Artillery

Eleventh Division— Brigadier General Philip H. Sheridan

35th Brigade— Lieutenant Colonel Bernard Laiboldt

44th Illinois

73rd Illinois
2nd Missouri
15th Missouri

36th Brigade— Colonel Daniel McCook

85th Illinois
86th Illinois
125th Illinois
52nd Ohio

37th Brigade— Colonel Nicholas Greusel

36th Illinois
88th Illinois
21st Michigan
24th Wisconsin
2nd Illinois Light Artillery
1st Missouri Light Artillery

Cavalry Brigade— Captain Ebenezer Gay (brevet brigadier general)
9th Kentucky
2nd Michigan
9th Pennsylvania

THE CONFEDERATE ARMY:
GENERAL BRAXTON BRAGG

Army of the Mississippi— Major General Leonidus Polk

Right Wing— Major General Benjamin F. Cheatham

Cheatham's Division— Brigadier General Daniel S. Donelson

1st Brigade— Colonel John H. Savage

8th Tennessee
15th Tennessee
16th Tennessee
38th Tennessee
51st Tennessee
Carnes's Tennessee Light Artillery

2nd Brigade— Brigadier General A.P. Stewart
4th Tennessee
5th Tennessee
24th Tennessee
31st Tennessee
33rd Tennessee
Stanford's Mississippi Light Artillery

3rd Brigade— Brigadier General George Maney
41st Georgia
1st Tennessee
6th Tennessee
9th Tennessee
27th Tennessee
Turner's Mississippi Light Artillery

Cavalry Brigade— Colonel John A. Wharton
1st Kentucky
4th Tennessee
8th Texas

Left Wing— Major General William J. Hardee

Second Division— Brigadier General J. Patton Anderson

1st Brigade— Brigadier General John C. Brown
1st Florida
3rd Florida
41st Mississippi
Palmer's Light Artillery

2nd Brigade— Brigadier General Daniel W. Adams
13th Louisiana
16th Louisiana
20th Louisiana
25th Louisiana
14th Battalion Louisiana Sharpshooters
Washington Light Artillery

3rd Brigade— Colonel Samuel Powell
45th Alabama

1st Arkansas
24th Mississippi
29th Tennessee
Barret's Missouri Light Artillery

4th Brigade—Colonel Thomas M. Jones

27th Mississippi
30th Mississippi
37th Mississippi
Lumsden's Alabama Light Artillery

Third Division—Major General Simon B. Buckner

1st Brigade—Brigadier General St. John R. Liddell

2nd Arkansas
5th Arkansas
6th Arkansas
7th Arkansas
8th Arkansas
Swett's Mississippi Light Artillery

2nd Brigade—Brigadier General Patrick R. Cleburne

13th Arkansas
15th Arkansas
2nd Tennessee
Calvert's Arkansas Light Artillery

3rd Brigade—Brigadier General Bushrod R. Johnson

5th Confederate Regulars
17th Tennessee
23rd Tennessee
25th Tennessee
37th Tennessee
44th Tennessee
Jefferson's Mississippi Light Artillery

4th Brigade—Brigadier General S.A.M. Wood

16th Alabama
33rd Alabama
3rd Confederate Regulars
45th Mississippi

15th Battalion Mississippi Sharpshooters
Semple's Alabama Light Artillery

Cavalry Brigade — Colonel Joseph Wheeler

1st Alabama
3rd Alabama
6th Confederate Regulars
2nd Georgia Battalion
3rd Georgia
1st Kentucky

APPENDIX III

The Inexperience
of Union Regiments

Of the 125 regiments and batteries that made up Beull's army, 35 were completely raw, having been mustered into the service at the start of the campaign. The new regiments, with dates of muster, were dispersed throughout his army as follows:

First Army Corps

Third Division

9th Brigade: 94th Ohio (August 22, 1862)

17th Brigade: 88th Indiana (August 29, 1862)

28th Brigade: 21st Wisconsin (September 5, 1862)

Tenth Division

33rd Brigade: 80th Illinois (August 25, 1862)
123rd Illinois (September 6, 1862)
32nd Kentucky (August 1862)
105th Ohio (August 20, 1862)

34th Brigade: 80th Indiana (September 8, 1862)
50th Ohio (August 27, 1862)
98th Ohio (August 20, 1862)
121st Ohio (September 11, 1862)

175

Second Army Corps

Fourth Division

10th Brigade:	84th Illinois (September 1, 1862)
19th Brigade:	110th Illinois (September 11, 11862)
22nd Brigade:	90th Ohio (August 29, 1862)

Fifth Division

11th Brigade:	79th Indiana (September 2, 1862)
14th Brigade:	86th Indiana (September 4, 1862)
23rd Brigade:	99th Ohio (August 26, 1862)

Sixth Division

15th Brigade:	100th Illinois (August 30, 1862)
20th Brigade:	73rd Indiana (August 16, 1862)

Third Army Corps

First Division

1st Brigade:	82nd Indiana (August 29, 1862)
2nd Brigade:	74th Indiana (August 21, 1862)
3rd Brigade:	87th Indiana (September 4, 1862)

Ninth Division

30th Brigade:	74th Illinois (September 4, 1862)
	75th Illinois (September 2, 1862)
31st Brigade:	101st Ohio (August 30, 1862)
32nd Brigade:	81st Indiana (August 29, 1862)

Eleventh Division

35th Brigade:	73rd Illinois (August 21, 1862)

36th Brigade: 85th Illinois (August 3, 1862)
                       86th Illinois (August 27, 1862)
                       125th Illinois (September 3, 1862)
                       52nd Ohio (August 25, 1862)

37th Brigade: 88th Illinois (September 4, 1862)
                       21st Michigan (September 9, 1862)
                       24th Wisconsin (August 15, 1862)

Cavalry Brigade: 9th Kentucky (August 22, 1862)

APPENDIX IV

Casualties

The reader may note that the casualty returns for the individual regiments do not always add up to the totals given. There are many reasons for this. Several Confederate regiments do not have returns; they may have been lost or destroyed at the end of the war. In both Union and Confederate records, discrepancies often appear because regimental returns were logged right after a battle, and in some cases, men listed as casualties or missing showed up a day or two later. Total casualty figures compiled from the regimental returns usually reflect adjustments that were made when more precise information was available.

THE UNION ARMY

Army of the Ohio

Headquarters Escort: Anderson Troop, 1 captured or missing; 7th Pennsylvania Cavalry, 4 wounded, 3 captured or missing.

First Army Corps — McCook
    Staff: 1 captured or missing.

Third Division — Rousseau

9th Brigade — Harris
        38th Indiana: 27 killed, 125 wounded.
        2nd Ohio: 27 killed, 77 wounded, 6 captured or missing.
        33rd Ohio: 21 killed, 78 wounded, 10 captured or missing.

94th Ohio: 7 killed, 17 wounded, 25 captured or missing.

10th Wisconsin: 37 killed, 109 wounded, 6 captured or missing.

Simonson's Indiana Light Artillery: 2 killed, 13 wounded, 6 captured or missing.

Brigade totals: 121 killed, 419 wounded, 53 captured or missing.

17th Brigade— Lytle

Staff: 1 killed, 1 wounded, 2 captured or missing.

42nd Indiana: 20 killed, 133 wounded, 21 captured or missing.

88th Indiana: 2 killed, 20 wounded.

15th Kentucky: 66 killed, 130 wounded.

3rd Ohio: 43 killed, 147 wounded.

10th Ohio: 60 killed, 169 wounded.

Loomis's Michigan Light Artillery: 1 killed, 6 wounded.

Brigade totals: 193 killed, 606 wounded, 23 captured or missing.

28th Brigade— Starkweather

24th Illinois: 28 killed, 79 wounded, 8 captured or missing.

79th Pennsylvania: 40 killed, 146 wounded, 30 captured of missing.

1st Wisconsin: 58 killed, 132 wounded, 14 captured or missing.

21st Wisconsin: 38 killed, 103 wounded, 56 captured or missing.

Bush's Indiana Light Artillery: 3 killed, 8 wounded.

Stone's Kentucky Light Artillery: 3 killed, 9 wounded, 1 captured or missing.

Brigade totals: 170 killed, 477 wounded, 109 captured or missing.

Tenth Division— Jackson

Staff: 1 killed

33rd Brigade— Terrill

Staff: 1 killed.

80th Illinois: 11 killed, 45 wounded.

123rd Illinois: 35 killed, 119 wounded.

101st Indiana: Losses unreported.

105th Ohio: 43 killed, 147 wounded, 13 captured or missing.

Parson's Light Artillery: 10 killed, 19 wounded, 20 captured or missing.

Garrard's Detachment: 6 wounded, 33 captured or missing.

Brigade totals: 100 killed, 336 wounded, 91 captured or missing.

34th Brigade— Webster

80th Indiana: 25 killed, 116 wounded, 16 captured or missing.
50th Ohio: 22 killed, 32 wounded, 79 captured or missing.
98th Ohio: 35 killed, 162 wounded, 32 captured or missing.
121st Ohio: 3 killed, 23 wounded, 16 captured or missing.
Harris's Indiana Light Artillery: 2 killed, 3 wounded, 3 captured or missing.
Brigade totals: 87 killed, 336 wounded, 146 captured or missing.

Second Army Corps— Crittenden

40th Indiana: 2 wounded.
Corps total: 2 wounded.

Third Army Corps— Gilbert

First Division— Schoepf

2nd Brigade— Fry

10th Indiana: 4 killed, 7 wounded.
Brigade totals: 4 killed, 7 wounded.

3rd Brigade— Steedman

Staff: 1 captured or missing.
87th Indiana: 2 wounded.
2nd Minnesota: 1 captured or missing.
9th Ohio: 1 wounded, 2 captured or missing.
35th Ohio: 4 captured or missing.
18th U.S.: 3 wounded.
Brigade totals: 6 wounded, 8 captured or missing.

Ninth Division— Mitchell

30th Brigade— Goodling

59th Illinois: 26 killed, 59 wounded, 29 captured or missing.
74th Illinois: No losses reported.
75th Illinois: 46 killed, 167 wounded, 12 captured or missing.
22nd Indiana: 49 killed, 87 wounded, 23 captured or missing.
Pinney's Wisconsin Light Artillery: 1 killed, 1 wounded.
Brigade totals: 122 killed, 314 wounded, 64 captured or missing.

31st Brigade— Carlin

21st Illinois: 6 wounded.
Hotchkiss's Minnesota Light Artillery: 4 wounded.
Brigade totals: 10 wounded.

Eleventh Division — Sheridan

35th Brigade — Laiboldt
44th Illinois: 1 killed, 11 wounded.
73rd Illinois: 2 killed, 33 wounded.
2nd Missouri: 18 killed, 51 wounded, 1 captured or missing.
15th Missouri: 1 killed, 7 wounded.
Brigade totals: 22 killed, 102 wounded, 1 captured or missing.

36th Brigade — McCook
85th Illinois: 5 killed, 38 wounded, 9 captured or missing.
86th Illinois: 1 killed, 14 wounded.
125th Illinois: 1 killed, 8 wounded.
52nd Ohio: 3 wounded.
Brigade totals: 7 killed, 63 wounded, 9 captured or missing.

37th Brigade — Gruesel
36th Illinois: 9 killed, 64 wounded, 4 captured or missing.
88th Illinois: 5 killed, 38 wounded.
21st Michigan: 22 wounded.
24th Wisconsin: 1 killed.
Brigade totals: 15 killed, 124 wounded, 4 captured or missing.

Cavalry Brigade — Gay
2nd Michigan: 4 killed, 13 wounded.
Brigade totals: 4 killed, 13 wounded.

Union totals: 846 killed, 2,819 wounded, 488 captured or missing = 4,153.

THE CONFEDERATE ARMY

Army of the Mississippi — Bragg

Cheatham's Division

1st Brigade — Savage
68 killed, 272 wounded, 7 captured or missing.

2nd Brigade— Stewart

62 killed, 340 wounded, 26 captured or missing.

3rd Brigade— Maney

136 killed, 517 wounded, 34 captured or missing.

Division total: 256 killed, 1,129 wounded, 67 captured or missing.

Anderson's Division

1st Brigade — Brown

Loss not individually reported.

2nd Brigade — Adams

6 killed, 78 wounded, 68 captured or missing.

3rd Brigade — Powell

Loss not individually reported.

4th Brigade — Jones

Loss not individually reported.

Buckner's Division

1st Brigade— Liddell

71 total killed, wounded, and missing.

2nd Brigade— Cleburne

Loss not individually reported.

3rd Brigade— Johnson

30 killed, 165 wounded, 9 captured or missing.

4th Brigade— Wood

Loss not individually reported.

Cavalry Brigade

Loss not individually reported.

Confederate totals: 510 killed, 2,635 wounded, 251 captured or missing = 3,396.

APPENDIX V

"The Charge of the First Tennessee at Perryville"

On October 8, 1884, there was a reunion of the 1st Tennessee Infantry. As this was the anniversary of the battle of Perryville, Captain B.P. Steele, of Company B, commemorated the event by paying tribute to his old comrades by penning a poem about the battle that was printed *in Southern Bivouac Magazine* for October of 1884:

> Far and wide on Perryville's ensanguined plain,
>   The thunder and carnage of battle resounded;
> And there, over thousands of wounded and slain,
>   Riderless steeds from battle's shock resounded.
> Cheatham's division was fiercely attacking,
>   And proudly from his men rose cheer after cheer,
> As before them McCook was sullenly backing,
>   Gallantly fighting as he moved to the rear.
> On Cheatham's left, Stewart's guns roared and rattled,
>   And in the center, Donelson onward bore;
> On the right, Maney's brigade charged and battled,
>   Valiantly driving the stubborn foe before.
> 'Twas there, held in reserve, impatiently lay,
>   The First Tennessee, the "Knights of the Kid Glove,"
> Eager and chafing to join the bloody fray —
>   Help their brave comrades, and their own powers prove,
> Soon was their impatient valor to be tried,
>   Soon they were to charge to the cannon's grim mouth —

Soon upon the battle's crimsoned wave to ride —
    Soon to prove themselvesworthy "Sons of the South."
For soon, at headlong speed, there came dashing down —
    His steed flecked with sweat and foaming at the mouth —
The warrior-bishop — he of the "Sword and Gown" —
    Who with like devotion served God and the South.
Every eye and ear of that gallant band,
    Was eager turned to catch the old hero's words;
On the guns more firmly clenched was every hand,
    And from their scabbards quick leaped two score of swords;
For all knew by the flash of the old chief's eye,
    That he had hot work for every trusty gun;
And ready was each man to fight and to die,
    In the bloody work then and there to be done.
A moment along their solid ranks he glanced,
    And with just pride his eagle-eye beamed o'er them —
Assured by their firm main, that when they advanced,
    No equal numbered foe could stand before them.
He noted the firm set lip and flashing eye,
    And on their sun-burnt cheeks the brave man's pailor;
And knew they had the spirit to "do or die,"
    For Southern honor and with Southern valor.
Then pointing towards the cannon-crested height,
    Where Loomis' guns volleyed in death-dealing wrath,
He seemed as a war-god gathering his might,
    To hurl missiles of destruction on his path,
And with a look that plainly said, "You must win,
    For the sake of the Sunny Land that bore you!"
He shouted above the battle's fierce din,
    "Forward! and carry everything before you!"
Forth they sprang, four hunderd, less fifty, all told;
    And as their ranks were thinned by iron and lead,
With true discipline, fearless courage, and bold,
    They closed their files and rushed on over the dead.
Towards the height, bristling in hostile array,
    With unwavering line the heroes rushed on —
Oh! truly was it a glorious display
    Of courage — worthy the fame the "Old Guard" won.
All dressed by the right with veteran skill,

They moved on their way with step steady and true,
And guns at the shoulder, to the foot of the hill,
As if on parade, for the "soldiers in blue."
But then, their muskets spoke, their wild shouts leaped,
As before them, in rout, a regiment fled;
Many of which their bullets halted and heaped
In bloody confusion, the wounded and dead.
Now more dreadful the carnage volleyed and roared,
A volcanic crater the hill's frowning crest,
Down whose bloody sides, death's fiery lava poured,
Sweeping the young and brave upon its breast.
Like sear leaves before the autumn blast they sank,
But their undaunted comrades pressed o'er them —
Pressed on, with quick, steady step and closed up rank,
Hurling death into the blue links before them.
Brave Loomis' support were veterans long tried,
And nobly did they second his fatal blows;
But their numbers and valor were all defied,
By the impetuous ranks of their Southern foes.
Loomis' gunners and horses went to the dust.
And his terrible war-dogs were hushed and still;
A few more quick bounds and a bayonet thrust,
And the "kid glove soldiers" had captured the hill.
But then came stern Rousseau, a Federal "brave,"
Rapidly sweeping down with his fine command,
And threw it like a torrent, wave upon wave,
Against the brave First's shattered and bleeding band.
But they met it as meets the breakers firm rock,
The wild, towering waves of the storm-lashed sea —
Met it to hurl it back with a fearful shock —
Back, like the foiled, rock-broken waves of the sea.
But just then the cry was passed along the line,
"They are flanking by the left! fall back! fall back!"
Ah! 'twas then more brilliant did their valor shine,
As with face to the foe, they retraced their track.
Proudly, their reluctant, backward way they bent,
With sullen, defiant mien, firm step and slow,
Sending back defiance and death as they went,
And moved more to the left in the plain below.

And then "forward!" was again the cheering cry,
    And quickly did those noble Southerners respond;
They again sprang forward, and their shouts rose high,
    As they swept the hill and the wide plain beyond.
And then, when the fierce, bloody conflict was o'er,
    The heroes sank down with fighting sore wearied;
And wept that of their brave comrades, full ten score,
    Were wounded or dead; but the height had been carried.

Captain B.P. Steele, "Charge of the First Tennessee at Perryville," *Southern Bivouac Magazine* (Louisville, Ky.), vol. 3, no. 2. October, 1884; pages 67–69.

Chapter Notes

Introduction

1. Sam Watkins, *An Adventure of General Leonidus Polk at the Battle of Perryville* (Southern Bivouac, May, 1884), 403.

2. Lt. Col. Charles Kerr, *Glimpses of the Nation's Struggle: Papers Read Before the Minnesota Commandery of the Military Order of the Loyal Legion of the United States, 1892–1897* (Wilmington, NC: Broadfoot, 1992), 266.

Chapter One

1. John P. Dyer, *From Shiloh to San Juan: The Life of Fighting Joe Wheeler* (Baton Rouge: Louisiana State University Press, 1961), 39.

2. *Ibid.*, 39.

3. Ezra J. Warner, *Generals in Gray: Lives of the Confederate Commanders* (Baton Rouge: Louisiana State University Press, 1959), 30.

4. Nathaniel S. Shaler, *Campaigns in Kentucky and Tennessee, Including the Battle of Chickamauga 1862–1864. Papers Read to the Military Historical Society of Massachusetts* (Boston: Military Historical Society of Massachusetts, 1905), 209; Warner, *Generals in Gray*, 221.

5. Dyer, 39–40.

6. Irving A. Buck, *Cleburne and His Command* (Jackson, TN: McCowat-Mercer Press, 1959), 103; Stanley F. Horn, *The Battle of Perryville* (Harrisburg, PA: Civil War Times Illustrated, February, 1966), 6; Lowell Harrison, *Perryville: Death on a Dry River Bed* (Harrisburg, PA: Civil War Times Illustrated, May, 1979), 5.

7. Warner, *Generals in Gray*, 280.

8. Col. Luke W. Finley, *Southern Historical Society Papers*, vol. 5 (Richmond: Southern Historical Society, 1902), 240.

9. Buck, 104–105.

10. Capt. Frank T. Ryan, *The Kentucky Campaign and the Battle of Perryville* (Nashville: Confederate Veteran Magazine, vol. 26), 158.

11. Buck, 105; Ryan, 210.

12. Buck, 105.

13. Buck, 106; Shaler, 210.

14. Shaler, 210.

15. Buck, 106.

16. Buck, 106–107, 110.

17. Ryan, 159–160.

18. Robert M. Frierson, *Gen. E. Kirby Smith's Campaign in Kentucky* (Nashville: Confederate Veteran Magazine, vol. 1, no. 4), 295.

19. Ryan, 159.

20. Buck, 108; John W. Rowell, *Yankee Cavalrymen: Through the Civil War with the Ninth Pennsylvania Cavalry* (Knoxville: University of Tennessee Press, 1971), 41, 77–79; W.E. Yeatman Memoir (Nashville: Tennessee State Library and Archives).

21. Buck, 108.

22. Buck, 108.

23. Ryan, 160.

24. Ryan, 160.

25. Robert Underwood Johnson and Clarence Clough Buel, *Battles and Leaders of the Civil War*, vol. 3 (New York: Castle Books, 1956), 65–68.

26. Basil W. Duke, *Reminiscences of General Basil W. Duke, C.S.A.* (Garden City, NY: Doubleday, 1911), 314–315.

27. Major E.T. Sykes, *A Cursory Sketch of General Bragg's Campaigns* (Richmond: Southern Historical Society Papers, vol. 11, 1905), 466.

28. Dyer, 42; Sykes, 466.

29. Don C. Seitz, *Braxton Bragg: General of the Confederacy* (Columbia, SC: State Company, 1924), 169–170.

30. J.P. Cannon, *Inside of Rebeldom: The Daily*

Life of a Private in the Confederate Army (Washington, DC: National Tribune, 1899), 54–55.
   31. Dyer, 42; Seitz, 170–171.

Chapter Two

   1. Alexis Cope, *The Fifteenth Ohio Volunteers and Its Campaigns 1861–1865* (Cincinnati: Published by the author, 1916), 185.
   2. Ezra J. Warner, *Generals in Blue: Lives of the Union Commanders* (Baton Rouge: Louisiana State University Press, 1964), 51–52.
   3. Dyer, 44–45.
   4. Dyer, 43.
   5. Seitz, 173–174.
   6. Seitz, 194.
   7. Major Henry M. Kendall, *The Battle of Perryville: War Papers Being Read Before the Commandery of the District of Columbia, Military Order of the Loyal Legion of the United States* (Wilmington, NC: Broadfoot, 1993), 376.
   8. General John T. Wilder, *The Siege of Munfordville: Sketches of War History 1861–1865 — Papers Prepared for the Commandery of the State of Ohio, Military Order of the Loyal Legion of the United States* (Cincinnati: Monfort, 1908), 296.
   9. Wilder, 296.
   10. Lowell Harrison, *The Battle of Munfordville* (Harrisburg, PA: Civil War Times Illustrated, June, 1974), 8; Wilder, 297.
   11. Wilder, 297.
   12. Sykes, 466–467.
   13. Harrison, 8; Sykes, 467.
   14. Sykes, 467.
   15. Wilder, 299.
   16. Wilder, 300.
   17. Wilder, 300–301.
   18. Wilder, 301.
   19. Sykes, 467–468.
   20. Harrison, 9; Sykes 468.
   21. Ephrim Allen Otis, *Recollections of the Kentucky Campaign of 1862: Military Essays and Recollections — Papers read Before the Commandery of the State of Illinois, Military Order of the Loyal Legion of the United States* (Chicago: Cozens & Beaton, 1907), 135.
   22. Harrison, May 1979, 8; Thomas M. Small, *Civil War Diary of Thomas M. Small* (Indianapolis: Indiana Historical Society), 3.
   23. Harrison, June 1974, 45.
   24. *Ibid.*
   25. *Ibid.*
   26. *Ibid.*
   27. Wilder, 302; Harrison, June 1974, 45–46.
   28. Harrison, June 1974, 46.
   29. Wilder, 302–303.
   30. Wilder, 303; Seitz, 178; Captain F.B. James,

Perryville and the Kentucky Campaign of 1862: Sketches of War History 1861–1865 — Papers Prepared for the Commandery of the State of Ohio, Military Order of the Loyal Legion of the United States (Cincinnati: Robert Clarke Co., 1903), 136.
   31. Cannon, 56.
   32. Charles M. Cummings, *Yankee Quaker Confederate General: The Curious Career of Bushrod Rust Johnson* (Rutherford, NJ: Fairleigh Dickinson University Press, 1971), 223.
   33. Seitz, 177.
   34. Capt. J T Patton, *Personal Recollections of Four Years in Dixie: War Papers Being Read Before the Commandery of the State of Michigan, Military Order of the Loyal Legion of the United States*, vol. 1 (Wilmington, NC: Broadfoot, 1993), 413; Bruce Catton, *Terrible Swift Sword* (New York: Pocket Books, 1967), 390–391.

Chapter Three

   1. Kerr, 272–273.
   2. Warner, *Generals in Blue,* 343–344; Joseph P. Fried, *How One Union General Murdered Another* (Harrisburg, PA: Civil War Times Illustrated, vol. 1, no. 5, June 1962), 14.
   3. J.M. Wright, *A Glimpse of Perryville* (Louisville, KY: Southern Bivouac, vol. 1, no. 3), 129; L.G. Bennett and Wm. M. Haigh, *History of the Thirty-Sixth Regiment Illinois Volunteers, During the War of the Rebellion* (Aurora, IL: Knickerbocker & Hodder, 1867), 237; Harrison, May 1979, 7–8.
   4. Warner, *Generals in Blue,* 115–116; Shaler, 246.
   5. Shaler, 246–247; Fried, 16.
   6. Fried, 16.
   7. Charles C. Gilbert, *Bragg's Invasion of Kentucky* (Louisville, KY: The Southern Bivouac, Volume 1, Number 4, September 1885), 221–222.
   8. Warner, *Generals in Blue,* 173–174.
   9. F.B. James, *Perryville and the Kentucky Campaign of 1862: Sketches of War History 1861–1865 — Papers Prepared for the Commandery of Ohio, Military Order of the Loyal Legion of the United States*, vol. 5 (Cincinnati: Robert Clarke Co., 1903), 162–163.
   10. Warner, *Generals in Blue,* 496.
   11. Rowell, 84–85.
   12. Harrison, May 1979, 8.
   13. H.B. Freeman, *Eighteenth U.S. Infantry from Camp Thomas to Murfreesboro and the Regular Brigade at Stone River: Glimpses of the Nation's Struggle — Papers Read Before the Minnesota Commandery of the Military Order of the Loyal Legion of the United States* (New York: D.D. Merrill, 1893), 121.
   14. Warner, *Generals in Blue,* 500.

15. Warner, *Generals in Blue*, 100, 294.

16. *The War of the Rebellion: A Compilation of the Official Records of the Union and Confederate Armies*, vol. 18, pt. 2 (Washington, DC: U.S. Government Printing Office, 1886), 360–361. Hereafter referred to as *O.R.*

17. Otis, 141–142; Harrison, May 1979, 8.

18. Henry Kendell, *The Battle of Perryville: War Papers Being Read Before the Commandery of the District of Columbia Military Order of the Loyal Legion of the United States*, vol.2 (Wilmington, NC: Broadfoot Publishing Co., 1993), 378; Bennett, 239.

19. Harrison, May 1979, 44; Joseph P. Glezen Diary (Indianapolis: Indiana State Library), October 1, 1862, entry.

20. Bennett, 240–241; James Lee McDonough, *War in Kentucky: From Shiloh to Perryville* (Knoxville: University of Tennessee Press, 1994), 208–209.

21. Bennett, 244–245.

22. Harrison, May 1979, 8; McDonough, 206.

23. Lancelot Ewbank Diary (Indianapolis: Indiana State Library), October 2 entry.

Chapter Four

1. Seitz, 180.
2. *Ibid.*, 179.
3. *Ibid.*, 180.
4. *Ibid.*, 184–185.
5. *Ibid.*, 184.
6. Horn, 8.
7. Grady McWhiney, *Braxton Bragg and Confederate Defeat*, vol. 1 (New York: Columbia University Press, 1969), 298–299.
8. Horn, 8.
9. McWhiney, 293.
10. Johnson, 14.
11. E.B. Long, *The Civil War Day By Day: An Almanac 1861–1865* (Garden City, NY: Doubleday, 1971), 274 275.
12. I..S. Ferrell, *Reminiscences of Fighting in Kentucky* (Nashville: Confederate Veteran Magazine, Volume 8, Number 1), 59.
13. Diary of Garrett Larew (Indianapolis: W.H. Smith Memorial Library, Indiana Historical Society), entry for September 30, 1862.
14. W.C. Gipson, *About the Battle of Perryville, Ky.* (Nashville: Confederate Veteran Magazine, vol. 9, no. 3), 163.
15. Unknown author, *The Kentucky Invasion of 1862* (Nashville: Confederate Veteran Magazine, vol. 34, no. 6), 409; Diary of John H. Tilford (Louisville, KY: The Filson Club Historical Society), October 7, 1862 entry; George D. Ewing, *General Bragg's Kentucky Campaign* (Nashville:

Confederate Veteran Magazine, vo. 34, no. 3), 214–215.

16. Daniel E. Sutherland, *Reminiscences of a Private: William E. Bevins of the First Arkansas Infantry, C.S.A.* (Fayetteville: University of Arkansas Press, 1992), 97.

17. Dyer, 50–51.

18. Colonel Red Reeder, *Sheridan: The General Who Wasn't Afraid to Take a Chance* (New York: Duell, Sloan and Pearce, 1962), 120–121.

Chapter Five

1. James, 143.
2. *Ibid.*
3. McDonough, 214–215.
4. *Ibid.*, 215.
5. McWhiney, 309.
6. McDonough, 216.
7. Kendell, 378–379.
8. Seitz, 193.
9. Board of Commissioners, *Minnesota in the Civil and Indian Wars 1861–1865* (St. Paul: State of Minnesota Press, 1889), 655; John H. Tilford Diary (Louisville, KY: Filson Club Historical Society), October 8 entry; Joseph P. Glezen Diary (Indianapolis: Indiana State Library), October 8 entry.
10. Captain H.C. Greiner, *General Phil Sheridan As I Knew Him, Playmate — Comrade — Friend,* (Chicago: J.S. Hyland, 1908), 202.
11. Horn, 1966, 42; W.H. Davis, *Recollections of Perryville* (Nashville: Confederate Veteran Magazine, vol. 24, no. 6), 554.
12. Col. Thomas Claiborne, *Battle of Perryville, Ky.* (Nashville: Confederate Veteran Magazine, vol. 16, no. 3), 225.
13. Claiborne, 45.
14. *O.R.*, 239.
15. Thaddeus C.S. Brown, Samuel J. Murphy, and William G. Putney, *Behind the Guns: The History of Battery I, 2nd Regiment, Illinois Light Artillery* (Carbondale: Southern Illinois University Press, 1965), 29–30.
16. McDonough, 222.
17. *O.R.*, 1158.
18. McDonough, 221–223.
19. *O.R.*, 1083–1084.
20. G.W. Brown Papers (Durham, NC: William R. Perkins Library, Duke University), letter from Brown to brother dated October 17, 1862.
21. McDonough, 224.
22. Johnson, 16.
23. McWhiney, 314.
24. Rowell, 88–89.
25. McDonough, 268.
26. Thomas, 226.
27. Letter of W.W. Carnes to Bishop (Durham,

NC: William R. Perkins Library), dated February 13, 1895.

28. *O.R.* 1039.

29. Solon Marks, *Experiences With The Ninth Brigade, Rousseau's Division, Army of Ohio: War Papers Being Read Before The Commandery of the Wisconsin Military Order of the Loyal Legion of the United States*, vol. 2 (Wilmington, NC: Broadfoot, 1993), 107.

30. *O.R.*, 1041, 1045, 1050; Marks, 108.

31. "Inside of Rebeldom," 57.

32. O.R., 1050–1051; Lt. Edward Ferguson, *The Army of the Cumberland Under Buell: War Papers Being Read Before the Commandery of the State of Wisconsin, Military Order of the Loyal Legion of the United States*, vol. 1 (Wilmington, NC: Broadfoot, 1993), 429; Shaler, 288; Buck, 112.

33. Yeatman, 4.

34. Gipson, 163.

35. McDonough, 239.

36. *Ibid.*, 243–244.

37. Thomas Lawrence Connelly, *Army of the Heartland: The Army of Tennessee, 1861–1862* (Baton Rouge: Louisiana State University Press, 1967), 263; Sykes, 469.

38. George D. Ewing, *General Bragg's Kentucky Campaign* (Nashville: Confederate Veteran Magazine, vol. 34, no. 3), 215.

39. McDonough, 243.

40. W.H. Davis, *Recollections of Perryville* (Nashville: Confederate Veteran Magazine, vol. 24, no. 6), 554.

41. Thomas L. Crawford, *The Battle of Perryville* (Nashville: Confederate Veteran Magazine, vol. 40, no. 4, 1933), 263.

42. Crawford, 263.

43. Davis Biggs, *Incidents in the Battle of Perryville, Ky.* (Nashville: Confederate Veteran Magazine, vol. 33, no. 2), 141–142.

44. L.S. Ferrell, *Reminiscences of the Fighting in Kentucky* (Nashville: Confederate Veteran Magazine, vol. 8, no. 1), 59.

45. O.R., 1059–1060; Paul Angle, *Three Years in the Army of the Cumberland* (Bloomington: Indiana University Press, 1969), 21.

46. Cummings, 226–227.

47. *O.R.*, 1060–1061.

48. O.R., 1060–1061; F.B. James, *Perryville and the Kentucky Campaign of 1862: Sketches of War History 1861–1865, Papers Prepared for the Commandery of the State of Ohio, Military Order of the Loyal Legion of the United States*, vol. 5 (Cincinnati: Robert Clarke Company, 1903), 149; McDonough, 254.

49. Thomas Euclid Magee Diary (Durham, NC: Duke University), diary entry for October 8.

50. Angle, 21.

51. McDonough, 279.

52. *O.R.*, 1066, 1068.

53. Marks, 108.

Chapter Six

1. Horn, 46.

2. Diary of Axel Reed (St. Paul: Minnesota Historical Society), October 8, 1862, entry.

3. Glezen Diary, October 8, 1862, entry.

4. McDonough, 273.

5. Bennett, 256–257.

6. *O.R.*, 1113.

7. *O.R.*, 1114.

8. *O.R.*, 1115.

9. *O.R.*, 1116–1117.

10. Bennett, 257; *O.R.*, 1033.

11. McDonough, 275–278.

12. Ferguson, 429.

13. Larry J. Daniel, *Cannoneers in Gray: The Field Artillery of the Army of Tennessee, 1861–1865* (Tuscaloosa: University of Alabama Press, 1984), 50–51.

14. Daniel, 280–281.

15. Buck, 113.

16. *Ibid.*, 114.

17. *O.R.*, 1123.

18. Rowell, 90–91.

19. *O.R.*, 1080.

20. *O.R., 1080.*

21. Shaler, 155.

22. McWhiney, 317.

23. Shaler, 286.

24. Axel Reed Diary, October 8, 1862, entry.

25. Marks, 108.

26. Horn, 46; Harrison, May, 1979, 46; *O.R.*, 1111.

27. Claiborne, 226.

28. McDonough, and Warner, *Generals in Blue*, 413.

29. Bennett, 259.

30. *Ibid.*, 260–261.

31. E. Hannaford, *The Story of a Regiment: A History of the Campaigns, and Associations in the Field, of the Sixth Regiment, Ohio Volunteer Infantry* (Cincinnati: Published by the author, 1868), 373.

32. Charles Gilbert, *Bragg's Invasion of Kentucky* (Louisville, KY: Southern Bivouac Magazine, vol. 1, no. 42, February, 1886), 551.

33. Charles Gilbert, *Bragg's Invasion of Kentucky* (Louisville, KY: Southern Bivouac Magazine, vol. 1, no. 40), 435.

34. Greiner, 204.

35. *Ibid.*, 203.

36. James M. McPherson, *Battle Cry of Freedom: The Civil War Era* (New York: Ballantine Books, 1988), 520.

37. *O.R.*, 1084–1086.

38. *O.R.,* 1084.
39. Greiner, 204, 207–208.
40. *O.R.,* 1121.
41. *O.R.,* 1033–1036.
42. James, 150.
43. Hannaford, 374–375.
44. McDonough, 287.

Chapter Seven

1. Sam Watkins, *An Adventure of General Leonidus Polk at the Battle of Perryville* (Louisville, KY: Southern Bivouac Magazine, vol. 2, no. 9, May 1884). 403.
2. Shaler, 286–287.
3. Cope, 206–207.
4. James, 153.
5. Diary of Johnson W. Culp (Louisville, KY: Filson Club Historical Society), entry for October 9, 1862.
6. McWhiney, 318.
7. Letter of Sam Shepardson, Shepardson Family Papers (Indianapolis: Indiana State Library), letter to "Dear Sister" dated October 16, 1862.
8. McWhiney, 319.
9. McDonough, 290–292.
10. Ferguson, 430–431.
11. Brown Papers.
12. Greiner, 211–212.
13. McDonough, 295; S.W. Peoples, *Graves of Our Dead at Perryville* (Nashville: Confederate Veteran Magazine, vol. 3, no. 5), 389.
14. McDonough, 292; James, 151.
15. Shaler, 287; Buck, 115–115.
16. Shaler, 287.
17. Unknown author, *The Kentucky Invasion of 1862* (Nashville: Confederate Veteran Magazine, vol. 23, no. 6), 409.
18. *Ibid.*
19. Wesley Thurman Leeper, *Rebels Valiant: Second Arkansas Mounted Rifles (Dismounted)* (Little Rock, AR: Pioneer Press, 1964), 117.
20. McWhiney, 321.
21. *Ibid.,* 321–322.
22. Sykes, 471
23. Dyer, 53–54.
24. *Ibid.,* 54–55.
25. Johnson, 19.
26. Dyer, 55.

27. W.E. Yeatman Memoir, 4.
28. James, 152.
29. Angle, 22.
30. Albert Hart, *The Surgeon and the Hospital in the Civil War: Papers of the Military Historical Society of Massachusetts, Volume XIII, Civil and Mexican Wars 1861, 1846* (Wilmington, NC: Broadfoot, 1990), 272–273.
31. Ewbank Diary, October 15 entry.
32. *Ibid.,* entries for October 19, October 20, October 25.
33. James, 163.
34. Cope, 208–209.
35. Cope, 209.
36. McWhiney, 322.
37. *Ibid.,* 323.

Chapter Eight

1. Cope, 209.
2. Otis, 133.
3. Harrison, 8.
4. Shaler, 289.
5. Warner, *Generals in Blue,* 52.
6. James, 164–166.
7. *Ibid.,* 166.
8. McWhiney, 323–324.
9. *Ibid.,* 325–326.
10. *O.R.,* 981.
11. Seitz, 199.
12. Dyer, 56–57.
13. Col. Luke W. Finley, *The Battle of Perryville: Southern Historical Society Papers,* vol. 30 (Richmond: Southern Historical Society, 1902), 240.
14. Dyer, 56–57.
15. *O.R.,* 1097; Larry J. Daniel, *Soldiering in the Army of the Cumberland* (Chapel Hill: University of North Carolina Press, 1991), 43.

Epilogue

1. Frank Vandiver, *Their Tattered Flags* (New York: Harper's Magazine Press, 1970), 162.
2. Unknown author, *Epithet to Fallen Confederates: War Papers Being Read Before the Commandery of the State of Wisconsin, Military Order of the Loyal Legion of the United States,* vol. 4 (Wilmington, NC: Broadfoot, 1993), 467.

Bibliography

Primary Sources, Manuscripts

Alabama State Department of Archives, Montgomery, AL
    James A. Hall Papers
    William J. Hardee Papers
Duke University, Durham, NC
    John Euclid Magee Diary
    Todd Quintard Papers
The Filson Club, Louisville, KY
    Johnson W. Culp Diary
Indiana Historical Society, Indianapolis, IN
    Lancelot Chapman Ewbank Diary
    Garrett Larew Diary
Indiana State Library, Indianapolis, IN
    Joseph P. Glezen Papers
    Leonard H. Mahan Papers
    Samuel Shepardson Papers
    Thomas M. Small Diary
Minnesota Historical Society, St. Paul, MN
    Axel Reed Diary
Tennessee State Library, Knoxville, TN
    John E. Gold Papers
    W.E. Yeatman Papers
University of Georgia, Athens, GA
    C.C. Platter Diary
Western Reserve Historical Society, Cleveland, OH
    Braxton Bragg Papers

Primary Sources, Books

Abbott, John S.C. *The History of the Civil War in America, Comprising a Full and Impartial Account of the Origin and Progress of the Rebellion, of the Various Naval and Military Engagements, or the Heroic Deeds Performed by Armies and Individuals.* New York: Henry Bill, 1865.

Allen, Brevet Colonel Theodore F. *Sketches of War History 1861–1865: Papers Prepared for the Commandery of the State of Ohio, Military Order of the Loyal Legion of the United States 1903–1908.* Cincinnati: Monfort, 1908.

Angle, Paul M. *Three Years in the Army of the Cumberland: The Letters and Diary of Major James A. Connelly.* Bloomington: Indiana University Press, 1969.

Aten, Henry J. *History of the 85th Illinois Volunteers.* Hiawatha, IL: Regimental Association, 1901.

Barnes, James A., James R. Cainahan, and Thomas H.B. McCain. *The Eighty-Sixth Regiment Indiana Volunteer Infantry.* Crawfordsville, IN: Privately published, 1895.

Bennett, L.G., and Haigh, Wm. M. *History of the Thirty-Sixth Regiment Illinois Volunteers, During the War of the Rebellion.* Aurora, IL: Knickerbockers & Hodder, 1876.

Brock, R.A. *Southern Historical Society Papers.* Richmond: Published by the Society, 1902.

Brown, Norman D. *One of Cleburne's Command: The Civil War Reminiscences and Diary of Capt. Samuel T. Foster, Granbury's Texas Brigade, C.S.A.* Austin: University of Texas Press, 1980.

Brown, Thadeus, Samuel Murphy, and William Putney. *Behind The Guns: The History of Battery I, 2nd Regiment, Illinois Light Artillery.* Ed. Clyde C. Walton. Carbondale: Southern Illinois University Press, 2000.

Buck, Captain Irving A. *Cleburne and His Command.* Jackson, TN: McCowat-Mercer Press, 1959.

Campaigns in Kentucky and Tennessee Including the Battle of Chickamauga 1862–1864: Papers of the Military Historical Society of Massachusetts. Boston: Military Historical Society of Massachusetts, 1908.

Cannon, J.P. *Inside of Rebeldom: The Daily Life of a Private in the Confederate Army.* Washington, DC: National Tribune, 1899.

The Comprehensive History of the Great War from Bull Run to Appomattox. New York: World, 1885.

Cope, Alexis. *The Fifteenth Ohio Volunteers and Its Campaigns: War of 1861–5.* Columbus, OH: Published by the author, 1916.

Davies, General Henry E. *General Sheridan.* New York: Appleton, 1895.

Davis, William C. *Diary of a Confederate Soldier: John S. Jackman of the Orphan Brigade.* Columbia: University of South Carolina Press, 1990.

Dodge, William Sumner. *A Waif of the War; Or, The History of the Seventy-Fifth Illinois Infantry, Embracing the Entire Campaigns of the Army of the Cumberland.* Chicago: Church & Goodman, 1866.

Duke, General Basil W. *Reminiscences of General Basil Duke, C.S.A.* Garden City, NY: Doubleday, Page, 1911.

Dyer, Gustavus W., and Moore, John T. *The Tennessee Civil War Veterans Questionnaires.* Nashville: Rev. Silas E. Lucas, Jr., 1985.

The Early Life, Campaigns, and Public Services of Robert E. Lee; With a Record of the Campaigns and Heroic Deeds of His Companions in Arms. New York: E.B. Treat, 1871.

Evans, General Clement. *Confederate Military History.* New York: Thomas E. Yoseloff, 1962.

Fisher, Horace Cecil. *A Staff Officer's Story: The Personal Experiences of Colonel Horace Newton Fisher in the Civil War.* Boston, 1960.

Floyd, David Bittle. *History of the Seventy-Fifth Regiment Indiana Infantry Volunteers.* Philadelphia: Lutheran Publication Society, 1893.

Gavin, William G. *Infantryman Pettit: The Civil War Letters of Corporal Frederick Pettit.* New York: Avon, 1990.

Graham, C.R. *Under Both Flags: A Panorama of the Great Civil War.* Chicago: W.S. Reeve, 1896.

Grant, U.S. *Personal Memoirs of U.S. Grant.* 2 vols. New York: Charles W. Webster, 1885.

Greiner, Captain H.C. *General Phil Sheridan As I Knew Him, Playmate — Comrade — Friend.* Chicago: J.S. Hyland, 1908.

Guernsey, Alfred H. and Alden. *Henry M. Harper's Pictorial History of the Civil War*. New York: Fairfax Press, 1966.

Hannaford, E. *The Story of a Regiment: A History of the Campaigns and Associations in the Field of the Sixth Ohio Infantry*. Cincinnati, 1868.

Harden, H.O. *Ninetieth Ohio Infantry*. Stoutsville, OH, 1902.

Hartpence, William R. *The 51st Indiana Volunteers*. Cincinnati, 1894.

Hazen, William B. *A Narrative of Military Service*. Boston, 1885.

Headley, J.T. *The Great Rebellion: A History of the Civil War in the United States*. Washington, DC: National Tribune, 1898.

Hight, John J. *History of the 58th Regiment of Indiana Volunteer Infantry*. Princeton, IN, 1895.
_____, and Gilbert R. Stormont. *Fifty-Eighth Indiana Infantry*. Princeton, IN, 1895.

Holmes, J. Taylor. *The 52nd O.V.I., Then and Now*. Columbus, OH: Berlin Print, 1898.

James, F.B. *Perryville and the Kentucky Campaign of 1862: Sketches of War History 1861–1865 — Papers Prepared for the Commandery of Ohio, Military Order of the Loyal Legion of the United States*, vol. 5. Cincinnati: Robert Clarke Co., 1903.

Johnson, Robert Underwood, and Buel, Clarence C. *Battles and Leaders of the Civil War*. New York: Century, 1888.

Kettell, Thomas P. *History of the Great Rebellion*. New York: N.C. Miller, 1863.

Kirkland, Frazar. *The Pictorial Book of Anecdotes of the Rebellion or the Funny and Pathetic Side of the War*. St. Louis: J.H. Mason, 1889.

Lathrop, David. *The History of the Fifty-Ninth Illinois Volunteers*. Indianapolis, 1865.

Military Essays and Recollections: Papers Read Before the Commandery of the State of Illinois, Military Order of the Loyal Legion of the United States. Chicago: Cozens & Beaton, 1907.

Minnesota in the Civil and Indian Wars 1861–1865. St. Paul, MN: State Board of Commissioners, 1889.

Neill, Edward D. *Glimpses of the Nation's Struggle, Papers Read Before the Minnesota Commandery of the Military Order of the Loyal Legion of the United States*. Wilmington, NC: Broadfoot, 1992.

Newlin, W.H. *A History of the Seventy-Third Regiment of Illinois Infantry Volunteers*. Hiawatha, IL: Regimental Association, 1890.

Perry, Henry F. *History of the 38th Indiana Regiment*. Palo Alto, CA, 1906.

Ridley, Bromfield L. *Battles and Sketches of the Army of Tennessee*. Mexico, MO, 1906.

Schmucker, Samuel M. *The History of the Civil War in the United States: Its Cause, Origin, Progress and Conclusion*. Philadelphia: Jones Brothers, 1865.

Shaver, Llewellyn A. *A History of the Sixteenth Alabama Regiment, Gracie's Alabama Brigade*. Montgomery, 1867.

Sheridan, General P.H. *Personal Memoirs of P.H. Sheridan: General United States Army*. New York: Da Capo Press, 1992.

Sherman, General William T. *Memoirs of General William T. Sherman by Himself*. New York: D. Appleton, 1875.

Stout, Dr. L.H. *Reminiscenses of General Braxton Bragg*. Hattiesburg, MS, 1942.

Sutherland, Daniel E. *Reminiscenses of a Private: William E. Bevins of the First Arkansas Infantry, C.S.A.* Fayetteville: University of Arkansas Press, 1992.

Tenney, W.J. *The Military and Naval History of the Rebellion in the United States*. New York: D. Appleton, 1867.

Thayer, William M. *A Youth's History of the Rebellion*. Boston: Walker, Fuller & Co., 1865.

Truesdale, Captain John. *The Blue Coats, and How They Lived, Fought, and Died for the Union, with Scenes and Incidents in the Great Rebellion*. Cincinnati: Jones Brothers, 1867.

Waddle, Angus L. *Three Years with the Armies of the Ohio and the Cumberland*. Chillicothe, OH: Scioto Gazette Book & Job Office, 1889.

The War of the Rebellion: A Compilation of the Official Records of the Union and Confederate Armies. Washington, DC: U.S. Government Printing Office, 1886.

War Papers: Being Papers Read Before the Commandery of the District of Columbia, Military Order of the Loyal Legion of the United States. Wilmington, NC: Broadfoot, 1993.

War Papers: Being Papers Read Before the Commandery of the State of Michigan, Military Order of the Loyal Legion of the United States. Wilmington, NC: Broadfoot, 1993.

War Papers: Being Papers Read Before the Commandery of the State of Wisconsin, Military Order of the Loyal Legion of the United States. Wilmington, NC: Broadfoot, 1993.

Watkins, Samuel R. *Co. Aytch.* New York: Macmillan, 1962.

Womack, J.J. *The Civil War Diary of Captain J.J. Womack, Company E, Sixteenth Tennessee Volunteers.* McMinnville, TN, 1961.

Primary Sources, Magazine

Confederate Veteran Magazine: volumes 1, 3, 8, 9, 16, 17, 23, 24, 26, 33, 34, 40.

Southern Bivouac: January 1883, February 1883, May 1884, October 1884, August 1885, September 1885, December 1885, January 1886, February 1886.

Secondary Sources, Books

Bowman, John S. *The Civil War Almanac.* New York: Gallery Books, 1983.

Catton, Bruce. *Terrible Swift Sword.* New York: Pocket Books, 1967.

Commager, Henry S. *The Blue and the Gray.* New York: Fairfax Press, 1982.

Connelly, Thomas L. *Army of the Heartland: The Army of Tennessee, 1861–1862.* Baton Rouge: Louisiana State University Press, 1967.

_____. *Autumn of Glory: The Army of Tennessee, 1862–1865.* Baton Rouge: Louisiana State University Press, 1971.

Cummings, Charles M. *Yankee Quaker Confederate General: The Curious Career of Bushrod Rust Johnson.* Rutherford, NJ: Fairleigh Dickinson University Press, 1971.

Daniel, Larry J. *Cannoneers in Gray: The Field Artillery of the Army of Tennessee, 1861–1865.* Montgomery: University of Alabama Press, 1984.

_____. *Soldiering in the Army of Tennessee: A Portrait of Life in the Confederate Army.* Chapel Hill: University of North Carolina Press, 1991.

Davis, William C. *The Confederate General.* Harrisburg, PA: National Historical Society, 1991.

_____. *The Orphan Brigade: The Kentucky Confederates Who Couldn't Go Home.* Garden City, NY: Doubleday, 1980.

Denney, Robert E. *The Civil War Years: A Day-by-Day Chronicle.* New York: Gramercy Books, 1998.

DeRosier, Arthur H., Jr. *Through the South with a Union Soldier.* Johnson City: East Tennessee State University, 1969.

Dowdey, Clifford. *Experiment in Rebellion.* Garden City, NY: Dolphin, 1946.

Dyer, John P. *From Shiloh to San Juan: The Life of "Fightin' Joe" Wheeler.* Baton Rouge: Louisiana State University Press, 1961.

Faust, Patricia L. *Historical Times Illustrated Encyclopedia of the Civil War.* New York: Harper Perennial, 1986.

Foote, Shelby. *The Civil War: A Narrative.* New York: Random House, 1958.

Funk, Arville L. *A Hoosier Regiment in Dixie: A History of the Thirty-Eighth Indiana Volunteer Infantry Regiment.* Chicago: Adams Press, 1978.

Garrett, Jill K. *Robert Smith "Confederate Diary."* Columbia, TN, 1975.

Garrison, Webb, Jr. *Friendly Fire in the Civil War.* Nashville: Rutledge Free Press, 1999.

_____. *Strange Battles of the Civil War.* Nashville: Cumberland House, 2001.

Hallock, Judith L. *Braxton Bragg and Confederate Defeat.* Tuscaloosa: University of Alabama Press, 1991.

Harrison, Lowell H. *The Civil War in Kentucky.* Lexington, KY, 1975.

Hicken, Victor. *Illinois in the Civil War.* Urbana: University of Illinois Press, 1966.

Hoenstine, Floyd G. *Military Services and Genealogical Records of Soldiers of Blair County, Pennsylvania.* Harrisburg, PA: Telegraph Press, 1940.

Horn, Stanley F. *The Army of Tennessee: A Military History.* New York, 1941.

Jones, Archer. *Confederate Strategy from Shiloh to Vicksburg.* Baton Rouge: Louisiana State University Press, 1961.

Kalman, Marsha E. *Civil War A–Z: An Illustrated Encyclopedia of Facts, Personalities, and Events of America's Bloodiest War.* New York: Gramercy Books, 2000.

Ketchum, Richard M. *The American Heritage Picture History of the Civil War.* New York: Doubleday, 1960.

Lanier, Robert S. *The Photographic History of the Civil War.* Secaucus, NJ: The Blue & Grey Press, 1987.

Leeper, Wesley T. *Rebels Valiant: Second Arkansas Mounted Rifles (Dismounted).* Little Rock, AR: Pioneer Press, 1964.

Long, E.B. *The Civil War Day by Day: An Almanac 1861–1865.* Garden City, NY: Doubleday, 1971.

Losson, Christopher. *Tennessee's Forgotten Warriors: Frank Cheatham and His Confederate Division.* Knoxville: University of Tennessee Press, 1989.

Lytle, Andrew N. *Bedford Forrest and His Critter Company.* New York: Minton, Balch, 1931.

McDonough, James L. *War in Kentucky: From Shiloh to Perryville.* Knoxville: University of Tennessee Press, 1994.

McPherson, James M. *Battle Cry of Freedom: The Civil War Era.* New York: Ballantine, 1989.

McWhiney, Grady. *Braxton Bragg and Confederate Defeat.* New York: Columbia University Press, 1969.

Parks, Joseph H. *General Leonidus Polk, C.S.A.: The Fighting Bishop.* Kingsport, TN, 1962.

Polk, William M. *Leonidus Polk: Bishop and General.* New York, 1915.

Pratt, Fletcher. *A Short History of the Civil War.* New York: Bantam, 1968.

Reeder, Colonel Red. *Sheridan: The General Who Wasn't Afraid to Take a Chance.* New York: Duell, Sloan and Pearce, 1962.

Rowell, John W. *Yankee Cavalry: Through the Civil War with the Ninth Pennsylvania Cavalry.* Knoxville: University of Tennessee Press, 1971.

Seitz, Don C. *Braxton Bragg: General of the Confederacy.* Columbia, SC: State Company, 1924.

Vandiver, Frank E. *Their Tattered Flags.* New York: Harper & Row, 1970.

Ward, Geoffrey C. *The Civil War.* New York: Alfred A. Knopf, 1990.

Warner, Ezra J. *Generals in Blue: Lives of the Union Commanders.* Baton Rouge: Louisiana State University Press, 1960.

_____. *Generals in Gray: Lives of the Confederate Commanders.* Baton Rouge: Louisiana State University Press, 1959.

Secondary Sources, Periodical

Civil War Times Illustrated: February 1966, June 1974, May 1979.

Index